TREASURES FROM PAUL

Colossians

KEN CHANT

TREASURES FROM PAUL

Colossians

KEN CHANT

Copyright © 2014 by Ken Chant

ISBN 978-1-61529-151-9

Vision Publishing
1672 Main Street E 109
Ramona, CA 92065
www.booksbyvision.com

All rights reserved worldwide. No part of the book may be reproduced in any manner without the written consent of the author, except in brief quotations embodied in critical articles of review.

A NOTE ON GENDER

It is unfortunate that the English language does not contain an adequate generic pronoun (especially in the singular number) that includes without bias both male and female. So, "he, him, his, man, mankind," with their plurals, must do the work for both sexes. Accordingly, in the following pages, wherever it is appropriate, please include the feminine gender in the masculine, and vice versa.

FOOTNOTES

A work once fully referenced will thereafter be noted either by "ibid" or "op. cit."

TRANSLATIONS

Unless otherwise noted, all scripture translations are my own.

TABLE OF CONTENTS

GO TO JAIL!..5
CHRIST HAS NO RIVALS 11
ONE: TUFFETS..13
TWO: HOPES..21
THREE: GUIDANCE..31
FOUR: HAPPINESS..45
FIVE: FAITH..55
SIX: PYGMALION..75
SEVEN: YESTERDAY..83
EIGHT: PRE-EMINENCE 89
NINE: FULLNESS...101
TEN: CONTINUE..111
ELEVEN: GLORY..119
TWELVE: IDENTITY...127
THIRTEEN: BAPTISM...139
FOURTEEN: POSITION 149
FIFTEEN: APPEARING 163
SIXTEEN: FORGIVING 177
SEVENTEEN: TRANSFORMATION..193
EIGHTEEN: CHOSEN 201
NINETEEN: PATIENCE..211
TWENTY: SINGING 219
TWENTY-ONE: HEARTILY 231
TWENTY-TWO: BLISSFUL 243
TWENTY-THREE: PARTNERS 259
TWENTY-FOUR: PRAISE 271
TWENTY-FIVE: BLAME 287
TWENTY-SIX: ARCHIPPUS 301
TWENTY-SEVEN: CHAINS 309
ADDENDA: HAPPY MARRIAGES 331
INDEX OF TEXTS 343
GLOSSARY...345
BIBLIOGRAPHY..349

ABBREVIATIONS

Abbreviations commonly used for the books of the Bible are

Genesis	Ge	Habakkuk	Hb
Exodus	Ex	Zephaniah	Zp
Leviticus	Le	Haggai	Hg
Numbers	Nu	Zechariah	Zc
Deuteronomy	De	Malachi	Mal
Joshua	Js		
Judges	Jg		
Ruth	Ru	Matthew	Mt
1 Samuel	1 Sa	Mark	Mk
2 Samuel	2 Sa	Luke	Lu
1 Kings	1 Kg	John	Jn
2 Kings	2 Kg	Acts	Ac
1 Chronicles	1 Ch	Romans	Ro
2 Chronicles	2 Ch	1 Corinthians	1 Co
Ezra	Ezr	2 Corinthians	2 Co
Nehemiah	Ne	Galatians	Ga
Esther	Es	Ephesians	Ep
Job	Jb	Philippians	Ph
Psalm	Ps	Colossians	Cl
Proverbs	Pr	1 Thessalonians	1 Th
Ecclesiastes	Ec	2 Thessalonians	2 Th
Song of Songs	Ca *	1 Timothy	1 Ti
Isaiah	Is	2 Timothy	2 Ti
Jeremiah	Je	Titus	Tit
Lamentations	La	Philemon	Phm
Ezekiel	Ez	Hebrews	He
Daniel	Da	James	Ja
Hosea	Ho	1 Peter	1 Pe
Joel	Jl	2 Peter	2 Pe
Amos	Am	1 John	1 Jn
Obadiah	Ob	2 John	2 Jn
Jonah	Jo	3 John	3 Jn
Micah	Mi	Jude	Ju
Nahum	Na	Revelation	Re

* *Ca* is an abbreviation of *Canticles*, a derivative of the Latin name of the *Song of Solomon*, which is sometimes also called the *Song of Songs*.

GO TO JAIL!

"Go to Jail. Go directly to Jail. Do not pass 'Go'. Do not collect £200." So said one of the "Chance" cards in the *Monopoly* game that was part of my childhood. The command was stern. The reluctant player was obliged to move his token to the Jail square, there to stay until the rules allowed an escape.

What does the *Monopoly* Jail have to do with *Colossians*? Nothing, except that I want to echo the Chance card and admonish you to do the same – "Go to jail!" – that is, go to the last sentence in Paul's short letter, and notice that he was in prison, in chains, in Rome, when he wrote to the church at Colossae. And he urged his readers not to forget his captivity – *"Remember my chains!"* he cried. (4:18)

I hope you will do that. As you read the letter, remember Paul's incarceration, and the harsh bonds that chafed him. They are salient to everything the apostle says. The dark walls of that Roman cell provide a background against which the letter itself shines with sparkling radiance, especially when we, like Paul, wear the chains of Christ with joyful thanksgiving!

As for myself, I was 19 in 1952, [1] when I began one morning to read Paul's *Letter to the Colossians*. I had done so before, but on this occasion I was mightily struck by the contrast between the lively Christianity Paul describes and my own comparatively dull experience. Oh! I knew and loved the Lord, and was serving him gladly – yet something was missing. I

---

(1) I am somewhat older now, as I write, in 2014.

resolved to find it. So, leaving my Bible opened on my bed, at *Colossians*, I began to pray, telling the Lord that I would not get off my knees until he had revealed the truth to me. I asked him to carry me into the vibrant Christian life those ancient people had discovered.

I won't tell you how long I stayed there, except that it was long enough to change me for ever! From that time on, *Colossians* has been my favourite portion of scripture. I love the whole Bible, but *Colossians* scores just a few more points!

Paul wrote his letters to the churches in Colossae and Ephesus around the same time, *circa* 60 A.D, but which letter was written first remains uncertain. Anyway, both letters contain ideas that had never before been expressed by anyone, anywhere. Imagine how extraordinary that is! For example, a thousand years prior to Paul, a world-weary cynic lamented the lack of anything new under the sun (Ec 1:9-10), and he was correct. It is indeed hard to say, "Here is something truly new!" Can there really be anything never seen or heard before? (2)

So much is it true that saying anything new is hard, even Jesus added little to human understanding of God and life. His religious, ethical, and moral teachings exist in the writings of earlier prophets. Sages, philosophers, and religious leaders who lived before him had already spoken most of what he taught. He often expressed those ideas differently, with greater pungency, and with vast authority – but the concepts themselves were not new. (3) Only in his death and

---

(2)   Even the amazing inventions and technology of the modern world are only extensions of ideas propounded in the myths, legends, predictions, and achievements of the past.

(3)   Opinions will differ as to what actually *was* new in the teaching of Jesus, although they would include the idea of God as a personal Father (Lu 2:49; Mt 6:9); the church (Mt 16:18); the inclusive nature of the gospel (Re 22:17);

resurrection did Christ alter the course of history and bring something radically different into human experience. If we had only his sermons he would be admired as a great moral teacher, and as a remarkably good man, but not as an innovative thinker, nor as the Redeemer of fallen humanity.

Yet suddenly, in Paul, a man appears who speaks what had never before been spoken, and whose head is filled with ideas that no one before him had ever conceived. Whence came the staggering grandeur of the revelation that fills the first two chapters of *Colossians*? –

> *Christ is the image of the invisible God, the firstborn of all creation. For by him all things were created, in heaven and on earth, visible and invisible, whether thrones or dominions or rulers or authorities – all things were created through him and for him. And he is before all things, and in him all things hold together. (1:15-17, ESV)*

Did Paul just conjure those exalted ideas out of a fevered imagination? Are his revelations nothing more than wild human invention, irresponsible fantasy? No one who has ever truly read the letter could deem it so shallow. No matter how improbable the vision Paul presents, it has about it the ring of truth, divine truth. To suppose otherwise is to supplant one miracle with another! That is, if Paul is not simply telling the truth about the supernatural Christ and the glory every believer may discover in him, then the letter itself becomes an inexplicable marvel. If *Colossians* is in fact a piece of human caprice, a literary contrivance, then it is a greater wonder than the wonders it purports to reveal! It is easier to accept that the

---

and one or two other ideas. But the greater part of what Jesus spoke and taught had been presented in the OT, or in the writings of other great thinkers, moralists, and religious leaders.

letter genuinely reports the real splendour of the gospel than to suppose that Paul concocted its treasures out of nothing.

Yes, the *Letter to the Colossians* is a miracle, but only because it is filled with Christ, who was revealed to Paul by the Spirit of God. It tells the awesome wonder of who Christ is and what he has accomplished for all who heartily believe in him. But the letter itself is simply a record of what Paul had seen, and heard, and knew to be the truth – Christ is pre-eminent and is our only Redeemer. (Cl 1:18, KJV)

Now, before leaving this preface, let me offer the caution that I have added to other books in this series – you are not holding a verse by verse commentary on *Colossians*. Several brilliant commentators have done a better job of that than I ever could. This book, as the series title proclaims, is a collection of "treasures" from Paul, and in picking out those several treasures, the book follows where they lead into many other parts of the Bible. Still, I hope that by the time you reach the last page, you will have a rich sense of all that Paul was striving to say.

You might also ask, "Why is there no comment here on some truly wonderful verses in *Colossians*?" In most cases, the answer will be that I have covered those passages in other books published by Vision College. [4] Usually, I do not repeat a commentary unless I have something important to add to remarks made elsewhere.

Also, do read the *Addendum* on "Church Governance" at the end of the book. It will explain itself and present some ideas that you may find provocative, but will nonetheless, I hope, stimulate you to think about some things a little differently. I hope, too, if you do not belong to the Pentecostal or

---

(4) For example, *Colossians 2:15*, which is expounded in Chapter 3 of my book The Cross and the Crown, Vision Publishing, Ramona California.

Charismatic movements, that as you read these pages you will forgive an occasional Pentecostal paragraph. They are few, but they do represent my sincerely held belief.

And a final word, reverting back to that Monopoly game that I so enjoyed as a child. Usually, I ended a game of Monopoly as a dismal bankrupt, sometimes helplessly imprisoned in the "Jail" square. But I remember one joyous occasion when, with ruthless tenacity, good luck, and much gloating, I managed to clean up the board, and walked away the proud possessor of everything – streets, properties, railway stations, utilities, bank reserves, and all!

I hope you won't emulate my gloating, except to boast of Christ; [5] nonetheless, may these pages truly enable you to see with delight and to embrace with rapture more of the treasures of Christ and of the gospel than you have ever known. Then you will be like Paul. He was incarcerated in a Roman jail; yet he saw himself as altogether a winner in Christ, rich beyond telling, destined for a throne, and in possession of supernal glory!

---

(5)   1 Corinthians 1:31; 2 Corinthians 10:17; Galatians 6:14; Philippians 3:3.

CHRIST HAS NO RIVALS

The city of Colossae was located in Asia Minor, and was a cosmopolitan commercial town. The Christian community probably consisted of a mixture of gentiles and converted Jews. The church was not founded by Paul, but by Epaphras (1:7; 4:12-13), who was probably a convert of Paul's, and an occasional companion with him in ministry. After pioneering three churches (in Colossae, Laodicea, and Hierapolis), Epaphras travelled to Rome to visit Paul (who was in prison), and he was still with the apostle when Paul wrote his letter to the Colossians, around 60 A.D.

The church at Colossae was generally strong and healthy (1:3, 4), and Paul was full of confidence for their future (vs. 5). Nonetheless, he was alarmed by reports of two insidious heresies that were creeping into the church and that might do irrevocable harm to their fresh young faith. The first error was being pressed upon them by certain Jewish teachers who wanted to impose the laws of Moses. (2:16-23) The second, and even more perilous error, was the intrusion of "gnostic" ideas about the heavenly hierarchy.

The "Gnostics" (whose beliefs came to full flower about 100 years later, and wrought temporary havoc among the churches) held that there were many layers of angels or demi-gods between humankind and God. These divinities ruled over the earth, but they could be controlled, or at least influenced, by acquiring the right kind of "knowledge" (Greek, *gnosis*). Within this teaching, Christ became just one of the higher orders of angels, and one of many other mediators who stood between God and his people. (2:8, 18)

Those false doctrines have risen again in our time. There are many who suppose that the best way to get to heaven is to pursue good works – that is, to build a quotient of self-made righteousness that will oblige God to admit the soul into eternal life (2:20-23). Then others, sometimes called "new age" followers, posit many spiritual beings who are reckoned to control human affairs, [6] but who can be made friendly, or even brought under command, by the proper rituals or by sundry magical formulae.

Against all such notions Paul wrote with passion, insisting on Christ's absolutely unique place in the cosmos, his irresistible authority, and his exclusive role as mediator between heaven and earth. (2:8-10)

The studies that follow will highlight Paul's teaching, showing that all the fullness of the Godhead is in Christ and all the fullness of Christ is in us. Christ has no rivals; we need no other Saviour. To add anything to the perfect work of Christ is folly. To depend on any other than Christ is idolatry. [7]

---

(6) One of the currently most popular, is the renewed pagan myth of an "Earth-Mother" (Gaia), the goddess of nature.

(7) This introduction was probably drawn from several sources. I compiled it many years ago for a set of lectures on *Colossians*, and have long since lost any notation of its origins.

ONE:

TUFFETS

We keep hearing about your faith in Christ Jesus and how much love you have for all God's people ... I rejoice when I hear that you are living as Christians, and that your faith in Christ is strong. Since you have embraced Christ Jesus as your Lord, keep following him, planting your roots in him, and making him the foundation upon which your life is built. (Cl 1:4; 2:5-7)

INTRODUCTION

Little Miss Muffet sat on a tuffet,
Eating her curds and whey; [8]
There came a big spider,
Which sat down beside her,
And frightened Miss Muffet away.

---

(8) "Curds and whey," the dish Little Miss Muffet enjoyed, was simply junket, a custard-like food made of sweetened milk, coagulated with rennet, and frequently served with fruit and cream. The dish is better known in Britain than in the USA. It got the name "junket", either because it was taken to market in little reed baskets, called jonquettes (from Latin *joncus*, reed.), or because it was served, either in such baskets, or on a reed mat.

During the last century (so I have heard) that famous nursery rhyme was published more often than any other, although its origins go back another 300 years.

Its meaning is unknown. Some claim that it refers to Mary, Queen of Scots (1543-87), who was said to have been frightened by religious reformer John Knox (1510-72). But that seems unlikely. In any case, the rhyme deals with a theme that is common in all literature – *the fears that may suddenly beset us without warning.* Among those fears and perils, against which Paul says we should present a strong faith, there is –

THE FEAR OF SICKNESS

A few years ago a Swine Flu epidemic laid a pall of anxiety upon the nation. That fear was a little irrational, since, on average, 3000 people die every year in Australia from ordinary flu! In any case, surely the first thing a believing Christian should do when confronted by serious illness is to hold fast to the promises of God. Here is one of them –

> *You should not fear terrors of the night, arrows that fly during the day, plagues that prowl the night, or epidemics that strike at noon. They will not come near you, even though a thousand may fall dead on one side of you and ten thousand on the other! (Ps 91:5-7)*

What a remarkable and all-encompassing promise! And we are certainly entitled to claim it for ourselves. Yet we must accept also that it states a general rule rather than an absolute fact. This we learn from, say, James, who acknowledges that sometimes illness, does overtake godly people –

> *If you are sick, call for the church leaders. Ask them to pray for you and anoint you with oil in the name of the Lord. Such prayers, offered in*

> *faith, will save* (9) *those who are sick and the Lord will make them well again." (5:14-15)*

Yet that promise of healing shows that we have a right generally to expect good health and prosperity from the Lord.

So let us be done with exaggerated fears that cause us to fall over! I say "exaggerated" because fear feeds on itself and has a tendency to grow ever larger. Miss Muffet is a good illustration of this. You may have noticed that in many illustrations of the rhyme, the spider is drawn much larger than life-size. (10) The artists, perhaps unconsciously, recognised that the girl's fear of spiders made the insect seem huge to her. Most of our fears are like that; they are much bigger than the actual peril.

So, while a degree of caution in the face of danger is always wise, panic is folly. Rather, the only valid response for a believer is to set yourself to trust the Lord with all your heart! Then it will be said of you as Paul said of the Colossians –

> *I rejoice when I hear that you are living as Christians, and that your faith in Christ is strong! (2:5)*

THE FEAR OF POVERTY

> *I have been young, and now I am old, yet I have not seen the righteous forsaken, nor their children begging for bread. (Ps 37:25)*

---

(9) The Greek word *sozo* can mean "save" or "heal", depending upon the context.

(10) Search for "Miss Muffet" under Google "Images", and you will find scores of examples.

Many commentators have problems with that text – it seems too good to be true! So they engage in pious evasions –

> It is not now universally true that the "righteous" are not "forsaken", in the sense that they do not want, or in the sense that their children are not constrained to beg their bread. (Albert Barnes)

> These temporal promises were more express to the Jews in the times of the Old Testament, than to Christians. (John Wesley)

> God promised Israel earthly blessings. He does not promise that to you and me. We are blessed with all *spiritual* blessings. You will be confused if you believe that God has promised you *earthly* blessings. (McGee)

> (That godly people never have to beg) is not my observation ... for I have relieved the children of undoubtedly good men, who have appealed to me as common mendicants. But this does not cast a doubt upon the observation of David, (for) he lived under a dispensation more outward and more of this world than the present rule of personal faith. (Spurgeon)

I find comments like those extraordinary. Did Israel under the law get a better deal from God than we do under grace? Does the promise of Moses have more power than the promise of Christ? Does the old covenant offer more prosperity than the new? Were they better off in the shadow of Sinai than we who live overshadowed by the Cross?

Hardly! Think, say, of *Hebrews*. Nine times the writer declares that the gospel is *"better"* than the law, saying that we have –

- A better Saviour (1:4)
- A better Hope (7:19)
- A better Covenant (7:22; 8:6)
- A better Promise (8:6; 11:40)
- A better Sacrifice (9:23)
- A better Property (10:34)
- A better Destiny (11:16)
- A better Resurrection (11:35)
- A better Salvation (12:24)

Jesus himself promised earthly blessings as well as heavenly –

> *Truly, I say to you, there is no one who has left (anything) for my sake and for the gospel, who will not receive a hundredfold <u>now in this world</u>, ... and in the age to come, eternal life. (Mk 10:30)*

What about the *"daily bread"* in the *Lord's Prayer*? Did he mean only bread? Or should we take "bread" to mean all those things that are necessary to good health and a joyful life? Indeed, if faith cannot reach out for daily needs of every sort, what use *does* it have?

Consider also –

> *God did not keep back his own Son, but gave him up for us. If God did this, won't he also freely give us everything else? (Ro 8:32)*

Are there no exceptions? Yes there are. Jesus himself added a warning about persecution to his 100-fold blessing (Mk 10:30). And think about the many *Psalms* of lament.

So there are exceptions to the general rule; but that does not make the rule less reliable. It means only that sometimes bold faith may have to appropriate the promise in a different manner, as, for example, Paul and Silas did in prison. They suffered anguish from having their legs cruelly forced apart in the stocks, yet they prayed and sang hymns in praise of God (Ac 16:24-25). In chains they may have been; defeated they were not. Paul was as sure of being *"more than a conqueror"* (Ro 8:37) when his hips were close to dislocation in the stocks as when he walked free. But such unusual situations do not lessen the right of every believer, under normal circumstances, to trust the Lord to meet every need richly.

Let us not be famous for fear but for faith, so that people will say of us, *"We keep on hearing about your faith, and about how much love you have for all God's people!"* (Cl 1:4)

THE FEAR OF WORLD EVENTS

Men's hearts will fail them for fear, and for looking out at those things that are coming on the earth: for the powers of heaven will be shaken. (Lu 21:26)

Note that "heaven" is *ouranos* = the sky, which gave its name to Uranus, the 7th planet from the Sun, which in turn gave its name to "uranium"! [11] Perhaps Jesus foresaw the present atomic age, splitting the uranium atom, with the consequent horrors of nuclear war?

But, said Jesus, when the rest of the world is *"looking out"* with terror, that is just the time that we should be *"looking up"*! –

---

(11) Uranus was discovered in 1781 and named after the Greek god who ruled the sky. Uranium was discovered by a German chemist 8 years later, and he named the new element after the new planet, little dreaming that his discovery did indeed embody the nuclear forces that shape the universe, and could also destroy our world!

> *But when these things start happening, then <u>look up</u>, and lift up your heads; for your redemption is drawing near. (vs. 28)*

Undoubtedly there is much to fear in this nuclear age, and nations rightly tremble at the prospect of an atomic war. But we Christians know that *"our times are in God's hands,"* (Ps 31:15) and we should live without fear, always confident that *"underneath us are the Everlasting Arms"*. (De 33:27) So, no matter what is happening around them, true Christians will remain focussed on Christ, allowing nothing to hinder them from *"following him, planting their roots in him and making him the foundation upon which their lives are built, and abounding in thanksgiving."* (Cl 2:6-7)

THE FEAR OF FALLING SHORT

This is perhaps the most prevalent and most secret fear of many Christians – "How can I be sure that I will not fall short of heaven?"

First, remember that you are God's own child, and he does not easily abandon his blood-born, blood-bought children –

> *Because you are God's children, God has sent the Spirit of his Son into you, so that you may now cry, "Abba! Father! You are no longer slaves but God's children, and since you are his children, God has also made you his heirs! (Ga 4:6-7)*

Second, you are filled with his Spirit –

> *You haven't received the spirit of slaves, which would take you back again into fear. Rather, you have received the Spirit of God's adopted children, so that now you can shout, "Abba! Father!" (Ro 8:15)*

So rise up in the power of the Holy Spirit, and cast off everything and anything that may be pushing you to backslide, to collapse in fear, to lose your inheritance.

We are doubly God's children, by **_birth_**, and by **_adoption_**, sealed by the Holy Spirit!

So long as you refuse to abandon that identity, so long as you cling to Christ, so long as you keep him as *"the foundation upon which your life is built"*, placing all your hope in him alone, you will be safe *for ever*! You will also be the kind of Christian Paul commends in our text: strong in faith; filled with the love of Christ; untroubled by fear; following Christ; deeply rooted in him; and radiant with joy! (Cl 1:4; 2:5-7)

TWO:

HOPES

When John F. Kennedy began campaigning for the USA presidency in 1959, he adapted the lyrics of a popular song and made it his campaign theme. He rode to victory in 1960 on the wings of that song, and became the youngest person and the first Roman Catholic to be elected president. The song was "High Hopes", which first appeared in the 1959 film, "A Hole in the Head", and sung by Frank Sinatra. (12) In part, it goes like this –

> Just what makes that little old ant
> Think he'll move that rubber tree plant?
> Anyone knows an ant can't
> Move a rubber tree plant.
> But he's got high hopes, he's got high hopes;
> He's got high apple pie in the sky hopes!

High hopes! If anyone has them, we do! –

> *Your **hope** in Christ is being safely kept for you in heaven. You discovered this **hope** when you first accepted the truth of the gospel ... You must never give up the **hope** you received when you heard the good news. ... Christ lives in you, and*

---

(12) "High Hopes" was sung by Mr Sinatra with a group of children, and it won an *Academy Award for Best Original Song*. The music was written by Jimmy Van Heusen, and the lyrics were by Sammy Cahn.

> *he is your **hope** that you will share in the glory of God. (Cl 1:5, 23, 27)*

The second most beautiful word in scripture, after "love", is surely "hope". As Paul said, there are three things that will endure for ever, *"faith, hope, and love, and the greatest of these is love."* (1 Co 13:13) "Faith" may come first, and "love" may be the greatest, but "hope" is in the middle, framed by faith and love.

We are a people of hope; but not just "hope", for we are truly gifted with "HIGH hope", far beyond any hope the song-writer could express. What is this *"**high** hope"*? It stands in contrast with an uncertain kind of "low" hope, which is fixed upon material things – a better job, new car, overseas holiday, luxurious home, fashionable clothing, and the like.

Such secular hopes have their proper place, but they are never more than a shadow of the *real* hope that should enthral our hearts in Christ.

Christian hope is fixed, not upon the ephemeral and elusive things of this world, but upon sure goals, things that we are certain to attain in Christ – victory, wholeness, triumph over death, paradise, the glory of God. But the low hope of this world is more akin to wishful thinking, a kind of yearning, so that even when it sparkles brightly it remains underlain with uncertainty. The very word "hope", in common use, is adverse to certainty, for it describes something that *might* happen, that we wish *will* happen, yet in the end, may *not* happen.

But not Christian high-hope. That high-hope is fixed on God's unshakable promises. We "hope" for those promises only in the sense that they are not yet fully ours. But undeniably, they *will* be ours in Christ! Thus there is a vast hiatus between secular hope and Christian high-hope. Whatever hope this world may conjure up will always be haunted by uncertainty. But we *know* in whom we have believed, and that he is able, and that he *will* honour all that he has spoken. (Ro 4:21; 2 Ti 1:12)

Furthermore, this high hope is the very reason for our salvation – *"for hope you have been saved."* (Ro 8:24) Many translations are uncomfortable with that rendering, and prefer either *"in hope"* or *"by hope"*. Yet Paul clearly wrote, *"for hope"*.

The grammatical structure is unusual, but Paul's meaning is surely plain enough. He cannot mean that we are saved "by" hope, for scripture strongly affirms that we are saved rather by "faith". After all, it is the gospel that gives us hope – *"Continue in your faith ... and never allow yourself to be moved away from the hope that comes to us in the gospel."* (Cl 1:23)

Nor can we be saved "in" hope, for this implies some doubt about our salvation, which in fact is utterly secure in Christ.

But we CAN be saved "for" hope — that is, God has saved us so that we might become a people filled with hope, high-hope, the very highest of hopes, hope that is certain of fulfilment, replete with unquenchable optimism!

WE HOPE IN CHRIST

"Hope" is "an expectation that something good will happen". In our case, that expectation is based upon the irrefragable promise of God. Our hope arises also from our union with Christ and from our knowledge that *"Christ is in us, the hope of glory."* (Cl 1:27) In this we differ from the people of ancient Israel. The Hebrew language lacked any exact equivalent to our word "hope". The Jews were indeed rich in hope, based upon their expectation of the Messiah, but they had to use other terms, such as confidence, expectation, assurance, and the like. (13)

By contrast, the New Testament has more than 80 occurrences of the Greek word *"elpis"*, which matches our "hope" – for only through the gospel can we have any *true* hope. The old covenant provided no such irrevocable hope, no such infrangible promise; but what the old lacked, the new has created in abundance. Anyone who is *"in Christ"* possesses an eternal high-hope, filled with the joy of salvation, the happiness of righteousness, the certainty of being part of the Bride of Christ, acclaimed by the angels of heaven! (Re 19:6-9)

Indeed, as we contemplate the Cross, we realise that even our own sins (so long as we are penitent and trustful) cannot disappoint us of this hope!

So we live *"in hope of eternal life, which God, who never lies, promised us before the world began."* (Tit 1:2)

WE HOPE IN HEAVEN

All true Christians can be described as *"looking for that blessed hope, the appearing of the glory of the great God and our Saviour Jesus Christ"* (Tit 2:13). Indeed, that expectation is one of the marks of a Christian. Without it, can a person really claim to be saved? We are already a people of eternity, standing on the edge of the dawning kingdom of God. We already hear the first echoes of the Trumpet of God, and of the Shout of the Archangel, (1 Th 4:16) and we see the first glimmers of the radiant return of Christ. In our heads we may

---

(13) The word "hope" occurs in many places in English translations of the Old Testament, but the Hebrew words so translated are not an exact equivalent.

think that the day is still distant; but in our hearts we can hardly help but feel that he is coming today!

Indeed, we cannot doubt that Christ will come again, and that every promise associated with his glorious return will be fully ours! That assurance is bound up with the church, which is his Bride, destined to be raptured spotless and beautiful for ever.

Furthermore, that day will also see the fulfilment of *"our living hope ... for an inheritance, incorruptible, and undefiled, ... which is reserved in heaven for us, who by the power of God are guarded through faith until we receive the salvation that is waiting to be revealed in the last day."* (1 Pe 1:3-5)

That magnificent promise is set by Christ before his Bride, the church. So I cling to the church. You can't get me out of it! For while I am in the church I know that when the church rises, I too will rise! So long as I am part of the church, my safety is absolutely secured.

But what do I mean by "church"?

I mean a *local* church, for in the end there is no other. The church is not some ethereal, invisible cloud, floating in the heavens. The church comprises the very visible and very tangible company of local congregations around the world, worshipping in a covenant relationship with each other and with Christ, and under his lordship. Inside such a church there is heaven; outside it, there is only hell.

So we are not only waiting for the promised prize, but we are waiting in <u>hope</u> – *high*-hope; that is, we cannot doubt that the crown will indeed be ours on that day! Nor even in heaven will hope vanish. For in Paradise there will still be unlimited opportunities for growth and achievement. And at each level of attainment the next will be confidently anticipated with high-hope. For indeed, *"Your **hope** in Christ is being safely kept for you in heaven."* (Cl 1:5)

WE HOPE IN THE THRONE

*When God wanted to prove for certain that his promise to his people could not be broken, he made a vow. Now we know that God cannot tell lies, so ... those promises should greatly encourage us to take hold of the **hope** that is right in front of us. This **hope** is like a firm and steady anchor for our souls. In fact, **hope** reaches behind the curtain and into the most holy place, where Jesus has gone ahead of us. (He 6:17-20)*

Jesus has gone ahead of us, and is enthroned at the Father's right hand, and scripture says that we will one day share that glory. This is our amazing and stunning hope!

But then, scripture also says that we are *already* God's new creation and we are *already* enthroned with Christ in the heavenlies! How can this be? Simply, by the biblical principle that many of God's promises are at once both true and not yet realised.

Our task is twofold — believe fiercely in the truth (in this case, that we are now enthroned with Christ); and yet never stop reaching out for its actualisation in our daily lives (cp. Ex 23:29-30; De 7:22), until eventually, in the world to come, the promise will be totally realised in us. In the meantime, we keep on striving to bring the promise into ever richer fulfilment in our daily lives. This means, day by day, that we seize more of the authority, riches, strength, and identity that the throne represents. And we do this by *faith* – that is, by growing in faith through thinking about the promises of God, praying over them, and by exercising such faith as we have to make them ever more real each new day.

Our case is like that of Israel – *"Little by little the Lord will drive out these nations as you advance. You will not be able to destroy them all at once, for, if you did, the number of wild animals would increase and be a threat to you."* (De 7:22)

Or again, *"I will not drive out your enemies within a year's time, for if I did, the land would become deserted, and the wild animals would be too many for you. Instead, I will drive them out little by little, until there are enough of you to take possession of the land."* (Ex 23:29-30)

So too it is with us. While the "land" is already altogether ours in Christ, our full possession of it must await his return. In the meantime, strive to possess as much as you can of all that the Lord has promised. How much? That will depend upon how much the believer grows in faith, maturity, spiritual understanding, relationship with God, and the like. But even if it is only *"little by little"* (as in Israel's case), we should not abandon the quest, but always keep pressing in for more.

So we are challenged never to despair but always to stand up and try again, and again, until the full victory of Christ is truly ours, even if that total triumph must await the rapture. Never lose hope that you will keep on grasping more and more of the reality of <u>who</u> (a child of God), and <u>what</u> (more than conqueror), and <u>where</u> (enthroned in the heavenlies) you are in Christ!

If we fall a thousand times, still we will cry, *"Rejoice not against me, O my enemy, for though I fall I will stand up again!"* (Mi 7:8)

And if at the end of life we are found face down in the dust, then the resurrection will carry us out of death and defeat and into the perfection of God!

But we must cling to Christ!

Sin cannot be ignored, but neither can it finally destroy the one who has resolved <u>never</u> to capitulate, nor ever to let go of the Saviour! That is why Paul, in our text, urged his readers with passion –

> *You must never give up the **hope** you received when you heard the good news. ... Christ lives in you, and he is your **hope** that you will share in the glory of God! (Cl 1:23, 27)*

CONCLUSION

Let me go back to the beginning of this chapter, and the song that helped to propel Jack Kennedy into the Oval Office –

> Everyone is voting for Jack,
> 'Cause he's got what all the rest lack,
> Everyone wants to back — Jack,
> Jack is on the right track.
> 'Cause he's got high hopes.

High hopes! What wonderful high hopes we have in Christ! And see! They will carry us, not to some paltry and temporary political office, but to the highest seat in the universe, the very throne of God!

That is why the apostle (He 6:17-20) urges us to do three things –

<u>Know that Christ has gone before us so that we can boldly follow him</u> — *"Jesus has gone ahead of us, behind the curtain and into the most holy place."*

<u>Never let go of the high hope that is already planted in us</u> — *"We know that God cannot tell lies; so his promises should greatly encourage us to take hold of the hope that is right in front of us."*

<u>Anchor that hope in the high heavens, where we are enthroned with Christ</u> — *"This hope is like a firm and steady*

anchor for our souls. In fact, hope reaches behind the curtain and into the most holy place."

Cast the anchor of high-hope and fix it in the Rock, Christ Jesus, so that you cannot be moved away, and then rejoice in the assurance of endless Paradise.

THREE:

GUIDANCE

> *We keep on praying for you, asking that with all spiritual wisdom and good sense you may truly come to know God's will. You will then be able to walk in a manner worthy of the Lord, pleasing him in every way, fruitful in every good work, and growing still more in your knowledge of God. (Cl 1:9-10)*

How willing is God to give us immediate and daily guidance? Philip Yancey began an article on that question in this way –

> The issues are immediate and clear-cut. Who do I marry? What job should I take? Should I go to a Christian or secular college? Which church should I attend? Ought I consider having another child? Should I move to Texas? . . . It would seem reasonable to expect God to be involved in such major decisions affecting our lives. And yet, try to make sense, if you will, of the most commonly heard advice on the topic of divine guidance . . . (14)

– then Yancey continues with a discussion of several common fallacies about divine guidance.

---

(14) *Christianity Today*, Sep 16, 1983; pg. 24.

I have my own list of fallacies, gathered across many years of both observation and personal experience. [15] But what about the main question? Is it always possible to obtain clear direction from heaven about what you should do in the important issues of life? The simple answer is – no! But there are many exceptions.

Of course, I am not talking here about moral decisions. How you and I should behave ethically and morally is spelled out clearly enough in scripture. No higher or better authority exists.

What about those practical matters upon which scripture is largely silent? We crave clear guidance from the Father; yet often it seems so difficult to find!

In reality, divine guidance is probably neither so easy nor so difficult to obtain as many people have suggested. Certainly Paul (in our text) was convinced that we *can* discover God's will, and do it, and so please the Father.

But there are errors to be avoided, and principles to follow –

TWO FALLACIES

Two wrong concepts keep on bringing frustration and disappointment to many Christians as they set out to serve God –

- the first is the idea that clear and certain guidance is available at all times;
- the second is that if one is doing the will of God then success is sure.

Both propositions are only partly true. That is –

---

(15) See my book *Discovery*, pub. Vision Publishing, Ramona Ca.

- clear guidance is only occasionally available; and
- success (in terms of statistical or material achievement) is nowhere guaranteed in scripture.

Let us then look at these two fallacies, beginning with

A FALLACY OF GUIDANCE

Many people expect that detailed guidance should be available from God on demand, and that to begin any project without a clear word from heaven is to court disaster. Yet see *Luke 10:10-11,* and notice how general was Jesus' instruction to his disciples. He left it to them to decide what town they would visit, and when. If he had thought it important for them to go only to such towns as they were commanded by God to visit, then he would have told them to be sure to ask for heavenly direction before they embarked on their missions.

What rule then should we follow?

GENERAL GUIDANCE IS ALWAYS AVAILABLE

See *Luke 10:1-4,* where the Lord left the disciples in no doubt that they were called into mission, and he laid down the broad parameters within which they had to work.

But the details were apparently left for them to determine each day, based on changing circumstances and the response (or lack of it) that they gained from their audiences (see again *vs. 10-11*). The Greek text of verse 5 reads, *"Into <u>whatever</u> house you enter... ,"* which implies that there was an element of accident in their choice of house. That is confirmed by the uncertainty of the response they might find there (vs. 6). Notice the complete lack of any suggestion that they should not go into a house unless they were specifically directed to do so by the Holy Spirit.

SPECIFIC GUIDANCE IS SOMETIMES AVAILABLE

To deny that God ever specifically guides his servants would be absurd, for scripture and life are full of examples of God doing just that, just as they are full of examples of people simply choosing what seems to be the best thing to do in each new situation. That is why Paul adds *"good sense"* to his admonition about seeking the will of God –

> *We keep on praying for you, asking that with all spiritual wisdom and <u>good sense</u> you may truly come to know God's will. (Cl 1:9)*

That is, don't be so pious that you discard all practical common sense, depending upon prayer alone; nor so earthbound that you have forgotten how to approach the throne of God and commune with the Lord face to face.

Both ideas, for example, are displayed by David. He declared that he had absolute confidence that the Lord would protect him from the savage attacks of his enemies; nonetheless, he took refuge in a cave! –

> *This is a poem David wrote, when he fled from Saul, and hid in a cave. "Be merciful to me, O God, be merciful to me! Do I not put all my trust in you? Yes, in the shadow of your wings, I will take refuge until the threatened disaster has passed." (Ps 57:1)*

Many similar passages could be cited, where trust in God and common sense are allied. Indeed, the entire *Book of Proverbs*, so filled with pragmatic counsel, is an example of the need to be practical as well as pious, sensible as well as saintly. Especially is this true in the matter of divine guidance – do not discard normal rules of diligence and caution.

Nonetheless, there are two settings in which specific divine guidance may be expected and trusted –

IN RESPONSE TO DIVINE INITIATIVE

That is, doubt is removed when God intervenes in some tangible way, making his purpose plain, either telling his servants exactly what he wants them to do, or preventing them from following some plan of their own. Both ideas, for example, are seen in *Acts 16:7-9*.

Godly hearts will be ever alert for such divine intervention (as Paul was), and willing and ready to obey instantly every word from God.

IN RESPONSE TO BELIEVING PRAYER

We should, of course, bring every day's activities before the Lord in prayer, whether or not the Lord chooses to speak into a situation himself. But especially, we should do so when we are unable to make a decision ourselves, or when there is no alternative to gaining some clear direction from heaven. At such times we are indeed instructed to ask for wisdom, and to ask in faith. (Ja 1:5-8) Thus Paul himself prayed for the Colossians, expecting his prayer to help them discover the will of God –

> *We keep on praying for you, asking that you may truly come to know God's will. (Cl 1:9-10)*

Note however, that certain things are *always* required of the children of God, and it is pointless to ask any further direction on these matters: *holiness, marital fidelity, integrity in word and action, loyalty to the church, regular worship*, and the like. We have already been told in scripture how to behave in many such circumstances, and the Lord will not change his mind merely to suit our convenience or wishes. (16)

A FALLACY OF PROSPERITY

Every believing Christian has a promise of prosperity. (3 Jn 2; Jn 15:16; 16:24; etc.) Most Christians can and should expect those promises to be fulfilled in this life; but if they are not fulfilled this side of the resurrection, then they certainly will be on the other side!

Yet though it is right for us to have a general expectation of prosperity, we have no absolute *guarantee* of it in any particular circumstance, or even in this world at all –

- thus, Jesus made it plain that his disciples will not succeed in evangelising every town in which they preach. Indeed, so uncertain is "success" that he warns his servants not to be too elated when they gain some great victory. Rather, said he, we should rejoice because our names are written in heaven, (Lu 10:17-20) for that will never change!

- times of persecution, of national or community collapse, or war, will normally impact Christians as much as they do the ungodly. When a bomb destroys a city, Christian homes and businesses will lie in the rubble, along with those of the ungodly, as also will Christian dead. Sometimes the Lord gives special protection to the righteous, but not often, and most certainly not always.

---

(16) I will, of course, allow that the terms do have to be defined. For example, what does a "holy" life mean; what ethical and moral parameters do we need to set; and so on?

- natural disasters (fire, flood, earthquake) do not usually bypass Christian homes, farms, businesses, or even lives; rather, Christians show the goodness of God not so much by divine preservation (although it does sometime happen), but by the manner in which they handle whatever crisis overwhelms them. Despite adversity, the true Christian will rejoice and give thanks to God. (Ha 3:17-18) Yet we cannot know what will happen –

  In times of prosperity be joyful, but in times of adversity consider this: God has made one as well as the other, so that no one can discover what the future holds. (Ec 7:14, NET)

- from some places, said Jesus, his disciples will be fortunate if they escape with their lives. (Mt 10:17-25; Mk 13:9,12)

And mark this – Jesus did not suggest that when his disciples were thwarted they should set themselves to "break through" with prayer and fasting (as many would urge today). On the contrary, he basically implied that "success" in ministry, or "failure" is something over which we have little or no control, for so much depends upon circumstances we cannot change or control –

I have seen this in human affairs – the swift do not always gain first prize; the strong do not always win the battle; prosperity is not always captured by the wise; intelligence does not always lead to riches; nor does success always come to those who are clever. Rather, time and chance may overcome them all. (Ec 9:11)

See also *James 4:13-16*; which declares that we ought not to boast about any achievement until it is actually done, for in the meantime a thousand things may prevent it from being done.

In harmony with the above, some pastors and missionaries, instead of battling along in an unresponsive environment, or struggling to make some ministry work when there is no reasonable chance that it ever will, would be wiser to follow Jesus' advice to *"shake the dust off their feet"* and go somewhere else. If they were to get out of the way, perhaps the Lord could send someone else, better equipped, into the situation. A new face, a new voice, might be able to accomplish a good work there. The same rule is true for any Christian in any area of life; there is no point in trying to sow seed on a bed of marble; go and find a more fertile field! [17]

AN UNHAPPY PREACHER

Sirach [18] speaks about two public speakers who had great gifts, yet still failed –

> Here is someone who is clever enough to teach many others, yet in the end he is useless to himself. Then there is the brilliant speaker who makes too many enemies and starves to death, because God did not give him popular appeal. (37:19-21)

Two men who were clever enough, and yet were not clever enough. Both of them were gifted public speakers, but one

---

(17) Over the years, I have seen several examples of pastors whose fortunes were radically improved simply by moving from an unfruitful parish to one where their ministry was valued and rewarded.

(18) Rabbi Joshua ben Sirach lived in Jerusalem during the early 2nd century B.C. He enjoyed a hardy, perilous, and adventurous life, and was probably around 80 years old when he wrote his book of Jewish wisdom, sometimes called *Ecclesiasticus* (the Book of the Church), because it was so popular with the Church Fathers.

lacked wisdom, the other, popular appeal. There is a mystery here. Why does the Lord equip people with many gifts, yet in the end withhold the one thing they need for true success? I don't know. It is one of the questions that await an answer in the life to come. But really, it is not important. Whatever we *have*, whatever we *lack*, we can still serve God to the best of our ability, and we can still devote ourselves to pleasing him in all that we are and do.

I once said to the Lord, and meant it, "Lord, I do not care if no eyes ever see one of my books, except yours and mine. I will still write them, and so long as you are pleased with what I have written, then I am satisfied!" Somewhat brash, no doubt, and I'm not sure that I would have had the courage or the tenacity to keep on writing if not one copy was ever sold! Happily, I was not put to the test. Enough readers like my work to encourage me to continue. Yet I'll never be renowned as a brilliant master of the English language, enthralling millions. Some measure of charm, some degree of skill, some level of eloquence, some facility with words, was never given me. But I do what I can with what I have, and hope indeed that what I do and what I am will please the Lord. Nothing else matters.

In the meantime, harking back to Sirach, teachers who ignore their own needs and so bring disaster upon themselves, could perhaps ameliorate their state by learning wisdom from others and from scripture. Preachers, whom the Lord has deprived of the gift of charm, may perhaps grow it by walking more humbly and producing the fruit of the Spirit. (Ga 5:16, 22, 23) And all who, like them, find that the Lord has blocked high achievement in one field, may find it is because he wishes them to succeed in another. Yet they need the experience gained in other less successful pursuits to boost their attainments in their major call.

At any rate, the old rabbi seems to be suggesting that life is a mixture of human and divine, so that what human nature lacks may be drawn down from heaven, and what heaven has failed to give, may be aroused by walking sensibly and wisely. That is, those two unhappy speakers may have had more reason to blame themselves for their failure than to shake a fist at God.

Yet many clever teachers will never gain enough wisdom to make their lives a success in human terms; and many brilliant preachers may never attract the crowds for which they yearn. Despite their best strivings, time and chance will drive them to disappointment. (Ec 9:11) That is when we should turn to the Lord and gain great comfort from knowing that our place in paradise, our reward in heaven, our status in the kingdom, do not depend upon how much the world acclaims us, but on how much Christ is revealed in us. Not what we *do*, but who we *are*, is God's criterion.

Had they followed that rule, those two failed public speakers – despite one falling apart and the other starving to death – would have found that they were actually a huge success in the eyes of the Lord!

PAUL'S INJUNCTION

Paul's prayer (heading this chapter) joins *"spiritual wisdom"* and *"good sense"* as keys to discovering the will of God. When those two virtues are properly united, the result will be people who are

> *able to walk in a manner worthy of the Lord, pleasing him in every way, fruitful in every good work, and growing still more in their knowledge of God. (Cl 1:9-10)*

We must recognise also that there is a difference between "success" viewed as statistical or material achievement, and "success" viewed as holiness in character and faithfulness in service. The first is not *guaranteed* to any of us; but the second is *required* from all of us! Thus, a pastor who labours fruitlessly in one town may enjoy a rich harvest in another. Was he then a failure in the first instance and a success in the second? No! But suppose he "fails" in both places? Even then he cannot be named a failure unless he has discarded his integrity, or become bitter and frustrated, or has stopped reflecting the beauty, grace, and love of Christ. So long as any pastor continues to behave Christianly, and truly preaches the whole counsel of God (Ac 20:27), and has striven to the best of his (or her) ability, he has no cause for shame, whether or not his labours attract a large congregation, or impact his community. Let the radiance of the Saviour beam from him (or her), and from any of us, and the plaudits of heaven will be deafening on that day, and we will be garbed in glory.

CONCLUSION

Why are these things so? Why doesn't God make it easy to get a "word" as often as we ask? Why does he seem to prosper some and not others?

- **_In the case of guidance_** it is because the Lord wants to bring us to wise maturity, to a capacity to make our own responsible decisions, not always needing to hold his hand like a toddler clutching its parent.

- **_In the case of prosperity_** it is because he wants to form character and strength, being far more concerned about who you **_are_** than what you **_do_** or what you **_have_**.

The Father's ultimate goal is to build a people who are fit to inherit, not this world, but the everlasting kingdom that lies on the other side of the grave. Statistics have scant attraction for God. His focus is not on the pile of beans we have laboured to accumulate, and are so busy counting. We could lose them all without troubling him over much. He is not concerned about the *count*, but the *counter*. Not *what*, but *who*.

On the day that is coming, you will be assessed not on how well you succeeded in some earthly enterprise, but on how well you succeeded as a *human being*. Even Paul was a little apprehensive about the possibility of failing this test –

> *I beat my body black and blue, and keep it under severe discipline, otherwise I might find that I have preached to others but am cast aside myself. (1 Co 9:27)*

Can a great and highly successful preacher find that his glorious work has all been for nothing? Yes, if he forgets that God does not care nearly so much about what he has *done* as about who he *is*.

So your works and mine, including the best and most noble, will have value on the Day of Judgment only insofar as they show the kind of person we are, and especially how well we have reflected the character of Christ.

This equality of destiny matched with the unpredictable vicissitudes of life should make any attentive person wary of putting too much hope in material things (see Mt 6:19-20; Lu 12:32-34). The grave consumes monarchs as readily as merchants; death has no favourites, makes no distinctions, and treats all human differences with disdain. As Horace said in one of his famous *Odes* (I.iv.13) –

> Pale Death kicks his way equally into the cottages
> of the poor and the castles of kings.

And a thousand years ago Omar Khayyam expressed his scorn of human pomp –

> I once bought a pot from a potter,
> Which told everything when it said,
> "I was an emperor and had a golden goblet,

Now I'm any drunkard's wine pot!" [19]

For the highest in the land as well as for the lowest, each new day is equally fraught with uncertainty. A ruler today can be a slave tomorrow, and a pauper may rise to be a king. (Ec 4:14-16)

These things are so self-evident it is amazing that anyone ever forgets them. Yet since most of us do forget, many prophets and divines, sages and poets, have striven to remind us of them, and to scourge the folly of loving this chancy world too much.

> O sudden grief that ever art near neighbour
> To worldly bliss! Sprinkled with bitterness
> The ends of joy in all our earthly labour!
> Grief occupies the goal to which we press.
> For your own safety think it is no less,
> And in your day of gladness bear in mind
> The unknown evil forging on behind! [20]

OUR HOPE MUST BE IN CHRIST

I once heard Billy Graham say that no one is ready to live until he or she is first ready to die. Is that a paradox of despair? No, for while I know that I must die, I also know that Christ has triumphed over the grave – therefore I shall never die! Death has lost its sting, the grave has lost its victory! (1 Co 15:55) Now, in the freedom of Christ, each new day weaves its richest texture, and each hour builds its most joyous frame.

---

(19) The Ruba'iyat of Omar Khayyam (12th century Persian mathematician, philosopher, poet); tr. Peter Avery & John Heath-Stubbs; Penguin Classics, 1983; Quatrains 41, 51, 208, 227. ("Ruba'iyat" simply means "quatrains".)

(20) The Canterbury Tales, by Geoffrey Chaucer (1345-1400); tr. by Nevill Coghill; Penguin Classics, 1977; pg. 151.

Is that how the fabric of your life is woven? Are these things its warp and woof? Is your heart fixed on obtaining *"the prize of the high calling of God in Christ"*? (Ph 3:14) Are you living for eternal values, ready for this world because you are ready for the next? Are you fit to live because you know how to die? Has earth become precious because heaven is more so? Are your possessions here touched with grace because your true affections are fixed above, where Christ is, sitting at the right hand of God? (Cl 3:1-4)

I do not see how anyone living in such a golden setting could ever lapse into dejection. Surely there is here an admirable cure for the bleakest depression, a panacea for the most melancholy soul, medicine to cheer the dullest heart! We're on the way to heaven. Christ awaits our coming. The angels are ready to herald our arrival with a thunder of acclamation. What is there in this brief moment of earthly existence that could possibly cloud such indestructible joy?

FOUR:

HAPPINESS

> *His glorious power will make you patient and strong enough to endure anything, and **you will be truly happy**. (Cl 1:11, CEV)*

I once heard a preacher say that the Bible nowhere offers *"happiness"*, but promises instead a better thing, *"joy"*. Perhaps the truth of that claim depends upon how "happiness" is defined; but, despite that preacher, the usual Hebrew and Greek words for "happiness" do occur often in scripture. Most translations render the word in our text as "joy" or "joyfulness", which makes the CEV a bit eccentric, but not inaccurate when it says that we will be *"truly happy"*.

Happiness, then, is a goal that the Bible endorses –

> *How beautiful upon the mountains are the feet of him who brings good news, who publishes peace, who brings good news of **happiness**, who publishes salvation, who says to Zion, "Your God reigns." (Is 52:7; ESV)*

So much is the *"good news"* of the gospel directed toward the happiness of those who believe, that Paul did not hesitate to ask God to exert *all his glorious power* to make the Colossians happy! Admittedly, that happiness came from learning patience and how to *"endure anything"*, but happiness it was, nonetheless. Indeed, the happiness a Christian knows is so real that not even brutal persecution can stifle it.

THE QUEST FOR HAPPINESS

I have heard it said that Aristotle argued that the quest for happiness is the supreme goal of life. If so, others have echoed his claim –

> O happiness! Our being's end and aim!
> Good, Pleasure, Ease, Content! whate'er thy name:
> That something still which prompts th' eternal sigh,
> For which we bear to live, or dare to die. (21)

> Every one of these hundreds of millions of human beings is in some form seeking happiness. (22)

Even a masochist, torturing his own flesh, is seeking pleasure, albeit twisted. Only a madman deliberately craves wretchedness; and perhaps even for him, in his insanity, misery alone can bring happiness.

So too, we Christians. Even if our main pursuit is holiness rather than happiness (He 12:14), we aspire to holiness because we know that without it there can be no happiness! Therefore, so long as we are pursuing happiness in the right way, and for the right cause, we have a strong right to grasp it. As the American *Declaration of Independence* declared in 1776 –

> We hold these truths to be self-evident, that all men are created equal; that they are endowed by their Creator with inherent and inalienable Rights; that among these, are Life, Liberty, and the pursuit of Happiness.

---

(21) Alexander Pope (1688-1744), *An Essay on Man*; Epistle 4, introductory lines.

(22) H. G. Wells (1866-1946), The Outline of History, ch. 40.

That is a Christian manifesto as much it is a political one. But despite their quest for happiness, most people discover that their sources fail them, and their quest is frustrated. The Bible, however, suggests three inexhaustible sources of perpetual joy that are open to every person who embraces Christ –

HAPPINESS IS FINDING GOD'S LOVE IN CHRIST

A young man once found Lord Bertrand Russell, the atheist philosopher, in a passive and troubled mood. The great thinker said: "I have made a strange discovery. Whenever I talk to a philosopher, I am convinced that happiness is no longer a possibility. Yet when I talk to my gardener, I become convinced of the opposite!" (23)

Modern psychology has discovered what the Bible revealed long ago: ***things*** cannot bring happiness outside of a sense of ***loving*** and of being ***loved.*** But where can one find this ***love***? If one looks for it in people, there are two problems –

- Even the best of people must at least sometimes fail to meet our expectations.
- Death remains the great mocker of even near-perfect human love.

William Barnes (1801-1886) was a country vicar, who was also an extraordinary scholar, possessing reading fluency in more than 70 languages. In addition, he was a gifted musician, a skilled wood and copper-plate engraver; and he wrote several books on philosophy. He is most renowned now for his

---

(23) I have lost the source of this anecdote.

wonderful evocation in poetry of the vanishing rural scenes of his childhood. [24]

In 1852, after 25 years of unsullied marital happiness, his wife Julia died. He wrote in his diary, "Oh, day of overwhelming woe. That which I greatly dreaded has come upon me. God has withdrawn from me his choicest worldly gift. Who can measure the greatness, the vastness of my loss? I am undone. Lord have mercy upon me!"

His tender poem, *The Wife A-Lost*, in the Dorset dialect, reflects the grief from which he never fully recovered. Across several stanzas, he tells how he cannot bear to sit or dine or walk in places that his wife had once frequented; instead, he will "go alone where the mist rides, through trees a-dripping wet, and sit beneath the darksome boughs" of the forest, "where she did never come". In the last stanza he says –

> Since I so miss your voice and face
> In prayer at eventide,
> I'll pray with one sad voice for grace
> To go where you now bide;
> Above the tree and bough, my love,
> Where you have gone before,
> And are waiting for me now,
> To come for evermore. [25]

As I write, my wife Alison and I have been happily wedded for 60 years. Neither of us can imagine life without the other. Yet

---

(24) For example, see http://www.poemhunter.com/william-barnes/poems/page-1/?a=a&l=1&y. See also the eponymous article in Wikipedia.

(25) *Folio Magazine*, Summer 1989; article by Ann Powell on "William Barnes;" pg. 23-24. I have anglicised the lines in the version given above. In the original dialect the lines read – Since I do miss your vace an' fece / In prayer at eventide, / I'll pray wi' woone sad vace vor grece / To goo where you do bide; / Above the tree an' bough, my love, / Where you be gone avore, / An' be a waten vor me now, / To come vor evermwore.

one day, possibly not far away now, one will be taken and the other left to sorrow. Like William Barnes, nothing will remain for the widowed spouse except to wait longingly for reunion in Paradise. All human love must one day be extinguished. In the end, the only unfailing source of love is in God, for he *is* Love. (1 Jn 4:8, 16)

But love is made futile if it is spurned, even the love of God. How much the Lord yearned to prosper his people! But they rejected his love and spurned his kindness. So he delivered them instead into the hands of their enemies –

> *I am the Lord your God, who brought you out of Egypt. I said, "Open your mouth, and I will fill it." But my people refused to listen to me; Israel rebelled against me. So I let them go their own stubborn way, and allowed them to do whatever they wanted. How I wish my people would listen to me; how I wish they would obey me! How quickly I would then overthrow their enemies and crush all their foes. You would see those who hate me bowing in fear before me; you would hear their sentence of eternal punishment. But I would feed you with the finest wheat and satisfy you with honey from out of the rock. (Ps 81:10-16)*

Is there a more chilling indictment in scripture than the fraught words the Lord spoke to Israel? – *"I let them go their own stubborn way, and allowed them to do whatever they wanted!"* God is no bully. If we choose to follow our own path, to ignore both his command and his promise, then he will help us to do so! But that was not his preference. Only listen to him, only obey him, and how quickly he will rout the enemy and feed you with the finest wheat and with sweet honey from the rock!

HAPPINESS IS FINDING GOD'S STRENGTH IN CHRIST

Much unhappiness has its root in

DEPRIVATION

– that is, the sense of being denied what you feel should be yours.

We would want much less, and be contented, if we only realised and appropriated all the riches we have in Christ! That wealth is well expressed by a Greek word, *ploutos*, which occurs some 20 times in the NT (see Ep 3:8; Ph 4:19; 2 Co 8:9; etc.). Several English words are based on *ploutos*, such as *plutocrat* (immensely wealthy) and *plutarchy* (rule by a wealthy elite); and *plutonomy* (the production and distribution of wealth).

The Greeks used *ploutos* to describe vast riches; and because most riches lie buried in the earth, the name of the god of the Underworld (*Pluto*) was also derived from it. More darkly, the Greeks had another reason for allying *ploutos* with the dread god – they realised that seldom is it possible to accumulate vast wealth without in some measure going into partnership with the powers of darkness.

But see the boldness of Paul, who takes this word, so redolent of idolatry and ill-gotten treasure, and applies it to Christ and to his church! As if he were saying that the only treasure that deserves the name is found in the riches that Christ brings to those who call him Lord.

INADEQUACY

When I was a young man, and had just preached in a local Baptist church, one of its elders told me that I was destined to be Australia's Billy Graham. Fortunately, I didn't take him seriously, although I won't deny that I had a few moments of giddy exultation! A year or two later, I got a promotion. An elder in a Pentecostal church told me that I would be Australia's *Elijah*! Billy Graham was marvellous; but *Elijah!* – that was really heady stuff! It might have ruined me, except, by the grace of God, I had enough sense to laugh it off.

Still, such comments did plant in me some ambition for greatness, which survived until I watched Billy Graham in action in Melbourne in 1959, when on one occasion more than 130,000 people were present at a crusade meeting. As part of a number of other meetings held during that crusade, about 1,000 pastors gathered for a morning session. The Melbourne media were also present, and Dr Graham invited them to question him in front of the crowd. Those hard-headed reporters and journalists attacked the evangelist from all sides, assaulting him with every tricky or accusing poser in their arsenal. Through it all, Dr Graham remained unperturbed, answering each question calmly, wisely, shrewdly, and effectively. I watched in awe. I knew that had it been me facing that ravening mob, they would have torn me to shreds. All ambition to be a national evangelist dissipated like a mist when the hot sun rises. I discovered some of my limitations that day! Among other things, it made me more resigned to my lot, content to be just what God wants me to be, no more, no less – which in itself is a great recipe for happiness!

Six decades have passed since then, and I do not regret never becoming a great evangelist or a rival to Elijah! It might have been fun, but I doubt it. Had I tried to fulfil any such dream, the demands and duties would probably have destroyed me. As it happens, sixty years of ministry proper for me, have left me still eager to serve Christ and the church, and happy to work within the framework the Lord has appointed for me.

I have learned this – when one is fulfilling the purpose of God (rather than human ambition) Christ freely offers his all-sufficiency (2 Co 3:5; 9:8), and living in a dependency upon his divine supply is a key part of a happy life. Thus our text –

> *His glorious power will make you patient and strong enough to endure anything, and **you will be truly happy**. (Cl 1:11, CEV)*

The presupposition behind that declaration, of course, is that it speaks only to people who are living in union with Christ, submissive to his will, and believing his promise. To such persons come patience, strength, and a quality of happiness that nothing on earth can undermine.

Does this mean that Christ is only a crutch? Hardly! Far from being a mere support, Christ is everything in life – not a crutch, but the very legs upon which we walk; not a breathing aid, but our lungs; not a pacemaker, but our heartbeat itself; not some medicine, but our entire health; not merely a part, but our all in all; not a prop for life, but the source of *all* life, and hope, and happiness!

HAPPINESS IS FINDING GOD'S HUMILITY IN CHRIST

How contrary the Christian quality of humility is to the world, and even, sadly, sometimes to the church! But it is the way of Christ, who set an example of self-denying service. (Ph 2:5-8)

Note these two strongly contrasting words in our language –

HUBRIS

which leads to Hell

Both the Greek word and its English derivative mean the same – excessive pride, unwarranted self-confidence, especially an arrogant defiance of heaven. Paul uses *hubris* with vehement passion to denounce people who hate God –

> *Since people do not see fit to acknowledge God, he allows them to debase their minds and to do what they should not do. They become filled with every kind of unrighteousness, evil, covetousness, malice. How eagerly they embrace envy, murder, strife, deceit, and malice! They are gossips, slanderers, haters of God, **haughty** (hubris), arrogant, boastful, ever dreaming up new ways to be wicked. They are disobedient to their parents; they behave like fools; they break their promises; they have no mercy, and they sin ruthlessly. (Ro 1:28-31)*

What a fiery tirade – it almost singes the paper! Dripping with scorn, burning with indignation, Paul leaves no doubt about his fury against people who wilfully ignore the evidence of God's existence and of his power and glory (vs. 18-20). The inevitable result of such hubris is eternal death (vs. 32). But then there is –

HUMILITY

which leads to Heaven

If we belong to Christ, let us hold to the mind of Christ, in true humility and grace. (Ph 3:13-15a) Then there will be no doubt about it – *"you will be truly happy!"* (Cl 1:11)

FIVE:

FAITH

> *You have heard before of the hope laid up for you in heaven. This hope is revealed in the word of the truth, the gospel ... (You) must stay deeply rooted and **strong in your faith**. ... I became a minister of the gospel for your benefit, and I am fulfilling the stewardship God gave me by making the word of God fully known ... I am glad to know that you are living as you should and that **your faith in Christ is strong**. ... Let the word of Christ dwell in you richly, so that you may teach and instruct each other with much wisdom. (Cl 1:23, 25; 2:5; 3:16)*

Mark in those verses the repetition of our dependency upon the Word of God, the need to hear the Word, and a demand to maintain strong faith, based upon the Word. The end result will be this – we will be a people who are *"living as we should"*, fulfilling God's purpose for us in Christ.

Let us start exploring those ideas by looking first at *faith*. There are three kinds of faith –

1. **Mental assent**
    - that is, belief in the fundamentals of the Christian faith; cp. *1 John 5:9-10*.

2. *Quiet confidence*

- that is, trust in the goodness and providence of God and in the integrity of his promises. (Is 30:15)

3. *Bold expectation*

This is an aggressive faith, which constantly looks for divine intervention. It is the *"strong"* faith that Paul mentions twice in our text just above. It expects signs, wonders, and miracles; see *Matthew 11:12; 17:20; 21:21-22*; etc. This bold expectation is the most advanced and the most demanding of the three kinds of faith; not many Christians attain to it. That is because the first two kinds of faith are largely *passive*, while the third is *active*. The first two are more akin to simple trust in the promises and providence of God; but the third is more akin to an aggressive, bold faith, the kind that Christ had in mind, when he said, *"The kingdom of heaven is being taken by storm, and those who are strong and forceful claim it eagerly for themselves."* (Mt 11:12) Paul calls it "strong" faith – tough, active, able to withstand attack and press on to victory; it knows how to possess the promises of God, and refuses to be denied.

This difference between the active and passive varieties of faith raises two questions –

1. How can you ***know*** when ***strong faith*** is called for?
2. How can you ***gain*** this ***strong faith***?

Our text passages suggest that the answer to those questions depends upon hearing from God (three times Paul mentions scripture – *"the Word of truth ... the Word of God ... the Word of Christ"*) (Cl 1:23; 2:5; 3:16) –

FAITH AND THE WORD ARE INSEPARABLE

Strong faith cannot exist apart from either an instruction or a promise from God. We cannot just "have" faith, as an entity in its own right, like holding an orange. Faith cannot stand alone.

Faith must always be linked with something else – a person, a promise, an action, or an undertaking. It is rather like love, which too cannot stand alone. To say that "I have love" is meaningless. The question would at once come – "Love for whom, or what?" Likewise, to say, "I believe" is pointless unless that belief is fixed in something. Love and faith disappear if there is nothing or no-one to love or to trust.

So, faith must have an object, which for a Christian is fixed upon the Lord and upon his promises. Faith finds its anchor in the Word of God, and its sure foundation in Christ himself.

This association of scripture with faith means that faith is never blind. It is not irrational, it spurns foolish superstition. Faith does not ignore the evidence; on the contrary, it rests upon the strongest proof of all, the promise of God!

Indeed, contrary to what most people feel, faith cannot survive if it is linked with the irrational. We cannot believe the unbelievable, nor make credible what is incredible, nor logically accept what is illogical. But at once someone might protest, "How then can we believe in a God who does the 'impossible', the 'incredible', things mysterious and amazing, and who often seems to mock human reason?" We can do so, simply because faith finds its *credible* basis in the assured promise of God –

- who cannot lie (Nu 23:19)
- whose promise has never failed (1 Kg 8:56)
- whose character is utterly trustworthy (Ja 1:17; He 6:17-19a); and
- whose power is adequate for his promise. (Ph 3:21b)

Thus, as we read, study, and accept the Word of God, we become persuaded that belief in God and in all his signs and wonders is not foolish, but deeply sensible. The more we are persuaded that it is rational to trust the Lord, even to the doing of miracles, the more faith will wax mighty in us. So keep on meditating each day in the Word of God. It is the source of all true life and prosperity. (Ps 1:2-3) I am a believer. But I am not a naïve simpleton, credulous, superstitious, and ignorant. I do not believe the impossible, the incredible, the ridiculous, or the irrational. On the contrary, my faith is credible, rational, and practical, because it is based upon the integrity of God and upon his irrevocable promise, undergirded by his limitless power! [26]

STAY STRONG IN FAITH

Twice our text urges us to stay *"deeply rooted and strong in faith"*, never presuming to call *impossible* what God has called *possible*! See *Matthew 17:20; 19:2; 21:21;* etc.

The rule is, only a word from God can banish uncertainty, and fill you with confidence that your prayers will be answered.

How can you get such a word from the Lord? It can come in various ways –

A SINGLE TEXT

God may speak to you at any time through a single verse, or even sentence, in the Bible. But beware: **"a text out of context may be a pretext!"** [27]

For example, Jesus said that we can have *"whatever we ask in prayer"* (Mt 21:22; Jn 14:13; etc.). But does that truly mean

---

(26) Someone might protest, "But you speak in tongues, and how irrational is that? (1 Co 14:14)" Yes I do, but glossolalia is irrational only in the sense that I do not know the meaning of what I am saying. It is the language of the spirit not the mind. The words may not be comprehensible to my mind, but the act itself is not irrational, for it is a work of the Holy Spirit.

(27) I have been unable to track down this well-known saying. It is attributed to different people, most, if not all, of whom are said to have spoken it long after I first came across it possibly six decades ago!

you can have *anything* you demand, whenever you demand it? Hardly, for the Master himself mentioned several things that prayer may not be able to change. For example –

- tribulation in this present world.
- persecution.
- opposition from family and friends.
- earthquakes, famines, wars.
- false prophets.
- plus other things that are beyond our control, and that God will be unlikely to change at your behest or mine.

Prayer cannot make you taller, or shorter, or change you from a blonde to a brunette, or turn you into a gifted artist, elevate you to Britain's throne, turn you into a golf champion, or enable you to do anything for which you lack skill, rank, or opportunity! You may say that God can do *anything!* Yes he can. He can even make Balaam's donkey talk. But he has done that miracle only once in history. Normally, the Lord abides by natural law. Also, he cannot deny himself; that is, he cannot do anything contrary to his own decrees. Even Jesus, when he was born, was subject both to natural and religious law. (Ga 4:4) Despite the real peril, Joseph and the heavily pregnant Mary, at Caesar's command, had to walk some 140 km from Nazareth to Bethlehem, where Mary was obliged to give birth in a stable and place her baby in a manger! Prayer could not remove from them the need to obey Caesar's command, or to accept housing in a cattle stall, but it could, and did, keep Mary and her baby safe from harm.

So, while the Lord no doubt does sometimes provide guidance from a single passage of scripture, be wary of placing more weight upon a verse than it can carry. But beyond a single text, there is perhaps a better way –

ABSORBING THE WISDOM OF SCRIPTURE

> Vain hopes delude the senseless, and dreams give wings to a fool's fancy. It is like clutching a shadow, or chasing the wind, to take notice of dreams. What you see in a dream is nothing but a reflection, like the image of a face in a mirror . . . Divination, omens, and dreams are all futile, mere fantasies . . . Unless they are sent by intervention of the Most High, pay no attention to them. Dreams have led many astray and ruined those who built their hopes on them. <u>Such delusions can add nothing to the completeness of the law; the wisdom spoken by the faithful is complete in itself</u>. (28)

Thus Sirach stresses the importance of the whole counsel of God, and of its rule over a single oracle. Indeed, the old rabbi sternly declares his preference for the ***law*** (that is, the whole Word of God) even over supernatural divination –

> No evil will befall the man who fears the Lord, but in trial he will deliver him again and again. A wise man will not hate the law, but he who is hypocritical about it is like a boat in a storm. A man of understanding will trust in the law; for him the law is as dependable as an enquiry by means of Urim. (29)

That wisdom of Sirach has never been improved upon. There is no guide so reliable as a thorough knowledge of scripture.

---

(28)　Sirach 34:1-8, NEB; emphasis mine.

(29)　33:1-3, RSV. The NEB reads, "A sensible man trusts the law, and finds it as reliable as the divine oracle." Cp. also 45:6, 8, 10.

AN ORACLE

Trusting in the word of God does not preclude you from hearing from God directly. Indeed, he may choose to speak to you by a _dream_, _vision_, _voice_, _impulse_, or some other revelatory means. But be wary! As Sirach said, many have been brought to real harm by being too credulous –

- like Charlotte, who read *Daniel 12:4* and felt that God was giving her permission to buy a car (which she needed for her church work), but it would have put her into ruinous debt. Happily, she heeded her pastor's warning, backed away from the purchase, and later a friend was prompted by God to *give* her a car!
- or Philip, who used *Proverbs 18:22* as justification (against all advice) for marrying a very unsuitable girl. Within two years the marriage collapsed, and the couple went through a bitter divorce.
- or Stephen, who split a church and destroyed his own ministry, by claiming that God had spoken to him through *Deuteronomy 28:13, 44*, telling him to take over the church from the senior pastor. He was sacked, and had to leave the town. [30]

Remember again the rule mentioned above: *a text taken out of context is a pretext!*

The author of the *Didaché* gave a sage warning to Christians in the early second century, telling them to be wary of always hunting for an omen or a sign –

> Do not keep on looking around for some omen, my son, because that will lead you to idolatry. Likewise, have nothing to do with witchcraft, astrology, or occult magic. Refuse even to watch

---

(30) The above names are fictitious, but not the incidents.

> such practices, for idolatry flourishes among them . . . Whatever happens to you, learn how to bring good out of it, in the knowledge that nothing can happen without God. (31)

The prophet Hosea, too, spoke scornfully about people being so desperate for a "sign" that they "*ask a piece of wood to give them a revelation! They actually trust a divining rod to provide them with guidance!*" (4:12). Then there are those who try to follow Gideon's poor example, by *"putting out a fleece"*.

But concerning all such revelations, such omens and signs, note –

- Sometimes God does speak to his people through sundry divine channels. (Jl 2:28; and cp. Da 7:1) So my remarks above are not intended to denounce signs, but rather to engender caution. God *may* guide you by an omen of some sort; but such things are more likely to be delusory than divine.

- Since the Holy Spirit is in us, we may rightly expect God to speak to us directly, giving us a word from heaven that is applicable to the situation we are facing.

- But do not gullibly accept every dream or vision as a revelation from God. It is easy to be deceived. Don't be foolishly ingenuous. Naïveté is sometimes nice; but more often, those who lack practical good sense will come to ruin. Test each oracle against scripture, and seek a critique from some wise and mature counsellor, whom you can trust to give you an honest response.

---

(31) The Didaché or *The Teaching of the Twelve Apostles*, is an anonymous instruction manual, written circa 100 A.D. It provided guidance to the early churches on several practical matters, such as baptism, the Eucharist, dealing with prophets, and the like.

TRUSTY COUNSELLORS

See *Proverbs 11:14; 24:6; 15:22*; etc.

Before you make any important decisions – especially decisions that relate to your spiritual life, to the church, or to your service for God – you should seek the advice of other reliable people.

But make sure to seek advice from those who really are counsellors. Only a fool turns to a fool for wisdom.

Beware also of those who may have a personal stake in the counsel they give. Be sure that you are getting objective, unprejudiced advice from a qualified and godly person. Thus Rabbi Sirach (*circa* 200 B.C.) wrote –

> Every counsellor says his own advice is best, but some have their own advantage in view. Beware of the man who offers advice, and find out beforehand where his interest lies. His advice will be weighted in his own favour and may tip the scales against you. He may say, "Your road is clear", and stand aside to see what happens. Do not consult a man who is suspicious of you or reveal your intentions to those who envy you. Never consult a woman about her rival or a coward about war, a merchant about a bargain or a buyer about a sale, a skinflint about gratitude or a hard-hearted man about a kind action, an idler about work of any sort, a casual labourer about finishing the job, or a lazy servant about an exacting task. Do not turn to them for any advice. Rely rather on a god-fearing man whom you know to be a keeper of the commandments, whose interests are like your own, who will sympathize if you have a setback. (37:7-12, NEB)

But even when you have sought advice from the best possible person, still remember that sometimes *"God sends counsellors away barefoot, and of judges he makes fools"* (Jb 12:17); which means that there are times when you will have to stand alone with the Word of God, drawing on the courage of your own convictions. In other words, be confident in your own sense of what is right, but not so much that you are too proud to seek advice. And when you do turn to a counsellor, make sure to choose the right one!

Who then should you consult?

A GODLY PERSON

> Rely rather on a God-fearing person whom you know to be a keeper of the commandments, whose interests are like your own, who will sympathise if you have a setback. (32)

A WISE PERSON

> If you love listening you will learn; if you lend an ear, wisdom will be yours. When you attend the gathering of elders, if there is a wise man there, attach yourself to him . . . if you see a man of understanding, visit him early, let your feet wear out his doorstep. (33)

That piece of advice I came across when I was in my mid-teens. I took it to heart, and across the decades I have constantly attached myself to people who were smarter than I, trying to absorb their wisdom. Some of them are still smarter than I, others I have long since transcended. No

---

(32) Ibid. vs. 12.
(33) Sir 6:32-37.

matter, I hunger to learn – from the old, from the young, from men, from women, from the learned and the unlearned, from anyone who can teach me what I do not know. The quest is lifelong, and, I suspect, will continue into eternity!

Yet there are times when even the wisest counsellors may fail you, and you will be obliged to trust the instruction of

YOUR OWN HEART

> But also trust your own judgment, for it is your most reliable counsellor. A man's own mind has sometimes a way of telling him more than seven watchmen posted high on a tower. But above all pray to the Most High to keep you on the straight road of truth. (34)

There they are, those seven sentries on their high tower; but they are looking the wrong way. They do not see the dust cloud of an advancing enemy horde. You are there too, on the ground, but you are looking in the right direction. The men on top of the tower keep saying that all is well, there is no enemy is sight. But you know better, and run off to sound the alarm!

Sometimes we can find ourselves in just that situation. All manner of good people may be telling you something, yet you know they are wrong and that you must stick to what you know is right. But again, be wise. Many people have been destroyed by stubbornness, refusing to accept wise counsel.

In this matter of trusting your own instinct, the peace of God can occupy the position of an internal referee or *"umpire"* (which is the meaning of the Greek word in Ph 4:7). This "peace" is not an infallible guide, but it is certainly an important one. However, it cannot stand alone, for as I have

---

(34) Sir 37:123-19.

already suggested, personal feelings are unreliable, and should be viewed with suspicion, or at least acted on with caution. Hence Paul adds two qualifications to the rule of the peace of God (vs. 6) –

- this peace cannot flourish in an environment of fear, or anxiety, but requires a heart that is fully trustful in the goodness, greatness, and wisdom of God; and

- this peace arises out of an environment of continual prayer, for it is when the soul is communing with the Lord that his will is most likely to be revealed.

GUIDANCE BY EXPERIENCE

The will of God is made known to us from both pleasant and unpleasant experiences. Some of our best lessons are born in failure (Pr 6:6-8; 10:4-5; 24:16; 27:12; Ps 34:19), which suggests that the Lord often allows things to happen that we wish would not happen! We expect good things to come to us from heaven (Ja 1:17), and we tend to think, when bad things happen, that we have lost our way. Which brings us back to the questions that opened this chapter – is divine guidance always available; does God wish to control every aspect of our lives, to make every decision for us? The answer would sometimes be yes; but not always.

Consider *1 Corinthians 7:25-28, 36-40*, which suggests that divine guidance is not usually available even in the very important matter of choosing a spouse. Paul simply says, *"Marry whom you will, but only in the Lord"* – that is, make sure that your spouse is a Christian. He was probably referring to *Numbers 36:6*, which gave a group of Israeli maidens' freedom to marry whomever they chose, so long as their husbands came from within the tribe. Neither the great lawgiver nor the apostle ever suggested that marriage cannot be entered until one's future spouse has been specifically identified by God. Therefore, it is not surprising if guidance cannot always be gained for matters of less importance!

Allow flexibility in the providence of God. He gives us a wide measure of freedom to choose our own path; seldom is there only one way that is acceptable. Just make sure that your choices are informed by scripture and arise out of a mature understanding of the issues.

BY EXAMPLE

"It is no secret what God can do, what he's done for others, he'll do for you!" (35)

One can often get a good sense of what the Lord wants to do by observing what he has done and is doing for other people.

---

(35) The title of a song composed by Stuart Hamblen, in the 1950s. Hamblen was perhaps the most popular man on radio in Los Angeles during the 1940s, as a singer and broadcaster, but he became an alcoholic. His life was nearly destroyed, until, in 1949, during a Billy Graham Crusade, he became a Christian. He was at once delivered from his craving for alcohol. The singer George Beverley Shea told this story about him – "Stuart Hamblen had accepted Christ at the Los Angeles meetings and he'd done some movies with John Wayne. One day, the story goes, John Wayne was walking along Hollywood Boulevard and the two met up. John Wayne had read about Stuart's conversion and asked him, 'What's this I hear about you going forward at Mr. Graham's meetings?' They apparently talked for a while and then Stuart said, 'It's no secret what God did for me. If he can do it for me, He can do it for anyone.' And the movie star said, 'That sounds like a song to me.' I'm not sure if that's true or not. And so Stuart Hamblen sat down at his Hammond organ at home and wrote this wonderful song that I still sing today at Mr. Graham's meetings." Billy Graham himself once said about Hamblen that his conversion was "the turning point" in the Billy Graham Evangelistic Association's ministry, where, before Hamblen accepted Christ, the crowds were rather small. Graham said Hamblen was the No. 1 radio personality in Los Angeles, which drew in crowds. That evening, in Graham's first coast-to-coast television broadcast, Hamblen shared about his faith and sang/spoke his signature hymn *It Is No Secret What God Can Do.*" (From the eponymous Wikipedia page, and from an article on George Beverley Shea in the *Assist News Service*, Feb 1st 2013, with some modifications.

Nonetheless, remember that God does not deal with all his children in the same way. Hence Jesus warned Peter not to place too much weight upon God's purpose for John. It was enough for both men to follow Christ, wherever and however he chose to lead them. (Jn 21:21-22)

CIRCUMSTANCES

"Open doors" often suggest the way the Lord wants us to go, but not always. Sometimes "doors" are "open" by mere chance, or by satanic wile. Also, as Solomon said: *"Those who wait for perfect conditions before they act, will never do anything!"* (Ec 11:4, paraphrased)

Note also the sarcasm in *Proverbs 22:13; 26:13*, where a lazy man uses the tiny risk of a lion waiting outside to keep him from going to work. Some people can always find a "sign" of some sort to decide for them what they should do.

It is sobering to reflect on the naturalism of *Proverbs*, the lack of any kind of supernaturalism in the collection. By "supernaturalism", I mean the attitude some people have of always expecting God to intervene in every circumstance, always ready with a miracle, an omen, a sign. The *Proverbs* are certainly not anti-supernatural, but neither do they advocate surrendering responsibility to a miracle. On the contrary, the book enjoins its readers to search after wisdom, which will teach them how to live wisely and well, and it bases the good life upon adherence to a collection of sound and practical maxims.

Further, before altogether allowing circumstances to guide us, we need to remember this – sometimes, to discover God's will, and to do it, one has to act against all comfort, and, in the teeth of bitter adversity, risk all. Sometimes you must press ahead, though every "door" seems to be closed.

GUIDANCE COMES BY DIRECT REVELATION

As Spirit-filled Christians, we are privileged to have access to the charismatic gifts of the Holy Spirit, including the gift of prophecy (which includes the twin gifts of tongues and interpretation), for by them God is able to speak directly either to the whole church or to individuals within the church.

There are numerous references in both Testaments to God providing guidance by a miracle, either of providence or of revelation. (Is 30:20-21; Lu 2:26-27; Ac 8:26,29; 9:10 ff; 10:19-22; 11:12; 16:7; 20:22; 21:4; 13:4; etc) But let this stand for them all: *"Paul went up to Jerusalem in response to a revelation."* (Ga 2:1-2)

The question however remains: was Paul always so directly guided, and what should our approach be to such supernatural dictates? And this is where we often encounter a fallacy, not in the idea of supernatural guidance (which is biblical), *but in the expectation that it must or will always occur –*

- You will be misled if your motivation is one of seeking infallible guidance at all times, and always by a miracle.

- Do not abrogate your personal volition. Sometimes people seek personal revelations because they feel that their mind and their spirit are at war with each other; but remember what we have already seen above, that Christ has restored us to personal integration.

And here is another worthy rule – the Holy Spirit is seldom in a hurry! If you are under pressure, it is probably not the Holy Spirit that is prompting you; God is never caught by surprise; events do not suddenly overtake him and find him unprepared! The Holy Spirit will not get angry if you test whatever revelation has come to you. (1 Th 5:19-22) You are far more likely to offend the Lord by accepting without question every prompting, impulse, whim, dream, or vision that comes your way. He will be pleased if you show proper caution, and are careful to do whatever is needful to confirm that you are truly hearing his voice.

It takes time to learn how to distinguish the true from the false. (He 5:14) But here again is a useful rule – the voice of the Holy Spirit never brings the kind of conviction of guilt that crushes hope. Always, even in rebuke, the Spirit brings a promise of redemption.

PROPHECY

On the spiritual gift of prophecy, note that it is a <u>*church*</u> gift, set in the church, to be exercised within the church and under church discipline. (1 Co 14:4, 24-25, 29, 31) Therefore, heed these warnings –

- Never attempt to gain guidance from God by prophesying to yourself, for that is a quick path to self-delusion.

- Never accept as divinely inspired any oracle that is contrary to the Word of God. While a true oracle does not actually have to quote scripture, it must never *misquote* it, nor speak against any biblical command, promise, or teaching.

- Never allow any prophetic utterance, no matter where or how it is given, to have *absolute* authority over you. Rather, as a member of God's royal priesthood, you have an inalienable right to decide for yourself how you will respond to any oracle. (cp. Ac 21:10-14)

- Even if a prophecy appears to be sound, accept its authority only if –
  - the church approves, and
  - it is confirmed by one or two other reliable witnesses.

Personal, or directive, prophecy may be a great gift from God, a miracle of divine revelation. But, if it is allowed to transgress the bounds of scripture, it can also become a fearful snare, a pitiful delusion.

But now, let me come back to –

THE WHOLE BIBLE

True and continual knowledge of the purposes of God arises out of constant meditation in the entire Word of God. True wisdom comes out of knowledge of the whole Bible, for it shows –

- ***God's Nature*** – that is, what he is likely or unlikely to do in each situation.

- ***God's Promise*** – that is, what he has already clearly undertaken to do.

CONCLUSION

God speaks: by his word; by good counsel; through pain and pleasure; favourable and unfavourable circumstances; supernatural circumstances; common sense; and in other ways.

We can be sure of God's will if we have a specific promise in scripture. However, we may still need to personalise that promise in relation to our present need. And if there is no clear promise, then we should put together as many indicators as possible.

None of those methods is perfect in itself: the more important the decision, the more you should look for a combination of factors. The best approach is to reach that place of maturity, of fusion with the mind and heart of God, where your thoughts and decisions will naturally reflect what God wants.

Nonetheless, there will be times when you will need a direct miracle of divine guidance; so always be ready for God to intervene in your life.

Successful guidance is based upon a relationship with Christ that is strong enough to keep you secure, no matter what your present circumstances may be. If you are in a close relationship with Christ, you will have little need to worry whether or not you are doing the will of God.

An important part of this process is a willingness to admit that you have made a wrong turn, and to ask God's help to get you back on the right path –

> It is pleasant to see plans develop. That is why fools refuse to give them up, even when they are wrong. (Pr 13:19, LB)

Another important part of supernatural guidance is this: don't be in too much of a hurry; even Jeremiah had to wait 10 days (Je 42:7; and cp 23:18); and Daniel faced a delay of 21 days. (Da 10:13)

The two greatest principles are as important in this matter of divine guidance as they are in every aspect of Christian life –

LOVE

If in every situation you do the most loving thing, that which best expresses your love for God and for your neighbour, you will not go far wrong. Philip Yancey comments that this is the difference between true religion and magic: magic attempts to manipulate the gods, to make heaven subservient to human will; but true religion gladly submits to the will of God. [36] Even better is the relationship the Father desires to establish

---

(36) I regret that I have lost the source of this fragment.

with us through Christ, out of which can spring a joyous partnership together in building the Kingdom, both now and for ever!

FAITH

To be in the will of God is primarily a matter of faith. If I am surrendered to God then I simply trust that the decisions I make day by day are good, and that what I am doing is approved by the Lord.

When complete certainty is lacking, and perhaps even when you do feel certain, you must be as well prepared for failure as you are for success. There is always a risk in the exercise of faith: *"Unwilling to fall, will always crawl!"*

If you have seized the promise of God; if you have gained a revelation of that promise within your spirit; if you are bold to proclaim that promise and assert its inevitable accomplishment, then it is probable that the promise will prove sure. And the apostle's encomium will apply to you – *"I am glad to know that you are living as you should and that your faith in Christ is strong!"* (Cl 2:5)

SIX:

PYGMALION

God rescued us from the power of darkness and brought us safely into the kingdom of his dear Son, by whom we are now set free! (Cl 1:13)

You may have seen the musical, *My Fair Lady* – either the theatre production, or the 1964 film, starring Audrey Hepburn and Rex Harrison. *My Fair Lady* was adapted from an earlier play by George Bernard Shaw, who drew his inspiration from an ancient Greek myth. The ancient story is about a young sculptor who fell in love with a gorgeous ivory statue he had carved of the goddess Aphrodite (Venus). The artist's name was Pygmalion, and he yearned for his lovely image to become a living woman. He decided to risk all for love. So he placed a sacrifice on the altar of the goddess, and prayed fervently for a miracle. When he returned home, he kissed the statue, and wonder of wonders (says the myth), the cold, hard ivory did indeed turn into an ardent and beautiful maiden!

She changed her name to Galatea; Pygmalion married her; and they lived happily ever after!

The oldest extant source of the story is Book Ten of Ovid's *Metamorphoses*, [37] and across the ages the myth of *Pygmalion and Galatea* has been used as a striking parable,

---

(37) The *Metamorphoses* is an epic poem, comprising 15 Books, and was written by the Roman poet Ovid just after the birth of Christ, perhaps around 8 A.D.

showing how the most unlikely things can change, and how the most amazing transformations can happen.

The happy couple (says the myth) had a son, who founded a city on the island of Cyprus, and called it by his own name, Paphos. The Pygmalion myth, of course, is nonsense, but the city still exists. Paul (along with Barnabas and John Mark) visited Paphos on his first missionary journey. (Ac 13:4-12)

At the time of Paul's visit, Paphos was still most famous for its connection with the Pygmalion myth, and also for a renowned Temple of Venus, the goddess who was sculpted by Pygmalion and then came to life when he kissed it. That story was enhanced by another myth, which tells how Venus herself arose from a sea shell among the foam at the shoreline of Paphos. (38)

It was there, in Paphos, that a series of real *transformations* began, metamorphoses (to use Ovid's word) that utterly demolished the old myths and changed the world for ever! –

FROM DARKNESS TO LIGHT

God has rescued us from the power of darkness! (Cl 1:13)

When Paul and his companions arrived at Paphos, three great changes occurred at once –

First, a Jewish sorcerer named Elymas, who was an advisor to the Roman governor of Cyprus, opposed Paul, and was temporarily struck blind. (Ac 13:6-11) This was Paul's first recorded miracle, and it was then that his name was changed from Saul to Paul. (vs. 9)

---

(38) This scene was the subject of a renowned painting by Botticelli in 1486. The painting hangs today in the Uffizi Gallery in Florence.

Second, Paul took over the leadership from Barnabas, and became the *apostle* Paul, and began his true ministry. (vs. 13) The governor and many others converted to Christ (vs. 12), and soon, crushed by the transforming power of the gospel, the pagan myths began to fade into obscurity. The glorious temple of Venus, too, and the governor's magnificent palace, in time crumbled into dust.

Third, Paul and his companions became men who went on to *"turn the world upside down"!* (Ac 17:6)

It is a striking irony that Paphos, the very city most renowned in the ancient world for the transformation myths of Pygmalion and Venus, was the place where the real metamorphoses of the gospel were launched! –

> *From his throne in heaven the Lord laughs, and holds the kings of the earth in derision!* (Ps 2:4)

He still rules the world! He is still bringing people from darkness to light, setting them free, and making them citizens of his indestructible kingdom!

FROM DEATH TO LIFE

We were as dead as Pygmalion's ivory sculpture – *"You were dead because of your sins, and you were outside of his covenant; but now in Christ, God has forgiven all your sins and made you fully alive!"* (Cl 2:13)

In a sense, Christ kissed the cold ivory of our dead selves, and lo! life poured into us, and we took on his own glorious likeness. That is a transformation beyond anything the ancient world ever dreamed of!

It is God's promise to everyone who believes, and rests upon grace alone apart from any work of ours –

> *Even we apostles must believe in Jesus Christ, so that we might be put right with God through*

faith in Christ, and not by keeping some sort of law – for by good works or by obeying a set of rules no one can ever be made right before God." (Ga 2:16)

Are you still hoping to gain a quotient of righteousness by following a list of regulations? Do you still suppose that good works will build up credit for you in heaven? Do you trust in obedience to biblical laws to establish your claim to eternal life? It is all a lie! Not even the apostles dared make any such claims! Mark again Paul's passionate assertion: *not even he or any of the other apostles* had any chance of gaining eternal life by any worth, sacrifice, or achievement of their own. They depended solely upon the atoning work of Christ. By the merits of Jesus alone they gained a right standing before God. We too must resolutely set ourselves to trust only in the blood and in the name of Jesus. Do as many good, noble, and righteous things as you can, for it is right for every Christian to do so. But whenever we approach the Throne of God, whether now or on the Day of Judgment, our plea must be –

> Nothing in my hands I bring,
> Simply to Thy cross I cling;
> Naked, come to Thee for dress,
> Helpless, look to Thee for grace:
> Foul, I to the fountain fly,
> Wash me, Saviour, or I die. (39)

FROM PAUPER TO PRINCE

You have been raised up with Christ, so fix your hearts on heavenly things, for that is where Christ sits, enthroned at the right hand of God.

---

(39) From the hymn, *Rock of Ages*, third stanza; by Augustus Toplady. The hymn was written in 1773, and first published in 1775 in a journal called *The Gospel Magazine*.

Keep your minds fastened in heaven, not chained to things here on earth. Have you not died? Is your life not hidden with Christ in God? (Cl 3:1-3)

He means that if Christ is enthroned at the Father's right hand, and we are united with Christ by faith, then we too must be enthroned!

This is how you should see yourself in Christ – reigning with him – which means –

- **_Overcoming the devil_** – for we are seated with Christ in the heavenlies, beyond the reach of all the powers of darkness. They may attack us on earth – they may even *"steal, kill, and destroy"*; but they cannot finally rob us of the abundant life we have in Christ. (Jn 10:10)

- **_Overcoming the world_** – for did we not overcome it when first we defied its wisdom and its scorn, and embraced Christ as Saviour and Lord? And shall we not continue to overcome it as we cling to our faith? Indeed, *"this is the victory that overcomes the world, even our faith!"* (1 Jn 5:4)

- **_Overcoming the grave_** – for we know that death in us has been destroyed, and even if we die we shall live again. The grave cannot hold us. The stone cannot confine us. Nothing but dust may remain, but still what has become corrupted will become incorruptible, and what was mortal will become immortal, and we shall rise in triumph and to supernal splendour!

FROM OUTSIDER TO INSIDER

God ... has brought us safely into the kingdom of his dear Son. (Cl 1:13)

We should never again see ourselves as being like those people of old who could go no further than the outer gate – *"If you are offering one of your cattle as a burnt offering, you must present it at the entrance of the Sacred Tent, so that the Lord will accept you."* (Le 1:2-3) None but priests could pass through the gate. The shimmering light of the candles in the holy places were banned to the people. No one but the high priest could ever pass the veil and enter the holy of holies.

But now, for everyone who believes, the way into the holiest is made open by the blood of the everlasting covenant! No statement ever written has ever been more glorious than that!

What resplendence those on the outside of the tabernacle missed! But we are now in Christ on the inside of the heavenlies! –

> *The Holy Spirit used those things to show that the way into the most holy place was not open while the tabernacle was still in use. ... But now, dear friends, we are completely free to go right into the holy of holies by the blood of Jesus!" (He 9:8; 10:19)*

And mark this, it is <u>only</u> by the blood of Jesus that we gain this entrance. You cannot earn it by any sacrifice, nor buy it at any price, nor attain it by any sort of labour. It is the free gift of God's grace, which leaves us with nothing to do except to believe and receive the promise with joy.

March in boldly, bravely, confidently, expectantly, and stand in the presence of God! As our text says, *"we have been brought safely in ... and by his dear Son we are now set free!* (Cl 1:13)

FROM BETROTHAL TO BRIDE

> *You are betrothed to one husband, to be presented as a pure virgin to Christ. (2 Co 11:2)*

This is one transformation that has not yet happened. We are betrothed, but the marriage feast of the Lamb is still to come. That joyous festival is our immediate goal beyond the rapture of the church.

Our present life is a time of preparation, for on that day the angels will sing, *"His Bride has made herself ready, for she has been given the privilege of wearing a gown of fine linen, bright and pure, woven out of the righteous deeds of the saints."* (Re 19:7-8)

Notice the anomaly – it is *given* to us; yet we must *weave* it!

We have no righteousness of our own – it must be given to us by Christ; yet if we are *made* righteous it is only so that we can *be* righteous. What comes to us by grace, must be worked out by faith. Yet still we depend upon grace, for even the best of our weaving will be knotted tangles! – *"I want to be found in Christ, not having any righteousness of my own built out of good works, but only the righteousness that comes from God through faith in Christ, and depends only upon faith."* (Ph 3:9)

If you are among those who have been transformed by the gospel of Christ, so that you have undergone the divine metamorphosis wrought by grace, then this is written to you (Rev 19:6-9) –

> *I heard what seemed to be the voice of a great multitude, like the roar of many waters and like the sound of mighty peals of thunder, crying out, "Hallelujah! For the Lord our God the Almighty reigns. Let us rejoice and exult and give him the glory, for the marriage of the Lamb has come." ... And then the angel said to me, "Write this: Blessed are those who are invited to the marriage supper of the Lamb." And he said to me, "These are the true words of God."*

SEVEN:

YESTERDAY

In Christ we have been given redemption, and the pardon of all sin. ... And we, who were spiritually dead because of our sins, and because we were not God's people, God has now made alive together with Christ. He was able to forgive all our wrongdoing, because on the cross he cancelled the record of debt that stood against us, along with all its legal demands. (Cl 1:14; 2:11, 13)

Just over 400 years ago, Thomas Heywood wrote a play which has been described as "the apex of dramatic achievement during the early 17th century." It is titled, *A Woman Killed with Kindness*, and at its heart is a wife who has betrayed her husband. In one place, the cheated husband laments –

> Take from th' account of time so many minutes,
> Till he had all these seasons call'd again,
> Those minutes, and those actions done in them . . . .
> But, oh! I talk of things impossible,
> And cast beyond the moon.

Ah! Those minutes and "the actions done in them"! How much we regret them! How we wish to recall them and remake them! But is it really so impossible? Are they truly "cast beyond the moon", and beyond all restoration, all cure?

INTRODUCTION

Human beings, alone among life on earth, are able to remember and record the past, and alone are obliged to live under the weight of it – for good or ill. Likewise, we alone can and must anticipate the future, an anticipation that is heavily influenced by our past. Among creatures on earth, only humans are aware that each day is bracketed by yesterday and tomorrow; we alone know that death overshadows all life. And so we carry a triple burden, unique to us, of yesterday, today, and tomorrow.

This study focusses on the first of the burdens, our past. We wish, like the poet, that we could wind back the years, and live them over again without fault. But our past cannot be changed, because, despite those time-travel novels, there is nothing to go back to. The past has no substance; it exists only in memory. Yet that does not destroy its reality, for the past is an essential element in our being. Is there then nothing we can do? How can we cast off the shackles? How can we undo what has been done, and create a new future out of the desolate ruins of yesterday?

THE GUILT OF THE PAST IS REMOVED

In Christ we have been given redemption, and the pardon of all sin. (Cl 1:14)

Thus speaks our text. Can this really be true? Can even God change what has become part of an unchangeable history? No, the story itself remains unalterable; but God _can_ remove our iniquities from the legal record, and declare null and void all charges. He _can_ (as our text says) find a way to discharge all our moral and spiritual indebtedness, and bring us into the liberty of the children of God.

He can do this through the substitutionary work of Christ on the cross. The moment I believe in Christ, that he died for my sins, and rose again for my justification, (Ro 4:25; 10:9) that moment all legal record of my past is obliterated. I am declared innocent, free of all the charges that were once raised against me. I can walk tall, head high, soul free, made into the very righteousness of God!

Theologians call this the *piacular* death of Christ – that is, no matter how awful the iniquity, the sufferings of the Saviour were even more terrible, and sufficient to eradicate the foulest sin, turning crimson sin into holiness whiter than wool. (Is 1:18)

THE MEMORY OF THE PAST IS TRANSFORMED

On the cross he cancelled the record of debt that stood against us. (Cl 2:13)

God says he will forget all our wrongdoing – *"I will never again remember their sins and their iniquities."* (He 10:17) Paul says the same thing differently, when he declares that every accusation that stood against us in the law courts of heaven has been expunged by the blood of Christ, so that no charges bearing your name or mine can be laid.

But what does that mean? God cannot actually forget anything that he knows; but he can choose the manner in which he remembers. He remembers sin now only as a battle that was won, a triumph gained, a victory secured for ever by Christ, and through Christ conveyed to us, who believe.

The memory of the past has also been transformed into the stairway that brings us to Paradise, for our redemption in Christ has gained us a better status than Adam unfallen could ever have gained. God, in the marvel of his grace, has turned even sin into a doorway to a higher and better life. Had I not sinned, I would have had no need of Christ. But needing Christ, desperately, I trusted him, and he has now brought me to a dimension of magnificence of which even Adam and Eve unfallen could not have dreamed!

THE POWER OF THE PAST IS BROKEN

We, who were spiritually dead because of our sins, and because we were not God's people, God has now made alive together with Christ. (Cl 2:11)

God does take a frightening risk when he offers through the gospel such free and seemingly easy pardon. But he warns us against using grace as a licence for sin by reminding us of the cost of that grace – *"on the cross he cancelled the record of debt that stood against us."* My *life* required his *death*. My freedom came because of his pinning to the cross. My healing came because he bore all my diseases at Calvary. It is *"in him"* and in him alone that I can rejoice in the hope of eternal life and of heaven.

So here is the safeguard against using grace as a licence to sin. No one can deliberately continue to live wickedly and still retain a grip on Christ. We have life only in Christ, and apart from him we are dead and doomed to perish for ever. But we can stay bound to Christ only by faith, and faith will wither and perish in the face of wilful iniquity.

But how can anyone who is truly redeemed, and loves the Redeemer, do other than strive to please him? Nor are we left alone to struggle against sin, for in the gospel there is not only cure for the grip of sin, but release also from its power –

> Rock of Ages, cleft for me,
> Let me hide myself in Thee;
> Let the water and the blood,
> From Thy riven side which flowed,

> Be of sin the double cure,
> Save me from its *guilt and power*. (40)

The last line of that stanza has been the source of some controversy. When he first composed the hymn, Toplady wrote the line as, "Save from wrath, and make me pure." But many people in the 18th century read those words as an endorsement of the Wesleyan doctrine of a "second blessing", that is, of sanctification as an experience that follows justification. I do not want to deny people an experience that for them was deeply meaningful; nonetheless, there can be no serious doubt that we are fully sanctified in Christ the moment we are justified in Christ. (1 Co 6:11) Toplady was appalled at the interpretation that had been placed upon his words, hence in 1776, when he produced his own hymn book containing *Rock of Ages*; he changed the line to the words above. He wanted everyone who gave voice to his song to recognise that *"from the riven"* side of Jesus flowed both rich grace to pardon and mighty power to deliver. Hide yourself in Christ, then, and in him alone, and that "double cure" for a double ill will be yours abundantly.

THE THREAT OF THE PAST IS RE-WRITTEN

> *Christ has erased all the legal demands that threatened us. (Cl 2:13)*

Behold, the day that augured a wintry cold, and offered a bleak prospect, now shines brightly with a clear blue sky! The future that once looked so gloomy, because of the past, now gleams with glad promise of eternal delights! The law has no hold upon us, no complaint it can make, no charge it can lay, no penalty it can exact. Instead, there is now set before us a new promise and a new future.

---

(40) Ibid. stanza one.

What will that future be like?

RAISED TO GLORY – *"There is one glory of the sun, and another glory of the moon, and another glory of the stars; for star differs from star in glory. So is it with the resurrection of the dead."* (1 Co 15:41-43)

MADE LIKE JESUS – *"It is not yet clear what we shall become. But we know that when Christ appears, we shall be like him, because we shall see him as he really is."* (1 Jn 3:2)

ENTHRONED WITH CHRIST – *"Everyone who wins the victory will sit with me on my throne, just as I won the victory and sat with my Father on his throne."* (Re 3:21-22)

REIGNING WITH CHRIST – *"I will give power over the nations to everyone who wins the victory and keeps on obeying me until the end. I will give each of them the same power that my Father has given me. They will rule the nations with an iron rod and smash those nations to pieces like clay pots."* (Re 2:26-27)

CONCLUSION

With the past undone and transformed in Christ, then at last we may rejoice because a new day has dawned for us. The lost minutes are not cast over the moon, but are returned to us in a new life in Christ. The lost seasons have been recalled and remade into steps toward Paradise. And now we look forward to that happy day when Christ will come to take us to be with him for ever. Then indeed, will the past be forgotten and be remembered never again, for *"God shall wipe away all tears from their eyes; and there shall be no more death, neither sorrow, nor crying, neither shall there be any more pain: for the former things are passed away."* (Rev 21:4)

EIGHT:

PRE-EMINENCE

Christ is the express image of the invisible God. He has sovereign rights over the entire creation. By him everything in heaven and on earth was created, whether they are visible or invisible, thrones or kingdoms, rulers or powers – whatever exists was created through him and for him. He himself was before all things, and everything holds together in him. He is the Head of his Body, the church; he is the beginning of the new creation; he is the first to rise from the dead, so that in everything he might have absolute pre-eminence. (Cl 1:15-18) [41]

How stunningly the resurrection of Christ impacted the disciples! They had known him as a man, seemingly with the same needs they themselves had. Even Paul, although he had never met Jesus the man, knew the stories about him well enough – that he had been born of a woman, had lived, preached, and died, as a man. Yet now Paul can describe him in words of almost unimaginable magnificence! – creator, ruler, sovereign, invincible, indestructible, the Author of

---

[41] This chapter is similar to Chapter Ten of my book *Emmanuel – Part One*, Vision Publishing, Ramona, California; except that this chapter contains material lacking from that, and that has material lacking from this. But the text is so much at the heart of *Colossians* that I felt an imperative need to include it here.

everything, so that all that exists is utterly dependent upon him for its continuance!

How could the disciples bring themselves to use such terms about a person they had known – one who, like they, was sometimes hungry, needing sleep, able to be wounded, even put to death? Indeed, they could not possibly have used such language about Christ if they had not been eye-witnesses of his *resurrection*. He had triumphed over death! He had ascended back to heaven! He had sent the Holy Spirit upon the waiting disciples! They had seen both his resurrection and his ascension, and they had also felt the power of his endless life, and of his Spirit. (Ph 3:10; Ac 2:1-4) So, although they had once known him as an ordinary man, now they could not, even at peril of their lives, assert him to be less than the universal Lord of all. They cried with the once-doubting Thomas, *"My Lord and my God!"* (Jn 20:28) Critics who wish to deny that Jesus ever conquered death need to find another explanation for this astonishing transformation of the disciples. From cowering and shattered doubters, they turned into unquenchable worshippers of the same Jesus whom they had seen die on the cross. But now they *knew* he was alive, enthroned in heaven, and without hesitation they worshipped him as Saviour and King!

But there were some, the *Gnostics*, who wanted to give Christ a lesser status.

The Gnostics [42] endlessly craved esoteric knowledge about the layered hosts of hidden demi-gods. They needed to know just what sphere of influence each spiritual ruler had. Malign spirits and beneficent ones alike, they said, could be propitiated and turned into allies. By knowing each power's name and function, and by discovering the correct ritual, their

---

[42] See my *Introduction* above, *Christ Has No Rivals*.

help could be secured. The spirits were more powerful on some days than others; certain seasons were auspicious while others had to be avoided.

The Gnostics believed that each heavenly authority had power to prosper or hinder different human enterprises; certain foods and drinks had to be avoided at particular times, and taken at other times. Some things were altogether taboo; others by contrast were essential. Thus the body of secret lore became ever more ponderous, posing an increasingly impenetrable barrier between the struggling worshipper and God.

Such nonsense was anathema to Paul, who exalted Christ to the highest heaven, driving out every other imaginable intermediary. Yet, in a wondrous paradox, the gospel also brings Christ into the closest possible bond with the humblest believer.

Here we examine what Paul meant by his powerful declaration — *"Christ must have pre-eminence in everything!"* (vs. 18)

CHRIST: PRE-EMINENT OVER ALL DEITIES

One of the down-sides of our modern multicultural experiment is a growing multi-religious spectrum. For example, in 1993 nearly 8000 people attended a *Parliament of World Religions* in Chicago. Among the delegates were Christians, Jews, Muslims, Hindus, Buddhists, plus people from the Baha'i Faith, the Fellowship of Isis, the Covenant of the Goddess, the cult of the Earth Goddess (Gaia), the Lyceum of the Venus of Healing, plus other sects, ancient and modern.

The Dalai Lama was there, and at least one Roman Catholic cardinal. (43)

Since then, the Parliament has been re-convened every few years, in different locations, with the next one (at the time of writing) being scheduled possibly for 2015. In the meantime, all these religions claim an equal place under the sun.

Evangelical Christians have rightly denounced such convocations because they deny the exclusivity of Christ. The diverse religions accord him just one place among a multitude of other supposed deities, divinities, and spiritual emanations.

The early church was given a similar opportunity to place Jesus among the mythical deities of ancient Greece and Rome. They passionately rejected the offer, saying that they would rather die than so demean the Saviour. And die they did. Many thousands of men, women, young people, and even children perished horribly. But suppose those early Christians had succumbed to the temptation to purchase social respectability at the cost of merging the gospel with other religions? Then the church would soon have vanished, or at best been mixed into a muddy religious sludge, lacking distinction, force, or glory.

That ancient pressure remains. Christians still face demands to syncretise their faith into some kind of universal religion,

---

(43) The first such Parliament was held in 1893, at which a young Hindu, Swami Vivekananda, greeted Americans as his "brothers and sisters" and caused a sensation by a powerful speech, which included the words: "I fervently hope that the bell that tolled this morning in honour of this occasion may be the death knell of all fanaticism, of all persecutions with the sword or with the pen, and of all uncharitable feelings between persons wending their way to the same goal." (*Christian Century*, Sep 22-29, 1993; pg. 886.) But of course, the Christian view is that the only proper goal to press toward is the one ordained by God; and the only Way appointed by God to reach it is through Christ, who alone is the Giver of eternal life.

with a multitude of gods, and almost limitless diversity. The world happily agrees that Jesus may be **one** way to eternal life, but loathes the claim that he is the **only** way to find God. Tell the world that there are many pathways to Paradise, and you will be proclaimed wise beyond measure. Insist that Jesus alone is the Way, the Truth, and the Life, (Jn 14:6) and you will be scornfully denounced as an ignorant bigot.

For this ongoing rejection of the Saviour, and especially the impulse toward some sort of syncretic religion, there are two main causes –

- *A loss of vitality in the church*. Where the church is lively, spiritually powerful, throbbing with the resurrection energy of Christ, even the world has to admit that there can be no compromise, that the gospel must be either loved or hated, that Jesus Christ is either the Rock of Ages or a stumbling stone of offence. (Is 8:14; 1 Pe 2:8; Ro 9:32-33; 1 Co 1:23; 2 Co 2:16) But where the church is worldly, spiritually dull, void of divine power, lukewarm and compromising, the world either ignores it, despises its claims, or urges it to join other faiths and present a harmless social religion.

- *Despair at the condition of the world*. Surging population growth; ecological decay; collapsing agriculture; the failure of materialism; bewilderment in politics; continuing religious hatreds – these all conspire to shake the faith of many. People feel that God, or at least religion, has failed them. The gospel of Christ is no longer seen as an adequate answer to life's dilemmas, and people hope that some sort of amalgam of all religions might better serve their needs.

But we must stand firm in the truth of the gospel. (1 Ti 2:5; Ac 4:12; 1 Jn 5:21) Indeed, there is salvation in no other than Christ, nor is there any other name under heaven given to us whereby we may be saved. (Ac 4:12)

Yet we may rightly ask, "Why must we limit ourselves to Christ?" What gives us Christians the right to say that the Christian faith alone is wholly true? The answer is simple – Christ, and Christ alone, is _risen_! Jesus has been declared the Son of God with power by his resurrection from the dead! The Holy Spirit has born witness to his holiness, and to the sole right of Christ to be the Redeemer of all mankind. (Ro 1:4)

So we must heed Paul's warning, and ignore anyone who wants to judge us because we don't emulate the false humility of the ascetics. We refuse to worship the spurious deities of the Gnostics, or to heed their delusory visions, but insist upon the exclusivity of Christ. (Cl 2:18)

Hence Paul declared –

> *People claim that many gods dwell in heaven and on earth; they insist on the existence of diverse gods and lords. But we say, "There is only one God, the Father, from whom everything came, and for whom alone we live. And there is only one Lord, Jesus Christ, through whom everything came into being, and from whom alone we have life." (1 Co 8:5)*

So heed the warning –

> *The Holy Spirit has clearly shown us that in the last days some believers will desert the Christian faith. They will follow false spirits, and they will accept doctrines spawned by demons. (1 Ti 4:1)*

Which leads to our second affirmation –

CHRIST: PRE-EMINENT OVER ALL DARKNESS

> *The Father rescued us from the authority of darkness and carried us into the kingdom of his dearly loved Son. (Cl 1:13)*

HE CONQUERED THE DARKNESS OF DEATH

Nothing in life is as harsh and full of dread as the certainty of death. From time to time my wife and I visit the graves of our parents, and of our baby son Gavin. We stand there, filled with loving memories — yet probably nothing remains of them but dust. We try not to think of that horror of corruption, decay, and dissolution. We want to remember only life and happiness, anticipating the joy of the coming day of resurrection, when our family circle will once again be unbroken.

Still, the questions arise: "How shall we view death? How shall we cope with it?"

Begin by noting that in the midst of life it is good to be reminded of death. Indeed, I am compelled to confront it often. I have to drive to and fro past a cemetery that is on one of my common routes. Seldom can I pass that garden of graves without thinking that I too will one day lie in the chilly damp earth, confined in a coffin, weighed down by marble, decaying to dust. It is an unhappy but healthy reminder!

We should all find ways to look squarely at death, and to remember our need to prepare for it. Thus, when a Roman general achieved a great military victory (so the story goes), he would be granted the right to an elaborate procession called a Triumph. He paraded in a gilded chariot – but not alone, for behind him stood a slave whose task was to keep saying, "Respice post te, hominem te esse memento! ("Look behind you; remember, you are only a man.") And, "Memento mori." ("Remember, you too will die.")

Similarly, it is said that Philip II, king of Macedon and father of Alexander the Great, was always accompanied by two men. Their duty was to say to him each morning, "Philip, remember that you are but a man;" and each evening, "Philip, did you remember that you are but a man"?

I hope you never forget it. You are presently alive. But you will surely die.

EMPEDOCLES AND ETNA

Sometimes people have tried to disguise the fact of their death. It is said that the followers of the great philosopher Empedocles (5th century BC) deemed him so wise that they began to proclaim him divine. He enjoyed being elevated to the rank of a god, and grew unhappy at the thought that death would rob him of this accolade. So he cast himself into the broiling crater of Mt Etna and was instantly consumed. He reckoned that no trace of him would remain to disillusion his worshippers. But he was tricked by an irony of fate. When his disciples went searching for him, they found one of his sandals had been coughed up by the volcano and was lying on its slope. They carried it home sadly, realising that their master was after all only a foolish old man.

In a way, every day we all have to confront some "sandal" of our mortality – the setting sun in the evening; the weariness that drives us to sleep; our need to breathe, to eat, to drink; the death of a friend; the onset of winter; and many other things. It is a wonder that anyone ever has to be reminded of the inevitability of death. Yet, strangely, we are all prone to push away the fact of our mortality, and to be surprised when the Reaper's sickle cuts us down.

It is illuminating to visit a cemetery and read the epitaphs. They can display everything from laughing scorn to utter despair. But the unshakeable foundation upon which the Christian faith stands is the fact of Christ's triumph over the grave. No other faith offers such a Saviour, who became one of us, then smashed our greatest foe! Indeed his triumph was so great that he was able to say –

> *"everyone who lives and believes in me shall never die!" (Jn 11:26)*

HE CONQUERED THE DARKNESS OF DESPAIR

One of the very greatest of English poets was John Keats, who died in Rome in 1821. He was only 26 years old. He left instructions that his name should not be on his headstone, but only the words: "Here lies one whose name was writ on water."

Keats recognised the ephemerality of life, and that even the most renowned man or woman must eventually be forgotten, washed in and washed out again by the tide of life, like a shred of foam on an ocean shore. Alas, most of us have to accept that we will be utterly banished from memory! Will anyone know about you, or care, a hundred years from now? Ask yourself; how far back through the generations does your own memory take you? I suppose you know something about your parents, even your grandparents? But what about your great-grandparents? Do you know even their names, let alone any details of their joys and sorrows, their defeats and triumphs? No, unhappily, in this life our main destiny is to be forgotten! A hundred years from now, apart from your immediate descendants, who will care, who will even know, that you were born, lived, and died?

So we carry a three-fold burden –

- the memory of past failure
- the necessity for present toil
- the obliteration of the lifeless grave.

Into that darkness of guilt and futility comes the passionate grace of God –

> *You were once alienated from God and each other, full of anger, and practising evil. But now Christ, by becoming a man and by his death, has reconciled you to God, so that you might stand before him holy, blameless, and without any blemish. (Cl 1:22)*

Whoever has such a hope, such an assurance, laughs at despair and at death, and faces life with eager confidence. I live. I will die. They are not important. What really counts is that one day I will *"stand before God, holy, blameless, without any blemish"*, surrounded by joy for ever!

CHRIST: PRE-EMINENT OVER ALL DAYS

The two great gifts of Christ are *life* and a *future*, which then place upon us the duty of finding and doing God's will, so that we shall receive heaven's prize. Can there be a higher happiness, a more satisfying life than this? See how it changes the dismal sense of *"a hundred years from now"*! Yes, before a century has passed, we will probably be forgotten on earth, but the saints in Paradise will care nothing for earthly renown. The citizens of the imperishable City of God live in the presence of the King. The entire universe lies before them as their inheritance in Christ! Whatever fame was lacking in this world will be unimportant to people who are lauded by angels!

Here is the Lord's solemn promise. Even now, while the world strives to obliterate all memory of us, our names are engraved upon his hand, never to be forgotten, but always remembered with love, delight, honour, and glory! –

> *I can never forget you! I have written your name on the palms of my hands. (Is 49:16, GNB)*

The allusion there is to an ancient practice of tattooing on the wrist or hand the name or mark of someone superior, or someone dearly loved. Thus, soldiers would mark themselves indelibly with the name of their general, at whose command they were willing to die. Or, to establish ownership, a slave would be tattooed with the name of his master. Often, idolaters would carve somewhere on their bodies the name of their favourite god. And sweethearts, just as some lovers do today, would mark themselves with the name or image of their beloved. And in the ancient world, some Jews too (but not all), marked themselves with the name of Yahweh –

> *Some of the people will say, "I belong to the Lord;" others will call themselves God's children; while still others will write upon their hands, "Yahweh's!" and thus show that they are true Israelites" (Is 44:5).*

So here is a lovely reciprocity. The people tattoo upon their palms the name of their God; and God in his turn tattoos their names upon *his* hands! (44)

Many early Christians read such passages literally, and, as the 6th century commentator Procopius of Gaza writes, "They marked their wrists, or their arms, with the sign of the Cross, or with the name of Christ." (45) Perhaps Paul had something of this in mind when he cried –

> *I have scars on my body that show how much I am the slave of Jesus! (Ga 6:17)*

I do not suppose that we should do the same in any literal sense – that is, I doubt that tattoos are a useful way to identify oneself as a Christian – but we should certainly carry the mark of Christ in a metaphorical or spiritual sense. There should be about us such a demeanour, such a reflection of divine grace that no one can doubt who our Master is. But each one will witness differently. As the prophet said, some, more

---

(44) You may protest that tattooing was forbidden by Moses (Le 19:28). Perhaps that rule had lapsed, or was ignored, by the time of Isaiah; or perhaps the people understood it as applying only to pagan or idolatrous tattoos. At any rate, Yahweh himself apparently had no compunction about carving their names on his hands, even though, of course, he could do so only metaphorically, not literally.

(45) This passage is often cited by commentators ancient and modern, but I have been unable to track its exact source, except that it comes from a tract written by Procopius.

extroverted, will boldly shout aloud that they belong to God. Others will depend upon their godly lives and loving character to tell the world that they serve the Lord. Others still, will be most effective in writing their testimony. That idea is brought out strongly in the Hebrew text, which says, *"this one ... and another ... and another."* (Is 44:5)

At any rate, everyone who lacks the mark of Christ upon them in some way (Re 7:3; 14:1; 22:4), will instead be obliged to bear *"the mark of the beast."* (Re 13:16; 14:9; and cp. 9:4; 20:4) This is your choice and mine. Which mark will we bear? It will be Christ or the Antichrist. And the choice must be made now, for after the resurrection, it will be too late.

But now let us return to our main theme. Whether time endures for a hundred or a thousand years before Jesus comes again, and whether we die known or unknown in this world, still our names are written before the Lord and our place in Paradise is assured. That confidence in its turn pre-supposes one great fact: that Christ reigns supreme over time, and can and does control every event toward fulfilling the Father's ultimate purpose. In our affirmation of Christ, this is the noblest expression of our faith –

> *Christ is before all things, and in him all things hold together. And he is the head of the body, the church. He is the beginning, the firstborn from the dead, that in everything he might be preeminent. (Cl 1:17-18)*

NINE:

FULLNESS

> *God was pleased to have all his <u>fullness</u> dwell in Christ. ... The <u>fullness</u> of the Godhead dwells in Christ bodily, and that same <u>fullness</u> has been given to you through your union with him. (Cl 1:19; 2:9-10)* ⁽⁴⁶⁾

With extraordinary daring, Paul applies the same word to us as he does to Christ – *"fullness"*. That is, as surely as Christ possesses all the fullness of God bodily, so we too bodily possess all the fullness of Christ.

The statement is so bold that many translators prefer to use one word for Christ and a different one for us –

> *For in him dwelleth all the fullness of the Godhead bodily. And ye are <u>complete</u> in him. (KJV)*

> *The full content of divine nature lives in Christ, in his humanity, and you have been given <u>full life</u> in union with him. (GNB)*

> *All of God lives in Christ's body, and God has made you <u>complete</u> in Christ. (GW)*

---

(46) Despite its similarity to Chapter 18 of my book *Emmanuel – Part Two* (Vision Publishing, Ramona, California), I have included this chapter because the text is such a key part of *Colossians*. A comparison of the chapters, though, will show many differences.

> *In Christ, in bodily form, lives divinity in all its fulness; and in him, you too find your own <u>fulfilment</u>. (JB)*

> *In Christ the Godhead in all its fullness dwells embodied; it is in him you have been brought to <u>fulfilment</u>. (REB)*

Those translations, and others like them, all recoil from the idea that we Christians are just as full of Christ as Christ was full of God. I suppose they do this because the idea is counterintuitive; it doesn't match reality. So the translators soften, or even change what Paul plainly wrote. They prefer to make scripture conform to daily human experience rather than compel us to rise up to meet the challenge of scripture. Well then, what *is* that challenge?

Paul plainly wrote, *"The <u>fullness</u> of the Godhead dwells in Christ bodily, and that same <u>fullness</u> has been given to you."* Or as the excellent ESV has it –

> *In Christ the whole <u>fullness</u> of deity dwells bodily, and you have been <u>filled</u> in him.*

The Greek word for "fullness" is *"pleroma"*, which has in it a sense of extravagant abundance. A good analogy can be found in the image of the ancient "Horn of Plenty", which is part of a Greek myth about a goat, *Amalthea*.

The myth says that Kronos, who was then the supreme ruler of all the gods on Mt Olympus, fathered a boy child by his wife Rhea. The child was called Zeus. But because an oracle had foretold that one of his children would supplant him, Kronos was in the habit of swallowing each baby as soon as it was born. Knowing this, Rhea hid the infant Zeus in a cave, giving him into the care of a young maiden. The maiden had a she-goat, named Amalthea, who provided milk for the baby, so that he grew in stature and strength. Eventually, Zeus became strong enough to overthrow his father Kronos and consign him to perpetual imprisonment in Tartarus.

While he was still young, but remarkably strong, Zeus accidentally broke off one of Amalthea's horns. Later, when he had consolidated his power, Zeus rewarded his foster mother by decreeing that whatever she desired would flow out of the horn. Consequently, it became famous as the "Cornucopia", or the "Horn of Plenty". It is usually represented as an elegant and hollow goat's horn, out of which tumble a profusion of fruits, grains, flowers, and, indeed, whatever the seeker desires.

Now the word Paul uses in our text, *pleroma,* was linked by the Greeks to the Amalthea myth, and its cornucopia of blessing. The sense is that there is nothing parsimonious in what God has done for us in Christ, but rather is so bountiful that it cannot be either measured or limited! Perhaps Jesus had a similar picture in mind when he used the expression *"more abundantly."* (Jn 10:10)

Somewhere I have heard *pleroma* translated as, *"we have been filled full"* in Christ; the idea being that we are not merely filled, but filled to overflowing, and filled yet again. Jesus caught the same idea when he described his friends as receiving from God *"good measure, pressed down, shaken together, and running over!"* (Lu 6:38)

How is this possible?

The speaker just mentioned said: "Fill a bucket with tennis balls; it is full, but it is not yet 'filled full', because you can add many marbles to the bucket, and after the marbles, small bearings; and after the bearings, sand; and after the sand, water, and after the water salt! Then it will indeed be 'filled full'!" (47)

So, says Paul to the Colossians and to us, as surely as Christ was *filled full* (*pleroma*) of God, so are we *filled full* (*pleroma*) of Christ. There is a vast mystery in that statement, one that we will never wholly comprehend in this life. Nor can we hope to access *all* those riches in daily life. But let us at least grasp what we can, always striving to understand better what this *fullness* means, and to utilise more richly what God has given us in Christ. In this study, though, I want to focus on just two areas where the fullness of Christ is sufficient for the emptiness that was in our souls –

THE RIGHTEOUSNESS OF CHRIST – SUFFICIENT FOR YOUR SIN

Perhaps the most pressing question in life is this: where lies the source of righteousness? For without a sense of righteousness the peace of God will be lost, nor will the soul be able to sustain any hope of heaven. So pressing is this inner urge for holiness that people in every generation and culture have resorted to extreme measures to gain it. In scripture, there is a tragic and terrible example of this, found in the several passages that refer to people burning their children alive as a sacrifice to some god. (Le 18:21; De 12:31; 2 Kg 17:17; 23:10; 2 Ch 33:6; Ps 106:38; Je 7:31; 32:35; Ez 16:20; etc) (48)

---

(47) I have lost the source of this illustration. I used it also in my book *Throne Rights*, which contains some of the ideas presented in this chapter, although expressed differently.

(48) Awful as it is to read of parents treating their children with such cruelty, I wonder if God might not almost find more to commend in those people than he does in many today, for two reasons – (1) at least those people had an awareness of sin, a sense of their need for heaven's pardon, a heart to pray, even if it was to Molech and not Yahweh, in contrast with the heedless

The prophets speak with revulsion about how the people banged drums in the Valley of Tophet to drown the shrieks of their dying infants. Those parents, desperate to placate the anger of heaven, were willing to cast their little ones onto the outstretched red hot arms of Molech, and watch them roll screaming into the idol's fiery belly.

But how terrible it all was, how loathsome in the eyes of God. How could holiness be found in such merciless cruelty?

The glory of the gospel is this, that it requires us to abandon all self-effort to placate God, and to put all our trust in just two things –

THE WORK OF CHRIST

That is, both his work at Calvary as our *Sacrifice*, where he made full atonement for all our wrongdoing, and his work at the Throne, as our *High Priest*, where he makes unbroken intercession on our behalf. (He 7:25) Thus he has become the source of *"uttermost"* salvation to all who trust in him.

And then, secondly, we must also place full trust in –

---

indifference to God and the crass earth-bound materialism of our time; and (2) the terrible toll that is being taken of young life today through (a) the holocaust of abortion on demand, and (b) the growing number of single-parent families. Surveys continually demonstrate how deeply children are hurt by family breakdown, and what fearful consequences develop in later life in people who were deliberately abandoned by one parent or the other in childhood. At the root of both problems (abortion and marital collapse) there often lies an ugly self-centredness, people whose highest concern is nothing beyond their own comfort and happiness. The cries of children in the 21st century must sound as dreadful in the ears of God as did the sobs of the little ones perishing hideously in the arms of fiery Molech of old.

THE WORD OF GOD

Scripture declares that we are already made the righteousness of God in Christ. There is nothing for us to do except gratefully receive the gift of God, by grasping his promise and rejoicing in it. Think, say, about *2 Corinthians 6:3-7*, where Paul lists many extraordinary achievements and sufferings upon which he might have based a claim of personal righteousness. But he rejects them all, suggesting rather that when he approaches the throne of God he will offer nothing to the Father except the righteousness of Christ. Paul resolved so to fill his left hand and his right hand with divine righteousness that no room would remain to hold *anything* else. (vs 7b)

Paul had and wanted no other plea but Christ.

When he needed to impress the <u>church</u> and to establish his apostolic credentials in the eyes of the people, he did not hesitate to boast about his many great works. But in the presence of <u>God</u>, at the throne of God, he abandoned *everything* except the righteous work of the Saviour, depending upon that alone to give him the right to approach the footstool of the Almighty.

This raises the question: "How do you know that you are saved? Upon what do you base your right to draw near to God?"

Do you place your trust in some good thing you have done, some great sacrifice you have made, or some religious experience you have had?

Many people do just that, but our song should always and only be

> My hope is built on nothing less
> Than Jesus' blood and righteousness;

> I dare not trust the sweetest frame,
> But wholly lean on Jesus' name!

– Edward Mote

THE RESURRECTION OF CHRIST – SUFFICIENT FOR YOUR VICTORY

The world has never heard any better news than this: *"Christ is risen!"* To us who believe, it declares that both death and the devil are deeply defeated, and that in Christ we are utterly victorious! But, only if we choose to live in the energy of Christ's resurrection. This is a major key to overcoming the strength of our fallen nature so that we discover a new and victorious life in Christ – see *Romans 8:11*.

How can we do this? In two ways –

BE FILLED WITH THE SPIRIT (RO 8:12-16)

It is the peculiar task of the Holy Spirit to impart to us in an ever-increasing measure the resurrection life of Christ. One way he does this is through the supernatural channel of glossolalia (of which the Aramaic diminutive *"Abba!"* seems to be a synonym, a kind of epitome of what the glossolalist is saying, or of how the Father hears glossolalia – as a loving parent hears the inarticulate cry of an infant.)

Glossolalia, too, is like an echo of the earthquake that shook open the tomb of Jesus; it is a channel through which his resurrection power can flow into and through the life of the Spirit-filled believer. But note that the manner in which the language is spoken is altogether under the control of the speaker (1 Co 14:14-15); which means that it will have no value unless it is spoken with fervour, love, faith, strength, joy. (1 Co 13:1)

But even as Spirit-filled Christians, victory will not be complete unless we also –

TAKE UP THE CROSS (RO 8:17-18)

What a paradox: we must die in order to live! But in the economy of God there has never been any resurrection unless the cross came first. Note how Paul himself exemplified both cross and crown. On the one hand, what zeal, what faith, what victory, miracles, authority, and sheer dynamic **life** we observe in the great apostle. Yet on the other, what suffering, what sacrifice, what endurance and toil, what ***dying.*** (see Ro 8:35-36; 1 Co 4:9-13; 2 Co 4:8-12; 6:4-10; 11:23-27)

So Paul demonstrated in himself this principle – as surely as there is no death without first there is life, so there is no life without first there is death. (Jn 12:23-26)

Does that mean that you and I cannot truly experience the love and life of Christ unless we suffer as Paul did? No, for God demands ***from*** each of us a level of obedience that will be ***for*** each of us like the crucifixion of our flesh. This will take a different shape for each believer – perhaps for some, a burden of prayer, or of persecution. Or perhaps for others a burden of service, of giving, of love, of ministry, and so on. Hence Jesus said: *"Take up your (own) cross, and follow me."* (Mt 16:24-25)

But always, Christ is sufficient, and in his fullness we can each fulfil the Father's purpose. For indeed, *"just as the fullness of the Godhead dwells in Christ bodily, so that same fullness has been given to you through your union with him."* (Cl 1:19; 2:9-10)

CONCLUSION

As you saw above, some translations render the text as, *"You are complete in Christ!"* That is, as surely as Christ was complete in God, lacking nothing to fulfil the Father's will, so are we complete in Christ, lacking nothing to fulfil the Father's will. In Christ we are now, today, the possessors of *complete* salvation, *complete* healing, *complete* victory, *complete* righteousness, and possessors of whatever else lies in the Father's purpose for us and in his promise to us. Since that is so, then, as much as lies within us we are called to *believe* the promise, to *appropriate* it to ourselves, and to *outwork* it in daily life – for nothing of God's gift is a licence to sin, but everything is a pathway to realised righteousness and to successful fulfilment of the Father's will.

Someone may protest, "But what advantage do I really have? I still have to struggle against sin; I still have to work this *pleroma* into my daily life; I'm still burdened with the weight of a corruptible and mortal frame! So where am I better off than a person who has never learned anything about being "complete" in Christ?"

What advantage? Simply this –

- it is the difference between a farmer knowing that he has an abundance in his barn even if the harvest fails, and one who has nothing to fall back on.

- it is the difference between a fisherman trying to pull in a net on his own, and one who has a strong man to help him.

- it is the difference between a shopper approaching the checkout unsure if he has enough cash, and one who knows he possesses more than ample credit.

- it is the difference between a lone soldier knowing that his enemy is stronger than he, and one who can instantly call a battalion to support him.

- it is the difference between being uncertain of victory, and knowing that win or lose, still you will emerge triumphant in Christ!

That is because, even if we do sin or fall short of divine glory in some way, yet still we remain *complete* in Christ, and in him on the day of resurrection we will cast off every shredded rag of this corruptible life. Then we will truly be made complete, both inwardly *and* outwardly, radiant with the shining splendour of the Saviour, beautiful in holiness, *complete* and fit to live and reign with him for ever!

That is something to *know*, and in it to rejoice with unquenchable joy!

TEN:

CONTINUE

Continue *in the faith, stable and steadfast, allowing nothing to move you away from the hope of the gospel that you have heard. (Cl 1:23)*

The greatest name in Old English literature is the Venerable Bede, who flourished in the early 8th century. He produced an enormous output of commentaries, biographies, hymns, histories, lesson books, and translations. His greatest work was his *Ecclesiastical History of the English People,* in which he included the line: "It is better never to begin a good work than, having begun it, to stop." [49] He lived by that rule himself. His very last work was a translation of the *Gospel of John,* which he completed in the final hours of his life. With the task almost done, and his strength exhausted, he paused for a long time, until finally his young scribe said, "There is still one more sentence, dear master, that we haven't written down" – whereupon Bede dictated the finishing words. After a little while the boy spoke again, "There, now it is written!" "Good," replied the aged priest; "It is finished; you have spoken the truth." Shortly after, he died. His work was done. His life was done. He had not only begun, but had finished well.

God wants finishers, not merely starters! (cp. Lu 9:62; Mt 10:22) Hence the key word in our text is ***continue***. Only those who continue will win the prize. Drop out of the race,

---

(49) Ecclesiastical History, by the Venerable Bede; Bk. One, ch. 23.

and the prize will be forever beyond your grasp. How can we avoid this? If you would be found at the end of your life still serving Christ and the church, there are certain things in which you must set yourself to persist –

CONTINUE IN FAITH

There is some doubt about how the opening injunction of our text should be read. Should it be –

- *continue in faith* – that is, "hold fast to your personal faith in Christ"; or, as I have it above,

- *continue in <u>the</u>* faith – that is, "hold fast to the truth of the gospel."

Since the Greek text clearly reads *"the faith"*, I take the latter reading as preferable, even allowing for the special ways in which Greek uses the definite article. The reference then will be to the doctrines of the gospel, not to your personal belief.

To *"continue"* in this faith means (as Paul says), to be *"established"* – that is, well grounded in doctrine. This countermands the foolish idea held by some, that doctrine is unimportant. What nonsense! Nothing more profoundly affects your life than what you believe. Even truer than the aphorism, "we are what we eat," is the maxim, "we are what we believe." No one can ever do or be more than what he or she both knows and holds to be true. Without sound doctrine, religion becomes a thing of sentiment, superficial, hollow, fragile.

Then we are told also

- to be *"steadfast"* – that is, resistant to all other ideas, dogmas, philosophies, while remaining firmly committed to the gospel.

A curse of the present age is the debilitating relativism that prevents anyone from claiming absolute truth. Our multicultural society demands that equal respect be given to all varieties of religious belief. Yet who is so flaccid, so lacking in vigour, as the person who always sees all sides of every question, but chooses none of them? (cp. 2 Ti 3:7)

The only trustworthy source of salvation truth available to us is the Bible. It follows then that continuing in the faith means also continuing in the Word – that is, constantly reading the Book, and meditating on its sentences. Can a physician succeed, or a mechanic, a lawyer, a dentist, or even a chef, without a thorough knowledge of their requisite text books? Neither can a Christian hope to gain any expertise in life, let alone in ministry and leadership, without constant immersion in scripture. (cp. Ps 1:2-3)

Notice how John associated ongoing good health and prosperity with the fact that his friends were *"continuing in the truth."* (3 Jn 2-3) Indeed, the idea is so important to him that he instantly repeats it. (vs. 4) For us Christians, compromise with the truth of scripture is impossible. *"Let God be true, even if it makes every man a liar,"* is our cry! (Ro 3:4) We believe the Word; we preach the Word; we stand on the Word; if need be, we will die for the Word – for here is the truth, the whole truth, and nothing but the truth! As the Texas politician and former US Vice-President John Nance Garner once said – "Ain't nuthin' in the middle uh thuh road but yeller lines and dead armadillers!" [50] We should of course respect the opinions of others and always admit the possibility that we may be wrong, or at least not wholly right; but withal there is a need to know what you believe and to maintain the zeal to contend for it.

To the command to be established and steadfast, Paul added the need

---

(50) I have lost the source of this quote. Mr Garner died in 1967.

- to be *"immovable"* – that is, unable to be shifted from your hope in Christ.

The greatest glory of the gospel lies in its future promise. (Re 21:1-22:5) In this life, at best, we can but *"taste"* the powers of the coming kingdom of God (He 6:5); but then, if we remain faithful, we shall enter into our full inheritance, toward which the entire creation is straining. (Ro 8:18-25)

CONTINUE IN GRACE

> *Paul and Barnabas, as they spoke with them, urged them to **continue** in the grace of God. (Ac 13:43)*

We all began our Christian lives with grace – that is, coming to the Father as sinners, we gained his unmerited favour through Christ, and were loosed from our guilt and from the grip of death. That same grace is the key to ongoing victory. Yet many, having begun well in grace, think to continue better by good works. No doubt true Christians _will_ hate sin and love righteousness; no doubt they will yearn to show the beauty of Christ, and they will strive to serve God, the church, and their neighbour. But they will never presume to use those works to make some claim upon God –

> *You stupid Galatians! I told you exactly how Jesus Christ was nailed to a cross. Has someone now put an evil spell on you? I want to know only one thing: how were you given God's Spirit? Was it by obeying the Law of Moses or by hearing about Christ and putting your faith in him? How can you be so stupid? Do you think that by yourself you can complete what God's Spirit started in you?" (Ga 3:1-3, CEV)*

Paul was not very polite, but he was certainly passionate! Why? Because this truth is irrefragable – we cannot begin with *grace* then end with *works*! It must be grace in the beginning, in the middle, and still grace at the end! For indeed, you can be sure of persevering, only if you trust wholly in Christ, and *never* in yourself. (Ga 3:1-5)

A group of saints were arguing in heaven about who among them was the greatest trophy of grace. They decided to put the question to a vote. All were eliminated one by one until only two remained. One was a vicious criminal who was saved on his death bed; the other, a person who had served Christ across a long life, after conversion as a child. The latter saint won the contest! Why? Because, while the converted criminal may have been a miracle of instant mercy, the long-enduring believer was a better example of the magnificent strength of the grace of God.

So make yourself entirely dependent upon grace. Leave no room for any human work to surreptitiously attempt to coerce God into giving it recognition. We must, of course do as many good works, godly works, righteous works as we can. But never think to offer them to God as a basis upon which he should pardon sin or welcome you to his footstool. Rather, we <u>do</u> good simply because we have been <u>made</u> good in Christ, not to build up some credit in heaven.

There is, I admit, a paradox here. Many scriptures do tell us that we *are* laying up treasure in heaven as we serve the Lord day by day, and that God will never forget what we have done in him and for him. (Mt 6:19-21; He 6:10; etc.) Yet, at least in this life, we should never try to come before God with an armful of good works. Come rather with your hands so full of the merits of Christ that no room remains for anything else. (2 Co 6:7) All our confidence must be in Calvary, and none in our own achievements. If, in the world to come, the Lord chooses to reward some or all of those works, then that is his prerogative. But we serve him simply because we love him, and we are happy to leave our ultimate end in his hands. And that is true. But scripture is realistic, so it also encourages us to have an eye to the breathtaking rewards that are offered to those who serve the Lord well. (Ro 2:10; 2 Ti 4:8; Ja 1:12; 2 Pe 1:10-11; Re 2:17, 25-28) We therefore have a double incentive. We serve the Lord in dependence upon his grace, first, because we love him, and second, because we deeply desire his promised reward.

CONTINUE IN PRAYER

> **<u>Continue</u>** *steadfastly in prayer, being watchful in it with thanksgiving. (Cl 4:2; ESV)*

The Greek word used here is an intensified form of the verb "to continue", and it means "to continue with strong purpose". It conveys an image of someone forcing his way through a jungle, or trudging determinedly across a desert. It was applied by the Greeks to anyone who set himself or herself dauntlessly to pursue and to obtain a passionately desired goal.

Christian people must each set their own habit and pattern of prayer, for no single approach can be mandated for everyone. But no matter how one prays, or with what style, all effective prayer will have a quality of forceful determination, of persistence, of refusal to allow any place for the devil. (Ep 4:27; 6:11) Also, while we all have different temperaments, gifts, personalities, circumstances, style, and the like, two things are essential components of prayer – *"watchfulness"* and *"thanksgiving"*. That is, successful prayer requires an alertness, a warmth of heart, and a stern commitment. And prayer is not complete without expressions of praise and gratitude to God. Those ideas, and others, I will explore more fully in a later chapter. [51]

---

(51) See *The Chains of Christ* below.

CONCLUSION

On May 17, 1587, Sir Francis Drake sent this message from the English fleet, which was engaging Spain's Great Armada in battle. It was addressed to Queen Elizabeth's Secretary of State, Sir Francis Walsingham: "There must be a beginning of any great matter; but the continuing unto the end until it be thoroughly finished yields the true glory."

The smaller English fleet kept on harrying King Philip's massive warships and eventually drove them so far up the coast that the winds carried them right away from England, and around the top of the British Isles. Most of them were wrecked on the wild shores of western Ireland, and only a shattered few finally reached Spain.

Queen Elizabeth caused a celebratory medal to be struck, which bore the words, "God blew and they were scattered – 1588." She and her subjects had not the slightest doubt that the Lord God had fought alongside the Protestant English seamen against the "heretic Catholics" of Spain!

Whether or not God loved England more than Spain is debatable, but the principle remains true – God certainly does support and give victory to his servants, especially when they have a heart to persevere bravely to the very end of their earthly pilgrimage. *"Continue!"* admonished Jesus. *"Continue!"* commanded Paul. *"Continue!"* instructs scripture. *"Continue!"* cry the angels. If your steps are faltering, then now is the time to renew your vows, stir up faith, and resolve that indeed you will not be merely a beginner but assuredly also a finisher. And in the meantime – *continue!*

ELEVEN:

GLORY

God has shown you the glorious riches of this mystery, which is <u>Christ in you</u>, the hope of glory. (Cl 1:27)

What an arresting expression! How can Christ be "in" us, and what does it mean? That depends upon how one chooses to translate the Greek preposition *en*. Does it mean *"among"* – that is, Christ is "in" the Church in the sense that wherever the people are gathered, he is there, in their midst. Or, does it mean *"in"* – that is, indwelling each and every believer?

Many scholars think that the primary meaning *en* should have here is "among". Others argue for "in". No doubt Paul would agree with all of them!

CHRIST IN THE CHURCH

Here *en* is taken to mean "among". If Christ is indeed standing among the company of his people, then the church is vastly more than a mere gathering of Christians. Rather we must see it as –

- *the <u>Body</u> of Christ* – of which we are all members.
- *the <u>Bride</u> of Christ* – by which we are eternally united with Christ.
- *the <u>Bethel</u> of Christ* – in which we are all safely housed.

And if Christ is in the Church, then this is its guarantee of GLORY! And this glory is

- <u>Invincible</u> – the Church cannot be overthrown.
- <u>Indestructible</u> – the Church will be glorious for ever.

- *Illimitable* – the glory of the Church will never stop increasing.

But then, other scholars insist that *en* should be translated simply as "in" – that is, Christ dwells in each believer. It seems unnecessary to be so restrictive. Surely the word may be readily taken in both its meanings. However, in this study I do prefer to focus on the amazing idea that Christ does indeed live within each of us –

CHRIST IN THE BELIEVER

In what sense is Christ *"IN"* each believer?

Certainly not in the sense that we each possess a bit of the Saviour! If Christ is in me, then he is in me <u>entirely</u> – that is, the <u>whole</u> of Christ is in each believer, everywhere and at all times. That is indeed a *"mystery"*, because who can explain the wonder of all the fullness of Christ indwelling every believing man and woman and of each of us being complete in Christ?

Yet that is the incredible assertion of scripture!

Thus Paul says a little later (Cl 2:9-10) that just as all the fullness of the Godhead dwells in Christ bodily, so all the fullness of Christ dwells in us!

Wuest translates it thus –

> *In Christ there is continuously and permanently at home <u>all the fullness</u> of absolute deity in <u>bodily fashion</u>. And you are in him, having been <u>completely filled full</u>, with the present result that you are in a state of <u>fullness</u>*

> *in Christ, who is the Head of every principality and authority.* (52)

As we saw a couple of chapters back, Paul uses there the Greek word *pleroma*, which was linked with the myth of Amalthea, the goat, with its fabled Horn of Plenty, the Cornucopia. You will (I hope) remember that *pleroma* means basically to fill a vessel or a hollow place right up; or, by extension, to bring something up to its fullest potential. So, we who believe are truly *"filled full"* with Christ, indwelt by him, and therefore rich in glory!

Paul calls this revelation of the indwelling Christ a *"mystery"*, not because it is something still hidden, nor because it belongs only to a few special initiates, nor because it is abstruse and hard to understand, but because for centuries the Jews had thought that salvation belonged to them alone. But now, through the gospel, *"the mystery that has been kept hidden for ages and generations is disclosed to the saints."* (Cl 1:26)

That "disclosure" shows how God has always intended that –

- <u>*The way to salvation should be open to everyone*</u>, not merely to the Jews.

Indeed, there were several suggestions of this in antiquity. For example, every person who became part of Abraham's household was also brought into the covenant God had made with the patriarch, unless they chose to reject it. (Ge 17:10-14)

Likewise, a large company of Egyptians chose to find shelter behind the blood and to be numbered with the people of God. (Ex 12:38)

---

(52) The New Testament: An Expanded Translation; by Kenneth S. Wuest; Wm. B. Eerdmans Publishing Co.

Then there was the Moabite maiden, Ruth, who became an ancestress of Christ himself. (Ru 4:18-22)

Despite such examples, and others like them, the common view remained that full salvation belonged to the Jews alone. But Calvary and the empty tomb showed that the doorway to eternal life has always been open to men and women of goodwill, who have decided to call the Lord their God and to worship him heartily.

- *The nation would be supplanted by the Church.*

Does God still have a plan for the Jewish nation? Some argue that he does; others, that he doesn't! Paul seems to state that the nation *will* have an important function in the future (cp. Ro 11:15); but he declares even more emphatically that the church is for the present the true Israel of God. (Ga 4:22-31; 6:16; Ro 9:6-8) I am content to wait and see what the Lord will do for and with the present Jewish nation. In the meantime his plan and promise are centred on the Church, the Bride of Christ, and of the Church I am resolved to be an integral part.

- *The Kingdom is spiritual, not earthly, and eternal not temporal.*

Therefore let us spurn the bewitchment of material things, fixing our eyes instead in the heavenlies, where Christ is, seated at the Father's right hand. There is our true treasure! There is our eternal destiny! There we are monarchs for ever on the throne with Christ! (Cl 3:1-4; Ep 2:6)

AN ACTIVE PRESENCE

Know that Christ in all his fullness is in you, not *passively*, but *actively* –

> *God raised Jesus from the dead. If his Spirit dwells in you, then he who raised Christ Jesus*

> *from the dead will also give life to your mortal bodies. He will do this through his Spirit who dwells in you. (Ro 8:11)*

Paul doubtless had in mind the quickening of our dead bodies in the resurrection. But the verse cannot be limited to our emergence from the grave on that great day. Rather, the context shows clearly enough that he was thinking mostly of the work of the Holy Spirit *now*, helping us to cast off the restraints of our mortality, and to live every day in Christ, vibrantly, joyfully, and victoriously.

That promise is good for all Christians; but it should be especially true of people who have enjoyed Holy Spirit baptism! We who have had our own personal Pentecost should above all others be able to draw upon his life-giving, empowering, and renewing grace.

If I truly *know* that Christ is in me, the hope of glory, how can my life be other than transformed? How could I be content to stumble along, burdened, groaning, crushed by inadequacy, wracked by doubts, and vulnerable to every fiery dart of the Wicked One? God forbid! Christ is in me! I have a sure hope of endless glory! In his adequacy I am more than a conqueror; in his strength I can do everything that lies in his purpose for me; by his might I can overcome every foe, seize every promise, enforce every victory, and on that last great day march through the Golden Gates in triumph!

A MYSTERIOUS PRESENCE

How this indwelling by all of Christ in every believer is possible, and how it is done, we are not told. We know only that it is true of every believer. In that sense, it remains a *"mystery"*. But that does not make it inaccessible. Many useful things are a mystery to me. My knowledge of the intricacies of an internal combustion engine is limited, but I have no trouble driving my car everywhere.

Don't ask me to explain the workings of this amazing computer on which I am typing these words, and which connects me to the world! But I can use it well enough, both for toil and pleasure, for learning and for amusement. Similarly, I cannot explain how Christ is as much in me as he is in you, but I know that I am *"filled full"* with him, both because scripture tells me so, and because I am deeply aware of his presence.

What treasure that knowledge brings! Paul trips over himself trying to express the inexpressible, piling words one on top of the other as he struggles to impact his readers with the truth –

> *(God has chosen) to make known <u>how great</u> among the Gentiles are the <u>riches</u> of the <u>glory</u> of this <u>mystery</u>, which is Christ in you, the hope of <u>glory</u>. (Cl 1:27, ESV)*

As someone has said, this mystery is not just a mystery but a <u>rich</u> mystery; not just a rich mystery, but a <u>gloriously</u> rich mystery; not just a gloriously rich mystery, but a <u>great</u> and gloriously rich mystery!

Paul is eager for his readers to grasp this truth. He wants to drill it into their souls. He is determined that they will not treat it as a casual saying, ephemeral, hardly worth noticing. No! This is sin-shattering, life-changing, God-honouring, divinely-given truth! So hear it, believe it with all your heart, get it working in your life, this great, rich, glorious mystery – *Christ is IN you, the hope of glory!*

A HOPEFUL PRESENCE

Because Christ is in us, we have a sure *"hope"* – which is not a wistful yearning for something that might not happen, but rather a joyful expectation of the certain fulfilment of God's promises, both now and for ever!

And for what do we hope? Nothing less than *"riches of glory"*, heaven's glory, the glory of holiness, the glory of righteousness, the glory of limitless wealth; and when Jesus comes again, the glory of the resurrection and of our rapture to Paradise. It is glory today, glory tomorrow, and glory in the shining City of God for ever!

But these things are not independent of our active appropriation by faith –

> *I pray that God may strengthen you with power through his Spirit in your inner being, so that <u>Christ may dwell in your hearts through faith</u>!" (Ep 3:16-17)*

Did you hear that? Christ dwells in our hearts *"<u>through faith</u>"*! Nothing else is needed; but faith is surely needed. Nothing else works; but faith surely works. Nothing else pleases God; but faith surely pleases him. (He 11:6) So *believe*.

The revelation of this mystery that Christ is in you, and of its greatness, riches, and glory, calls for a faith response from you, the hearer. It is a truth so powerful, so energised by the Holy Spirit himself, that no believer should rest until he or she has grasped its reality, and can stand up shouting, "Yes! I know it! Christ really is in ME, and he is all my hope of glory, both today, tomorrow, and for ever!"

TWELVE:

IDENTITY

I struggle, so that your hearts may be encouraged, knitted together in love, and that you may discover all the riches of full assurance that come from knowing and understanding God's mystery, which is Christ. (Cl 2:2)

Just who do you think you are, anyway? Don't you know what you is? You ain't what you're not. So, let's see what you got. How you gonna turn failure into success? Listen up! You isn't who your friends say you are. You ain't what your family says you is. And you're not who you think you is – <u>unless you dig what the Lord God says you are</u>! (53)

Both the text and the American saying focus on the same idea – do you know who you really <u>are</u>? Why? Because until you do know just who you are, and what you have, and where you are going, life will never have any real meaning. Paul says that in Christ you can come to *"know and understand"* both yourself and God's purpose for your life, and from that you will be wonderfully *"encouraged"* and will gain *"all the riches of full assurance"*!

So let us "dig what the Lord God says you are"! And "let's see what you got"! And base your opinion, not upon what friends say, or family, or the devil, or even what you may think about

---

(53) Anonymous American.

yourself apart from Christ, but only upon God's word about you.

Here are some excellent affirmations that every believer can make – (54)

I AM <u>WHO</u> GOD SAYS I AM

If that heading is true, then you are not what many people think they are –

- You are *not* alone in the world, without friends or companions.
- You are *not* someone unloved and unlovable.
- You are *not* the failure you think you see in the mirror each morning.
- You are *not* ugly and undesirable!
- You are *not* lost and without purpose in the world or the church!
- You are *not* wicked beyond redemption!
- You are *not* too timid or anxious to become someone wonderful!
- You are *not* a person without any gifts or useful capabilities!
- You are *not* lacking, either in a destiny or an eternal purpose!

You are in fact *only* what God says you are – <u>*his new creation in Christ*</u> !

---

(54) Sometime in the 1980s, in what was then the Crystal Cathedral, in Orange County, Los Angeles, I heard Dr Robert Schuller preach a sermon with headings similar to those in this chapter. But I think my headings are different, and the body of text under each of them certainly is. Nonetheless, I want to credit Dr Schuller with a message that greatly encouraged me at the time. I may have forgotten the detail of its contents, but not its impact.

> *Anyone who is in Christ is a <u>new creation</u>, for everything that was old has passed away, and now the new has come! (2 Co 5:17)*

"All that was old has passed away!" – therefore, you *should* be saying of yourself –

- I was a child of Satan; now I am a son of God.
- I was a slave of sin, and all my works were death; but now I am forgiven and my actions are all touched with holiness.
- I was destined for hell; now my end is everlasting life.
- I was full of pride, malice, and wrath; now I seek true humility.
- I dreamed only of earthly wealth; and lived for this world alone; now I have God for my portion, and I look not at those things that are seen, but at those that are eternal. Truly, I AM A NEW CREATION!

But this becoming "new" depends upon actually *believing* that you *ARE* new! *"Without faith it is impossible to please God!"* (He 11:6)

Also, it is true only of tho*se* who are *"in"* Christ, which includes the idea of a close union with his *"body"*, the local church, of which he is the Head. Indeed, every person for whom it is possible to be an active member of a local church is rightly expected to join one. The church *IS* the *"body of Christ"* on earth, and it is surely absurd to claim a relationship with the Head of the Body without also relating to the Body. No young swain has ever yet carried only his sweetheart's head to the altar of marriage. It's a package deal. All or nothing!

But remember always that Paul is not talking so much about the believer's <u>practice</u> as about our <u>position</u> in Christ. Not an outward work of reformation but an inward principle of grace. Not an *achievement*, but an *identity*. The one should lead to the other, but they should never be confused. Only at the resurrection will the two become perfectly aligned.

But in the meantime, who you are in Christ as his new creation is the REAL you, whether or not you manage to live it out day by day! Believe it! Affirm it! Strive to live it! "I AM God's new creation in Christ!"

I CAN DO WHAT GOD SAYS I CAN

> *I can do everything through Christ who strengthens me. (Ph 4:13)*

He does not mean that we can do *anything*. Rather, we can do *everything* that lies in God's purpose for each of us – that is, I can do whatever he wants me to do, I can be whatever he wants me to be or to become. But in doing this, we must depend upon the enabling strength of Christ. Therefore, let us never emulate Moses in his stammering timidity –

> *"I have never been a good speaker. I wasn't one before you spoke to me Lord, and I'm not one now. I am slow at speaking, and I can never think of what to say." But the Lord answered, "Who makes people able to speak or makes them deaf or unable to speak? Who gives them sight or makes them blind? Don't you know that I am the one who does these things? Now go! When you speak, I will be with you and give you the words to say." (Ex 4:10-14, CEV)*

What the Lord promised Moses is equally true for us – *"I will be with you!"* Against that reality, so long as you cling to Jesus, and _know_ who you are in him, nothing that happens in this life can have any lasting significance! Like Paul, even if we are shipwrecked, beaten, stoned, starving, naked, imprisoned, still we cannot help but sing with joy –

> *If God is for us, who can be against us? ... Who can separate us from the love of Christ? Will it be affliction, hardship, persecution, famine, nakedness, danger, or a sword? ... Never! In all these things we are more than conquerors through Christ! ... For I know that neither death, nor life, nor angels, nor demons, nor the present, nor the future, nor evil forces, nor stars, whether at zenith or nadir, nor anything else in all creation, will be able to separate us from the love of God that is in Christ Jesus our Lord! (Ro 8:31-39)*

Observe how Paul clung to faith even when everything around him declared that God's promise was false! Instead of peace and prosperity, good health and happiness, he was obliged to endure *"affliction, hardship, persecution, nakedness, danger"* and a threatening sword. But still he rejoiced that God was for him!

Or think about Blandina (a slave girl, who was martyred in 177, in Lyons). Eusebius (Book 5:2) writes that she was "tortured by turns from morning till evening in every manner", so that her tormentors acknowledged that they were conquered, and could do nothing more to her. –

> They were astonished at her endurance, as her entire body was mangled and broken; and they testified that one of these forms of torture was sufficient to destroy life, not to speak of so many and so great sufferings.

Some days later, she was tied to a stake in the public arena and scourged, thrown to wild animals that tore her flesh, scorched by being strapped into a red hot chair, tortured again, several times, and then –

> After the scourging, after the wild beasts, after the roasting seat, she was finally enclosed in a

> net, and thrown before a bull. And having been tossed about by the animal (she was then put to death). ... And the heathens themselves confessed that never among them had a woman endured so many and such terrible tortures.

Blandina, and countless other brave men, women, young people, and even children died unshaken in their love for Christ and in their trust in his sure promise. None of them wished for their lives to end so horribly; nevertheless, they endured bravely. Their inspiration was Jesus, who set us an example. He knew who he was, and for the joy that was set before him endured the cross, and despised its shame, being sure of the crown promised him by the Father.

Nothing can discourage the person who *knows* who he or she is in Christ, and knows also that in the strength of Christ all things are possible, that they can most certainly do whatever the Lord has commanded.

I AM <u>WHERE</u> GOD SAYS I AM

God says that every believer is *"enthroned with Christ in the heavenlies."* (Ep 2:6)

At once we touch on a principle of war – <u>always occupy the higher ground</u>! This means that by faith you should position yourself where God says you are – with Christ in the heavenlies, enthroned by God.

The Greek Orthodox Church has a marvellous word that exactly describes who Christ is and who we are in him – *pantocrator* – one who possesses absolute power and total authority! (cp. Mt 28:18) In particular, it does not describe so much what the Lord *can* do as what he *is* doing. It is active, not passive. He is acting, and always does so, as the one who is Almighty. Never in weakness, but always and only in limitless power. Which does not mean that the Lord roughly sweeps aside every foe and every obstacle, that he behaves with remorseless might, but only that whatever he chooses to do, no one and nothing can successfully oppose him.

The Greeks got the word from Paul –

> *"I will be a father to you, and you shall be sons and daughters to me," says the Lord <u>Almighty</u>."*
> *(2 Co 6:18; the Greek word is pantokrator)*

The only other place it is found in the NT is in the Apocalypse, where John uses it 9 times to describe God in his *almighty* power. (1:8; 4:8; 11:17; 15:3; 16:7, 14; 19:6, 15; 21:22)

This is the same God who raised Christ from the dead, enthroned him at his own right hand, and now, in Christ, also raises us to the same lofty dominion.

It is hard for us to imagine the impact such ideas made upon Paul's first, very superstitious, readers. Having lived from the day of their birth under the oppression of countless dreads, and especially fear of the malign influence of the stars, their heavenly enthronement in Christ suddenly showed them that they had

- nothing to fear from the zodiac
- nothing to fear from demons
- nothing to fear from time
- nothing to fear from death!

But, you say, I am not on a throne, but struggling here on earth!

Yet once a monarch has been crowned, it matters not if he is absent from the palace, or at war – he still retains his royal power! Is the British queen less royal when she travels, say, to Australia, and walks the streets in ordinary garb, far removed from the pomp of her palace? Or, think about Richard the Lionheart (12th century). He spent almost no time in England during the 10 years of his reign, yet he is renowned as the nation's greatest warrior king!

Someone else may say, "How do you know that Paul is not talking about our future state?" John Wesley, the great 18th century preacher, echoed that idea – "This (enthronement in the heavenlies) is spoken by way of <u>anticipation</u>. Believers <u>are not yet possessed</u> of their seats in heaven; but each of them has a place prepared for him." (55)

But notice the way Paul uses the past tense in three places –

- "God <u>made</u> us alive with Christ" (vs. 5)
- "God <u>raised</u> us up with Christ" (vs. 6)
- "God <u>enthroned</u> us with Christ" (vs.6)

Are you *<u>already</u>* made alive and raised up? Then you are already *<u>enthroned</u>*!

Others say that in this life we have only partial access to the throne – we are only part-way there. But a king cannot be half-crowned, or half on the throne – it is all or nothing!

What is lacking is only our seizure of all that the throne means and offers.

Since the beginning the Angel of God has been calling the people of God to *"come up higher!"* (Rev 4:1) That is, carry yourself by faith to where you already are in Christ, on the throne, at the Father's right hand! This does not mean a life free of any pain or struggle – think again about Paul –

> *I have toiled harder than any other apostle. I have been more often imprisoned, whipped more savagely, and near death more often.*

---

(55) <u>John Wesley's Explanatory Notes on the Whole Bible</u> – *Ephesians 2:6*. The emphasis is mine.

> *Five times I suffered thirty-nine lashes by the Jews; three times I was flogged by the Romans; and once I was stoned. I have been in three shipwrecks, and once I spent twenty-four hours in the water. ... I have been in danger from floods and in danger from robbers, in danger from my own people and in danger from strangers; in danger in the cities, and in danger in the country. I have faced danger on the high seas, and danger from false friends. I have worked to exhaustion, often going without sleep. I have endured hunger and thirst, and my life has been imperilled by a lack of food, shelter, and even clothing! (2 Co 11:23-28)*

Was he a defeated man? Did he lack faith? Was Satan walking all over him? Hardly! In the middle of all those miseries Paul pronounced himself more than a conqueror in Christ! He knew that he was a member of God's new creation, enthroned with Christ in the heavenlies, and that he could not finally be overthrown! So let this, too, be your constant bold vision and brave affirmation – "I am where God says I am, on the throne with Christ in the heavenlies!" Then, even if you have to endure all the hardships of Paul, and more, you will still be a winner!

I AM <u>WHAT</u> GOD SAYS I AM

Immeasurably wealthy, limitlessly strong, incredibly able, and entirely whole!

The trouble is, of course, we're not like that at all! Yet there are many scriptures that do say we are all those things –

> *God has blessed us with every spiritual blessing in Christ (Ep 1:3) ... We are made strong with the very strength of Christ (Cl 1:11; Ep 6:10) ... We can do anything in Christ (Ph 4:13) ...*

> *Everything is possible for the one who believes (Mk 9:23) ... We are dead to sin and alive to God (Ro 6:11) ... God's immeasurably great power is at work in us (Ep 1:19-20) – and many more!*

So how can we resolve this paradox? We have to accept two realities –

1. <u>We live in an imperfect world, so that things don't always happen as we wish they would</u>.

Think about Paul again, who, if a choice had been given him, would surely have preferred peace and prosperity to starvation and torture. But he had to accept, and indeed embrace, what life and the purpose of God thrust upon him.

And consider passages like these, among many others –

> *Then I said, "What hurts me most is this – that God is no longer powerful." (Ps 77:10, GNB)*

> *O God, you keep on deceiving me. You are like a brook that promises refreshment, but then dries up in summer. (Je 15:18)*

Is it right to say that God is a liar? Is it true that he is no longer powerful? Of course not. But we are people looking through a dark glass, catching only glimpses of reality, and living in an unfair and tumultuous world. Life frequently fails to work out as we think it should. Things happen that we do not like and do not want. (Ec 9:12-13) So long as we are in this mortal frame, we must remain in a state of imperfection. Nonetheless –

2. <u>The promise of God remains true, and I must and will echo the apostle</u> –

> *When God wanted to prove for certain that his promise to his people could not be broken, he*

> *made a vow. God cannot tell lies! And so his promises and vows are two things that can never be changed. (He 6:17-18)*

Likewise, we too must insist upon the truth of God's word. Whatever storms we may be sailing through, we can find an epicentre of calm in the unshakable promises of God. So let us go through that previous list again, and personalise it –

> *God has already blessed <u>me</u> with every spiritual blessing in Christ (Ep 1:3) ... <u>I</u> am now made strong with the very strength of Christ (Cl 1:11; Ep 6:10) ... <u>I</u> can do anything in Christ (Ph 4:13) ... Everything is possible if I set myself to <u>believe</u> (Mk 9:23) ... <u>I</u> am dead to sin and alive to God (Ro 6:11) ... God's immeasurably great power is at work in <u>me</u>! (Ep 1:19-20) – and many more!*

Is it permissible to change scripture like that? Most certainly it is. Scripture itself tells us to do this – *"God has said, 'I will never leave you nor forsake you;' so then, <u>we should boldly say</u>, 'The Lord is my helper; I will not fear; what can man do to me!'"* (He 13:5-6) Do you observe the process? God makes a promise. In response to it, we boldly affirm that it is true; and we do that by re-stating the promise in our own words, applying it to our present need.

So too, with every promise of God, do the same – re-state the promise and personalise it, never doubting that in God's time it will be fully realised.

Grasp as much of the heavenly reality as you can now, in this life, while always rejoicing in the extravagance that is yet to come! And it is indeed true, for even if we don't gain our heart's desire in this present world, we most assuredly will in Paradise! And in the meantime, so long as we have one breath remaining, we should strive to see the promise fulfilled now!

Who then are you? You should answer –

- "I am WHO God says I am (his new creation in Christ);
- "I am WHAT God says I am (more than a conqueror in Christ);
- "I am WHERE God says I am (enthroned with Christ in the heavenlies); and therefore,
- "I can DO all that God says I can do, and BE all that God says I can be!"

THIRTEEN:

BAPTISM

You were buried with Christ in baptism, and you have risen with him too, through your faith in the power of God, who also raised Jesus from the dead. (Cl 2:12)

In the Great Commission (Mt 28:18-20) water baptism is set against a thrilling and majestic background. The drama began with the passion of Christ a few weeks earlier, followed by his staggering resurrection and emergence from the tomb and his several striking post-resurrection appearances to different people. Then the disciples were commanded by Jesus to walk 150km from Jerusalem to a certain mountain in Galilee, where he promised to show himself to them. More than 500 people trekked to the top of the mountain, (1 Co 15:6) an arduous and wearying climb. (56)

All the time, they were asking one another, "What will the risen Christ say and do; what miracle will he show us; what marvellous sign will he display; what prodigy will he perform?"

How excited they must all have been when he appeared to them!

Yet, probably to the great disappointment of many who were there, he did no more than commission them to go out into the world, preach the gospel, and baptise those who believe!

---

(56) Probably Mount Tabor, 1843 feet or 560 metres high.

Why did he not commission them in Jerusalem? Why did he impose upon them that long and seemingly unnecessary walk to Galilee, and the toilsome climb to the top of the mountain? Why the frustrations of the wearying walk back again, after such a brief encounter with Christ?

Many reasons for those remarkable scenes might be found; but among them, Christ certainly intended to highlight the importance of baptism as a part of Christian initiation. Jesus was determined that they would never forget his two commands – go and ***preach***; go and ***baptise*** !

Baptism cannot be relegated to an afterthought of Christian life. Christ himself maximised its importance, and thus enhanced its value in the life of faith. He tried to ensure that the church could never sensibly treat baptism as a mere ritual. By surrounding baptism with majesty, dignity, spiritual power, and fervour, he intended to make such an impact that baptism would ever after maintain a vital place in the life of each Christian and of the entire church. And so it has. Christians have diverse views about baptism, (57) but there is no denomination that does not practise it in some form or other!

A GREAT POWER

There is nothing insignificant about baptism; it has extraordinary importance in the life of the church. Does anyone still doubt that? Then, beyond the dramatic setting of the command to go and baptise everyone who believes, consider how Jesus himself associated baptism with a declaration of *"All power ... !"* (Mt 28:18)

---

(57) Is it essential for salvation, or not; by sprinkling or immersion; for children or only those old enough truly to repent and believe; in running or still water; is it a sacrament (conveying divine grace) or an ordinance (merely a memorial); and the like?

Every baptised believer can and should merge with that glorious might!

It also includes the idea that everything belongs to Christ, and that he can do whatever he pleases, including turning the simple act of baptism into a dynamic spiritual force!

At once we confront a strange paradox. How can it be that this seemingly innocuous and apparently irrelevant ceremony of plunging people into water, or even just sprinkling them, is one of the major foundation stones of the Christian church? How can it be a channel of the very life and power of the risen Christ? Yet, so great is its value, that *where there is no baptism, there is no church*!

Some have tried to argue against that proposition, but it is surely true. (see Mt 28:5-7, 16-20; Mk 16:15-16; and cp. Ac 2:37-3; He 6:1-2; etc.)

Here then is one of the fundamental doctrines of the gospel, which should stand at the very beginning of true Christian life. (cp. He 6:1-2, *"teaching about baptisms"*)

It is the first doorway for a new Christian into the multiplied blessings of the Father. [58] And if this was not your experience when you were baptised, whether as an infant, child, teenager, or adult, then reach back in faith and grasp it now in Jesus' name! There is extraordinary spiritual power inherent in the waters of baptism for those who believe the promise of God

---

(58) I am making no argument here for one method of baptism above another. My personal preference is for baptism of believers only, by full immersion (I was, after all, brought up in the Baptist Church!). But I freely allow that there are other ways of reading and interpreting the biblical injunctions concerning baptism. The *form* of baptism has less importance than the *faith* of the person looking back on it. Were you sprinkled as a child? Look back to that. Were you immersed as a believer? Look back to that. *All* who are baptised should embrace their baptism, believe the promise of God, and rise up to walk in *"newness of life."* (Ro 6:4)

boldly and embrace it joyfully. This aspect, lively faith, is emphasised by Paul in our text. (Cl 2:12) Without it, baptism is a futile and probably ridiculous public bath. But with faith, and through faith, says Paul, baptism gives us access to the resurrection life of Christ and to all the power of God!

The same ideas are expressed by Paul again in *Romans 6:4b, 17*, where he says that we who have been baptised were raised to new life by *"the glory of the Father"* (vs 4). But once again, the promise belongs only to those who believe and *"obey"* (vs 17). There is a Bible way to gain the blessings of the Bible, and no other will do. So, this *"new life"* belongs to people who are *"baptised"*, and it belongs to *"all"* of them (vs. 3).

Note that the water has no power in itself; it is no more than a means ordained by God whereby, through faith, we may absorb his divine strength. The water remains just water; but the entire ceremony, wrapped around with worship and the word, energised by faith and the Spirit, opens the way to the same power that raised Jesus from the dead! (Cl 2:12)

A GREAT POSSESSION

The Greek text of the Great Commission reads, *"baptise into the name ..."* (vs. 19-20a)

It is actually a Hebrew (not Greek) idiom, which has the meaning, *"into possession of the name"* (cp. Ps 124:8; Is 30:27-28) –

> *Behold, the Name of the Lord comes from afar. It is burning with anger, and the smoke of his fury rises thickly. His mouth is full of fury, and his tongue is like a devouring fire. His breath is like a river in flood, carrying everything before it. He shakes the nations in a sieve, to separate those that are destined for ruin. He places hooks in the jaws of the people and drags them off to destruction."*

There, as in many other places in scripture, the Name of the Lord is personalised, it stands as a surrogate for God. All that the Lord is, so is his name. To possess one, is to hold the other. In the case of baptism, it means that our obedience to the command should bring us into a new kind of union with the Godhead, for we are baptised –

INTO THE NAME OF THE FATHER

That is, baptism marks and publicly announces us as the children of God who may rightly reckon that they merit all his favour. Being baptised, and called his children, we have a claim on all that his fatherhood means – nurture, care, supply, protection, training, discipline, inheritance, and much more.

INTO THE NAME OF THE SON

By baptism we are brought into spiritual union with the death, burial, and resurrection of Christ, so that we may deem ourselves dead, buried, risen, ascended, and now enthroned with Christ and in Christ and for Christ for ever. (Ep 2:4-6; Ro 6:5-11) From this advantageous position we may exercise spiritual authority over all the principalities of darkness, treading on *"serpents and scorpions"* and voiding their power, so that *"nothing can by any means hurt us."* (Lu 10:19, KJV)

INTO THE NAME OF THE SPIRIT

Baptism marks us as the true temples of the Holy Spirit, fit now to be equipped with supernatural power. As Peter said, in the first Christian sermon ever preached –

> *Repent, and be baptised every one of you in the name of Jesus Christ, for the remission of your sins, <u>and you will receive the gift of the Holy Spirit.</u> (Ac 2:38)*

To those who have received the heavenly gift comes the right to seek and to use the diverse charismata of the Spirit, (1 Co

12:7-11; 14:1) and to embrace one of the many ministries and service functions that are available in the local church.

A GREAT PROMISE

Those who are baptised in water in fulfilment of the Great Commission receive also this promise from the risen Christ – *"I will be with you <u>day by day</u>."* (Mt 28:20)

The usual translation, *"always,"* is too distant, too abstract and vague. Jesus' actual promise was concrete, dramatic, specific – *"each day, every day, all day!"* Which he also said would continue, *"to the end of the age."* So there is also an eternal dimension in baptism – it is an affirmation of our confidence that time will one day end and the everlasting kingdom of God will begin.

In conjunction with this, baptism is an affirmation that death will be destroyed, for whether on this side of the grave or the other, the promise remains sure – *"<u>I am and always will be with you</u>!"*

A GREAT PASSION

By baptism we are **<u>crucified</u>** with Christ. (Cl 2:12; and cp. Ro 6:3) That is, we publicly show our confidence in the value of his death, and we are brought into a mystical union with that death. By faith, in baptism something <u>dies</u> in us (Ro 6:6-7) and we are freed from sin, both its guilt and its power. It is a kind of consummation of our new birth, in that it brings into public view what was formerly internal. I do not mean that a person must be baptised to be saved. On the contrary, any person who truly believes in Christ at once receives both the pardon of God, and access to the resurrection power of Christ. But baptism seals this, and becomes a catalyst to release the full dimension of salvation into the believer's life.

Then, by baptism we are **<u>buried</u>** with Christ (vs 4). That is, all that belongs to the old is carried down into the grave. But, what about later sin? Faith constantly renews baptism, as though I had been baptised but a moment ago, and my sins buried but a moment ago, and myself now risen to endless life in holiness and in Christ.

Then, by baptism we are **_raised_** with Christ (vs 4b-5), sharing in his resurrection life and in his promise of Paradise. The *"glory of the Father"* (vs. 4) is at work in baptism! It is the glory of –

- **_Victory Over Death_** (vs 8-9)

Baptism is a re-enactment of the Passion of Christ, with its promise of a future resurrection and enthronement in the heavenlies! But notice the *"if"* in vs 5a, 8a. I suppose I cannot say that the unbaptised have no access to the life of Christ, although some would construe the *"if"* to mean just that. But I *will* say that people who refuse baptism do deny themselves a marvellous channel of the richest blessings of *"the glory of the Father"* (vs. 4). It is worth noting that the phrase *"the glory of the Father"* is used only here and in the two places where Jesus talks about the day when he will come again *"with all his holy angels and in the glory of the Father."* (Mk 8:38; Mt 16:27) So baptism shines with the radiant splendour of that marvellous coming day, reflects its magnificence, and helps to make each baptisand ready for it!

- **_Victory Over Sin_** (vs 10-11)

The emphasis in baptism is always upon *"life"* and victory over sin (vs 4b, 11b). There are two keys to this victory –

   1. _Commitment_ – that is, a resolve to live a new kind of life in Christ and to abandon the old.

   2. _Confession_ – that is, a bold and firm affirmation, as you *"reckon yourself dead indeed to sin, but alive to God in Christ Jesus"*.

CONCLUSION

Here then is a summary of the meaning of baptism – *"you were buried with Christ in baptism, and risen with him too."* (Cl 2:12)

Buried with Christ.

Do you believe that? All that belonged to your old self – its fears, doubts, angers, corruption, rebellion against God, and the like – are now deeply buried, to be left behind as you emerged from the waters into a new life in Christ. It takes an act of faith to make it a reality. And that faith has to be sustained, perhaps renewed from time to time, for the old nature is prone to resurrect itself. We find ourselves sometimes like the child in the fairy tale –

> Once upon a time there was a stubborn child who never did what his mother told him to do. The dear Lord, therefore, did not look kindly upon him and let him become sick. No doctor could cure him, and in a short time he lay on his death bed. After he was lowered into his grave and covered with earth, one of his little arms emerged and reached up into the air. They pushed it back down and covered the grave with fresh earth, but that did not help. The little arm kept popping out. So the child's mother had to go to the grave herself and smack the little arm with a switch. After she had done that, the arm withdrew, and then, for the first time, the child had peace beneath the earth. [59]

---

(59) The Complete Fairy Tales of the Brothers Grimm, tr. & ed. Jack Zipes; Bantam Books, London, 1987; Story 117; pg. 422.

What a ghastly story! I suppose its original purpose was to teach the necessity of proper discipline in raising a child. But I see it as a parable of our old self, which keeps trying to shake its way out of grave after we have buried it in baptism. The only cure is a swift blow with the rod of faith! In the name of Jesus, drive it back into the grave and keep it there, buried with Christ in baptism!

Risen with Christ

Scripture affirms that we who are baptised were *"raised into life with Christ"*. Do you see that as merely some sort of ethereal or heavenly life? No! It should be a *felt* life, a life *experienced;* not theoretical but practical; not dogma, but deed. All who are baptised into the name of Christ should seize the promise of God and unite themselves by faith with the power that raised Christ himself from the dead. (Cl 2:12) The Greek text lends itself to two ideas –

- We were raised with Christ through faith *in* the power of God.
- We were raised with Christ through faith aroused *by* the power of God.

In the first case, our faith apprehends the power of God; in the second, the power of God energises our faith. I like to think that both are true. Yes, I do reach out to the Lord with all the faith I can muster, striving to make the fullness of his resurrection life my own; but I'm also delighted to know that the Lord reaches down to me and packs my faith with divine force, so that it cannot fail to triumph in Christ!

In baptism we replay the passion and victory of Jesus our Lord. We share his agony in the garden when we repent and submit, body, soul, and spirit, to the command of God to be baptised. We share the cross, and the death, burial, and resurrection of the Saviour. Coming out of the waters (or away from them), we share his rising from the dead into a new dimension of life in the heavenlies. We ascend with him to the Father's throne, where we reign with him, exercising authority over the enemy and quenching his fiery darts. And at the end, our baptism points the way to the final rule of God, when at the return of Christ we share the rapture of the church and enter into his eternal joy and his sovereign dominion for ever.

No matter what form your baptism took, seize the fact that you have been baptised, wrap that fact in faith, believe the promise of God with all your heart and its reality will be yours. Amen!

FOURTEEN:

POSITION

> *Have you been raised with Christ? Then seek those things that are above, where Christ is, enthroned at the right hand of God. Set your minds on heavenly things, not on things that are on earth. For you have died, and your life is hidden with Christ in God. When Christ, who is your life appears, then you too will appear with him in glory. (Cl 3:1-4)*

If your desire is to live victoriously in Christ, then one of the most helpful ideas you can grasp is the difference between your **_standing_** (which describes your true position in Christ in the heavenlies), and your **_state_** (which describes your actual condition on earth) –

THE TWO REALITIES

YOUR STANDING

This describes your **_legal position_** in Christ in the heavenlies, before the throne of God. It is a position of imputed righteousness. That is, because of Calvary, you are now treated by God as if you had never sinned. And in Christ you have been elevated to the throne in heaven. This is how God sees each of us in Christ – redeemed, holy, exalted, enthroned, eternal. This is true of every person who is united with Christ by faith, regardless of how well or how poorly he or she may be behaving. Sin cannot affect it, either for better or worse. (60)

Do you believe in Christ? Are you born again? Then your heavenly standing is unassailable. No demon can defile it; no angel can change it; no human hand can wreck it!

But this lofty standing exists in a state of tension with –

YOUR STATE

This describes your **actual <u>condition</u>** on earth; that is, the degree to which you have managed to appropriate the fullness of Christ in your daily life. It is based upon recognising that you will never in this life be wholly free of sin, although we must keep striving to rid ourselves (by faith) of all iniquity.

Plainly, there is a *gap* between our secure **standing** in heaven and our fluctuating **state** on earth. That is, our actual **condition** on earth never equals the amazing **position** of full righteousness God has given us in heaven in Christ. Two of Paul's letters, *Ephesians* and *Colossians,* are built around this theme. In each letter, the first half is devoted to the believer's **<u>standing</u>**, and the second half to the believer's **<u>state</u>**. This was the apostle's unvarying approach – always he wanted people to know **<u>who</u>** they were in Christ before he told them **<u>what</u>** to do as Christians. Yet how often that pattern is reversed today! The sorry result is seen in the frustrated experience of God's people, who are thereby brought under law instead of into grace. Paul provides an answer to the

---

(60) Except, of course, that wilful persistence in wrongdoing will undermine faith and eventually break the bond between the sinner and Christ. We are safe only so long as we are still "in Christ", which we will always be, if we steadfastly acknowledge him as Saviour and Lord, and continue to embrace his pardon and redemption by faith. You will find more on this just below.

problem in the passage that heads this chapter, (Cl 3:1-4) where he tells us that –

- we are _now_ glorified with Christ;
- this glory is not yet _visible_;
- until it becomes visible at the rapture, we must _appropriate_ it by faith.

The remainder of this chapter is an explanation of what those propositions mean in the daily life of a Christian. My plan is to explore the differences between our **standing** and our **state** in Christ, and how to handle the tension between the two.

KNOWING THE DIFFERENCE

YOUR STANDING

In the first half of *Colossians*, Paul says that in Christ you are already –

- an heir of God (1:12)
- a citizen of heaven (1:13)
- redeemed (1:14)
- reconciled and perfect (1:21-22)
- indwelt by divine glory (1:27)
- complete in Christ (2:10)
- risen with Christ (2:12)
- dead to the world (3:3)

All that, and more, just from the first part of *Colossians*; and you could find much more in *Ephesians* and elsewhere. Those things are true NOW of every believer. That image shows how we appear *"in his sight."* (1:22) The Father has resolved to see us only as we are in Christ, which is the status we have before him in heaven. This status is wholly based upon the work of Christ, to which we can _add_ nothing, and from which we can *take* nothing. It is a free gift of God's grace to every believer in Christ.

Now comes the paradox. This legal *standing* does not automatically, or instantly, become true in a Christian's daily experience. In fact, most people find that their actual *state* on earth is very different from their legal *standing* in heaven.

How can that difference be reconciled? How can we bring the two together? Before those questions can be answered, we need to look at –

YOUR STATE

Paul lists a number of sordid offences that the people in Colossae (or, at least, some of them) were committing –

- sexual immorality, impurity, passion, corrupt desire, greed, idolatry, anger, wrath, malice, slander, obscene language, and lying! (See Cl 3:5-9; and cp. Ep 4:17-22)

Would you call those people Christians? If you went into a church and learned that was how many of the people were behaving, how would you respond? What wretched sins they were committing! Can such people truthfully claim to be Christians, holy, enthroned with Christ in the heavenlies?

Paul certainly *wanted* them to live righteously; but **he refused to make human action dominant over divine grace**! He understood (as someone has said) that the gospel is the four-letter word **_DONE!_**, not the two-letter word **_DO!_** So, before he corrected their faults, he showed them the way of faith; he gave them *revelation* before he administered *rebuke*; he brought them *inspiration* before delivering *instruction*; he set them in the *heavenlies* before he gave any attention to what was happening in the *earthlies*. In other words, he planted them securely in a *heavenly <u>position</u>* before he attacked their *earthly <u>condition</u>*. (61)

Yet the tendency in many churches is to reverse the gospel; as if scripture said, "When I see you <u>*doing*</u> righteously, then I will say that you <u>*are*</u> righteous." But that is law, not grace. The gospel method is always to declare the believer already thoroughly righteous in Christ, and only then to say, *"Now that you <u>are</u> righteous, you should begin to <u>live</u> righteously!"*

The great thing to notice here is that a poor *state* does not change a Christian's high *standing;* or, a lowly *condition* does not change a Christian's exalted *position*. Just how important that idea is becomes clear when it is realised that *none* of us is ever entirely free from sin, and that future offence is certain. If our *standing* were insecure, if it could be changed hourly by our earthly conduct, then none of us would ever know security in Christ. We would never know whether or not we are acceptable at the Father's throne. We would never be able to obey the scriptures and walk *"boldly into the holiest"*, there to make our requests known to God. (He 10:19-23; 4:16; Ph 4:6) Hence, though some of the Colossians were guilty of vile sin, Paul still gives them an astonishing commendation. He says –

> *(You are) God's holy and faithful people, our brothers and sisters, who are united with us in Christ ... Goodwill and peace from God our Father belong to you in Christ! ... Set your heart*

---

(61) Because of this contrast between our *position* and our *condition*, this doctrine is sometimes called *Positional Truth*. Be careful, however, to sever this doctrine from any connection with the heresy known as *antinomianism*, which argues that Christians are free from any obligation to keep the moral laws of God. On the contrary, the aim of *Positional Truth* is the same as Paul's, to bring people to a place in Christ where they will be able, readily and joyfully and in the strength of their secure position in the heavenlies, to keep every moral and ethical principle taught in the gospel. You will find more on this just below.

> *upon the things that are above, where Christ sits enthroned at the Father's right hand. You have died, and your life is hidden with Christ in God. Christ is now your life, and when he appears, then you, too, will appear with him in glory. (Cl 1:2; 3:3-4)*

Does Paul then not care that they were sinning? Is he indifferent to their evil? Did he reckon that impiety and wrongdoing could be overlooked? Hardly! His _goal_ was to entice them into godly, holy, and virtuous living. But his _method_ was to make their unchanged _standing_ in the heavenlies in Christ the basis for his appeal for an improving _state_ on earth. So this message of a secure standing gives no license to sin, though some have taken it that way, both today and in the past. (Ro 6:1-4)

As for Paul, although he had no tolerance for sin, he also knew that people could never rid themselves of sin by struggling against it. Victory is gained by positioning yourself in the heavenlies and by giving yourself a new identity in Christ. Then, from the vantage point of the throne, each Christian should take authority in Jesus' name over sin, the devil, and all the works of the flesh.

When people learn how to claim their legal *standing* in Christ BEFORE they make any attempt to alter their actual *state* on earth, they soon discover three delightful benefits –

- they find themselves in a place of unbroken peace with God, a peace achieved, not by their own merits (for we have none), but by those of the risen Christ. (Ro 5:1)

- they escape the feeling that they must "work their way back" into God's favour after they have committed some sin. But how *can* you "work your way *back*" when you are *already* standing there in heaven, before the throne, complete in Christ, and already *highly favoured* by the Father for Christ's sake? (Ep 1:3)

- they gain an unbroken right to speak and act in the authority of Christ, especially in the realm of taking control over Satan and destroying sin.

The simple gospel truth is this – the only way to *become* righteous is to declare that in Christ you *are* already righteous; there is no other way that is acceptable to God. The principle is plain – the ungodly behave ungodly; the unrighteous behave unrighteously. They cannot do otherwise! Can this be changed? Yes! Make the ungodly godly, and the unrighteous righteous, then they will naturally do righteously and live in a godly manner. (Mt 7:16-19; 12:33-35; Lu 6:43-45; Ja 3:11-13) A thorn tree cannot produce an orange; nor will hanging oranges on its branches do any good. But turn it by a miracle into an orange tree, and it will produce the golden fruit naturally. Can a blind man see by striving and struggling? No, no matter how hard he tries his eyes will remain dark. But restore his sight by a miracle and he will see without trying! Sight will become natural for him, even if he takes a while to become familiar with all that surrounds him. Likewise, make a blind sinner a saint, and he will at once begin to see heaven and behave saintly.

Sinners cannot make themselves righteous, nor can they produce the fruits of godliness. But let them be transformed by the supernatural power of the gospel, and they will then grow an abundant harvest of sweet fruit. Godly people behave godly. Righteous people behave righteously. People who truly *know* they are Christians will behave Christianly. But the ungodly never can do any more than hang plastic fruit on a dead branch. It may have the outward appearance of a living tree, but it is an illusion. Can a cat bark like a dog? Perhaps one could be trained to do so, but it would still be a cat. However, turn it into a dog by a miracle, and it will bark naturally!

So, once again, how do you get a person to act Christianly? You can't. But let that person become a Christian, then he or she will naturally act Christianly. The unrighteous do unrighteously, no matter what they do, because whatever they do is darkened by sin. But make that sinner righteous, then he or she will behave righteously, so much so that even sin becomes overwhelmed by grace.

That is what God has done for us in Christ. He has torn out the root of sin and replaced it with a root of righteousness. We have but to let that root grow and flourish and produce its proper fruit in our lives. In the meantime, our legal standing remains that of people who are deemed entirely righteous in Christ in the heavenlies. (Ep 1:1-3)

Let us then recognise what God has done for us in Christ, and affirm it boldly, by faith. You may then declare in the name of Jesus – "I am now the very righteousness of God in Christ, enthroned with him in the heavenlies, able in his strength to do righteously and to display godliness in every way!"

NARROWING THE GAP

You can now see that Christian life is primarily a matter of *narrowing the gap* between your *standing* (of unblemished righteousness in heaven) and your *state* (which still contains dregs of the old self). This is a process into which we must all enter with goodwill and with unshakeable faith, because –

- continuation of our legal standing depends upon continuation of our union with Christ by faith;
- but that union cannot be sustained in the presence of wilful and un-repented sin. (Cl 3:6; Ep 5:3-7; He 10:26-31)

Sin, un-repented and deliberately continued, is a deep poison to faith, eroding it and eventually destroying it. But union with Christ cannot be sustained apart from faith, so that when faith goes away that union is sundered. The sinner is once again on his own with sin, and without hope of redemption. (He 6:4-6; 12:15-16; Ga 5:19-21; 2 Pe 2:22) Does that mean that any and every sin will cut us off from Christ? Of course not! We all sin and must depend upon the blood of the covenant to hide that sin and keep us pure in the sight of God. (1 Jn 1:8-10) What then? If you happen to sin, you should *repent*, claim *pardon*, (1 Jn 2:1-2) and at once *reaffirm* your legal standing in Christ. That affirmation of your heavenly position should then become –

- the greatest *incentive* to avoid sin, the greatest impulse toward holiness; and
- the best *method* of overcoming sin.

After all, there are only two choices for changing yourself –

- you can *look ahead*, set up an image of what you want to be, and then struggle to achieve it, which is what most people do; or
- you can *look up*, see what you already *are* in Christ, and set yourself simply to bring that into fruition by faith.

SOME ILLUSTRATIONS

Think about a tone-deaf person struggling to learn the piano, and finally having the good sense to give it up. Compare him with a gifted person who senses music pulsating in every fibre of his being, and simply dedicates himself to bringing out and perfecting his innate skill.

Or, think about an ungifted person trying to turn a lump of marble into a lovely sculpture. The result is likely to be more graceless than the original lump. But hand that person a splendid image covered in mud, even concrete, so that he needs only break away the overlay to reveal the underlying beauty, and he will do quite well. He can't create the statue, but he can reveal it.

So we, who are made in the image of Christ, still wear a veneer of flesh. We should be steadily removing that veneer, so that we show more and more of the loveliness of Christ.

Removing that veneer, or bringing out that inner beauty, or "narrowing the gap", is neither a matter of works, nor of fierce struggle, nor of sheer determination. Even less does it depend upon tear-drenched prayer, or some bitter sacrifice.

Rather, revealing the beauty of Christ who is in you should be a natural product of the means of grace, such as – the lively word of God, believing prayer, supportive fellowship, anointed ministry, and the like. Just as a farmer plants his seed and then allows nature to take its course, so we, making diligent use of those tools of divine grace, may expect that God himself will bring out of that "seed" the harvest of righteousness.

USE YOUR HEAVENLY STANDING

Since we have now made this marvellous discovery, that any true grip of the _standing_ God has given us in Christ will irresistibly create in us a hunger to bring our _state_ into conformity with that standing, we should make good use of it.

TO DEFEAT SIN

Peter puts it like this –

> *Live like people who are free, but not using your freedom as an excuse to do evil, but rather to serve God. ... Do not join those who promise freedom while they themselves remain slaves of corruption. For whatever you allow to rule you has made you its slave. (1 Pe 2:16; 2 Pe 2:19 ff.)*

So your legal standing does not remove from you the need to serve God and to practice self-discipline, although it does change both the _reason_ and the _motivation_ for doing so. That is, now, as a person declaring yourself righteous in Christ, and refusing any lesser affirmation, you will turn toward obedience and holiness – for the righteous do righteously! They cannot do other! If you have been made righteous by grace through Christ alone, and you _know_ it, and you _affirm_ it, then you will do as the righteous do. And you will do this –

- as an _expression_ of your God-given standing, not in an effort to _earn_ heaven's favour; and
- in _recognition_ that faithful service now will gain you an inheritance in the coming kingdom.

So we need to understand this rule – God will not permit us to work for his favour in *this* world, for he has decreed that we can have that favour only as a gift of his grace. But we *are* encouraged to work for reward in the coming kingdom.

Then, too, you should use your heavenly standing as the basis upon which

TO DEFEAT SATAN

Once you have fully realised and confessed your legal standing in heaven, you should use that standing, not only as the best remedy against sin, but also as the sole basis upon which you resist Satan, whether he attacks you by word or deed –

> *The weapons we use in our fight are not the world's weapons _but God's powerful weapons_, which we use to destroy strongholds. We ... pull down every proud obstacle that is raised against the _knowledge of God_; we take every thought captive and make it obey Christ. (2 Co 10:3-5, GNB)*

Notice that the devil's attack is concentrated upon our "*knowledge of God*". Why? Because, that knowledge is the chief source of our victory over the devil. That is why Paul tells us to *"take captive every thought"*, never allowing them to wander into pathways of error, but focussed always on Christ and on what he wrought for us by his Passion, his resurrection, and his ascension. Keep a vision before your eyes, not of your wrongdoing, your faults and failures, but of your heavenly enthronement, utterly righteous and victorious in Christ. (Ep 2:5-6; Cl 3:1-3)

And with that vision deeply engraved upon your inner spirit, you should use your legal standing as the sole basis upon which

TO APPROACH THE THRONE

of God boldly in prayer. (He 10:19-23) Never allow anyone or anything, in heaven, on earth, or beneath the earth to rob you of your unassailable right in Christ to draw near to the Lord and speak your requests with confidence, sure that he will hear you and answer you generously.

Or consider all that is hidden in this marvellous statement –

> *God did all these things in agreement with his eternal purpose, which he has achieved through Christ Jesus our Lord, so that <u>because of our union with Christ</u> and <u>through our faith in him</u>, we may now <u>go boldly into God's presence with all confidence</u>. (Ep 3:11-12)*

Did you mark Paul's arresting fourfold affirmation? God has wrought so marvelously for us in Christ, that now

- through our **union** with Christ (and only because of that union); and
- through our ***faith*** in him (and solely and exclusively by faith); we may now
- go **boldly** to the throne of God (presenting no other claim than the merits of Christ); and there

- we may **pray** with confidence, knowing that the Father will welcome us, hear us, and respond to our requests.

Such is the assurance that belongs to those who truly know, believe, and confess <u>who</u> they are in Christ, <u>what</u> they have in Christ, and <u>where</u> they stand in Christ!

CONCLUSION

Christians who have found security in the righteous standing God has given them in Christ, and who refuse to be moved away from that position, not even by their own sin, will be able calmly and steadily to bring their state on earth closer and closer to their standing in heaven.

This way of life is built upon two things –

A CONTINUING SPIRIT OF REPENTANCE

There is never any room for arrogance in Christian life, for God honours a contrite and broken heart. (Ps 34:18; 51:17; Is 57:15; 66:2)

People make four mistakes about repentance –

- they act as though it were <u>unnecessary</u> – but repentance is the pre-condition of every aspect of our relationship with God, followed at once by confident faith.

- they act as though it were <u>spasmodic</u> – but repentance is not so much an *act* as it is a *condition*, an unchanging attitude, a constant aspect of our approach to God. [62]

---

[62] I do not mean that we must for ever be dragged down by gloomy thoughts of our sin. How appalling! On the contrary, we are called to a life of endless delight and perpetual praise. But underlying all our joy and happiness in the

- they act as though it were a _good work_ – but repentance is simply the channel through which we express our sorrow for sin and our claim upon the inexhaustible grace of God. It has no merit in itself, except in attaching us to Christ.

- they act as though it were an _emotion_ – but repentance is not a matter of tears or passion (although on occasion they may be appropriate). It is rather a *choice*, an act of *will*, whereby we declare ourselves sinners in need of the grace of God and depending only upon that grace to bring us pardon and restoration.

Emotion, even deep emotion, *may* be involved in repentance, but it is not necessary. No more is required than that sin be sincerely confessed, abjured, and placed under the blood, followed by unwavering trust in the mercy and love of the Lord. *Then* emotion will always be appropriate, in the joy of sins forgiven, the happiness of peace with God, and the delight of renewed fellowship.

A CONTINUING AFFIRMATION OF FAITH

Remember these things, and never let anyone push you off _the bedrock of your faith_. Strive to excel in everything you do for the Lord ... Stay alert. Stay _firm in your faith_ in Christ. Stay full of courage and be strong in Christ! (1 Co 15:58; 16:13)

Lord, there should be a tender spirit of repentance, acknowledging that we remain sinners in absolute need of divine grace, never free of fault, always depending upon the cross.

FIFTEEN:

APPEARING

When Christ who is your life appears, then you too will appear with him in glory. (Cl 3:4)

Everybody loves a military parade – the prancing horses, the rumbling tanks, the drums, the pipes, a thousand marching feet shaking the earth – how it stirs the blood! But the greatest parade ever seen will be driven from memory when Christ returns, coming in the glory of the Father, accompanied by all his holy angels, while the heavens resound with the strident blare of the Trumpet of God and the thunderous shout of the Archangel! (1 Th 4:16) Nor can it be supposed that the millions of the redeemed, as they rise to meet their Lord in the air, will be bashfully silent. No! Their glad cries, their rapturous praise, will subdue even the acclamations of the angels!

Who is this One who is coming? Who else but the glorified Christ, <u>who is our life</u>! What a beautiful expression! For he is truly our life, both now and forever. He quickens our whole being, spirit, soul and body; he is the surety that every part of us is included in his redeeming work; he is himself the guarantee that we will be kept safe and blameless until the day of his coming. (1 Th 5:23)

And <u>he is our life</u> because he has saved us from death, *first*, by his own atoning death that rescued us from the curse of the broken law; and *second*, by smashing the strength of Satan who for so long had held us in his thrall. Then <u>he is our life</u> because we live only to please him in all that we do and say. We desire that he should be preeminent in all things. As the eye of a servant is fixed upon his master, and as a handmaiden's eye looks to her mistress, so is our gaze fastened to the Lord (Ps 123:2). *He is our life* because his touch transforms the most mundane activities into pathways to Paradise, sanctifying each task, and giving it eternal value. And *he is our life* because only in him do we have any assurance of eternal life in the coming New Heaven and New Earth. And so, because *he is our life*, we seek his honour, we exalt his name, and our desire is so to live that we become more like him in every way.

This life we have in Christ is remarkable because "it is eternal in its duration; it does not prevent physical dissolution, but survives it; it is part of the Divine life; therefore age cannot enfeeble its powers, disease cannot impair its beauty, and death cannot terminate its existence" (J. T. Woodhouse). Hence, because Christ who is our life dwells in us, we know that we too cannot ever actually die; we simply step from earth into heaven, from mortality into immortality, from a physical form to one that is spiritual, and from time into eternity! (Jn 11:25; 1 Co 15:51-53)

One day this Christ, who is our life, will *"appear"*. He is presently hidden from normal view, discernible only by the eye of faith. But then he will be blazingly visible to every eye, for *"every eye shall see him."* (Re 1:7) We too, whose glory in Christ is presently hidden from the view of the world, will appear with him in glory. The splendour that is already ours in Christ will then be openly revealed. How the peoples of the earth will greatly wail when they discover what they have lost! How they will mourn when they learn too late that that they do not know him whom they should have known! They will see his church sharing his endless life, in which they will never be able to delight. They will see the wrathful judgment that faces them, while his beautiful church turns joyfully to its celebration as the Bride of the Lamb.

Thus the coming of Christ will reveal to the world whom he truly is; and it will also reveal us to the world, as his transfigured people, clothed with his glory. That effulgent magnificence will shimmer with our triumph over the grave, and emanate from the radiant new bodies the resurrection will bring us, and blaze with all the shining promise of our reign with Christ as crowned monarchs.

Let us look at some aspects of that promise –

THE PROMISED THRONE

> *To him that overcometh will I grant to **sit with me in my throne**, even as I also overcame, and am set down with my Father in his throne. (Re 3:21)*

I reverted in that text to the Authorised Version [63] of the Bible, because I love the word, *"overcometh"*! John uses it 8 times in connection with the believer overcoming the world, the flesh, or the devil, and each time he adds a different stupendous reward –

- *To him that overcometh will I give to eat of the tree of life, which is in the midst of the paradise of God. (Re 2:7)*

- *He that overcometh shall not be hurt of the second death. (vs. 11)*

- *To him that overcometh will I give to eat of the hidden manna, and will give him a white stone, and in the stone a new name written, which no man knoweth saving he that receiveth it. (vs. 17)*

- *He that overcometh, and keepeth my works unto the end, to him will I give power over the nations. (vs. 26)*

---

(63) Commonly abbreviated as either AV or KV (for *King James Version*). First published in 1611.

- *He that overcometh, the same shall be clothed in white raiment; and I will confess his name before my Father, and before his angels. (3:5)*

- *Him that overcometh will I make a pillar in the temple of my God and I will write upon him my new name.* (vs. 12) And then, our text –

- *To him that overcometh will I grant to sit with me in my throne, even as I also overcame, and am set down with my Father in his throne. (vs. 21)*

- *He that overcometh shall inherit all things; and I will be his God, and he shall be my son. (21:7)* [64]

One could easily write an entire book just expounding those eight divine promises, but let them all be summarized under the saying, *"We will be enthroned with Christ, reigning with him from the Father's throne!"*

Our authority will be invincible; our command, irresistible; our right to rule, unassailable; our dominion, universal; and our throne, that of the King of kings and the Lord of lords.

There is only one pre-condition – we must be known as *"overcomers"*. What does that mean? Many suggestions have been made, some of them so rigorous that it is hard to believe anyone will qualify! But surely, unless most of us are to be stripped of any claim upon the promise, an *"overcomer"* is simply a born-again and faithful believer. We who believe overcome the world by refusing all its blandishments, and by ignoring its jeering scorn. We overcome the world, the flesh, and Satan when we repent and turn to Christ as our only Saviour. And we keep on overcoming the world when we resist

---

(64) You will, I hope, include the feminine with the masculine in these references, and pardon the chauvinism of the AV translators!

all temptation to behave like a dog going back to its vomit (2 Pe 2:21-22), but instead press faithfully on, serving the Lord joyfully to the end of our lives!

So, I do not agree with those who claim that one cannot be an "overcomer" unless one has display some extraordinary quality of courage, or reached some astonishing level of achievement. In my opinion, any ordinary Christian who sticks to Christ, refuses to backslide, is an active member of a local church, and trusts wholly in the grace of God for righteousness and salvation, fully qualifies as an "overcomer". They will gain the throne on that great coming day.

I will concede only, as Jesus himself said, that there will different ranks in the kingdom, and different levels of royal authority (Lu 19:17-19); but *all* who are faithful to the end will have *some* measure of dominion, some degree of royal authority in the kingdom.

But there *does* seem to be another principle at work – only those who reign **now** will reign **then**! Or, we shall possess **then** only as much of our inheritance as we succeed in possessing **now**! That is, what we now grasp **spiritually** in Christ we will then possess **openly** on the throne. So, if you would have high authority in the coming kingdom, you should begin **now** to capture and use as much of your throne rights as you are able to grasp by faith.

THE PROMISED CROWN

Four crowns are offered to every overcoming Christian –

THE CROWN OF RIGHTEOUSNESS

> *Henceforth there is laid up for me **the crown of righteousness**, which the Lord, the righteous judge, will award to me on that Day, and not only*

to me but also to all who have loved his appearing.
(2 Ti 4:8)

Plutarch (*circa* A.D. 46-120) wrote a book about famous people of his time, including the renowned Macedonian warrior, Alexander the Great, who in the 4th century before Christ carved out the largest empire the world had seen to that time. Plutarch tells this story about him –

> (Before he embarked upon his campaigns, Alexander decided to provide for his friends, who were abandoning all to follow him. So he) supplied what they wanted, by giving good farms to some, a village to one, and the revenues of some hamlet or harbour-town to another. So that at last he had apportioned out or engaged almost all the royal property; which giving Perdiccas an occasion to ask him what he would leave himself, he replied, "His hopes!" "Your soldiers," replied Perdiccas, "will be your partners in those," and refused to accept the estate he had assigned him. Some others of his friends did the like. [65]

Toward the end of those long campaigns, and with many of the friends killed in battle, some of them may have begun regretting turning aside the king's generous gifts and choosing instead to share in his hopes! But among those who survived the wars, and Alexander's death, some did indeed inherit a crown. His vast empire was broken up (into four monarchies, Egypt, Syria, Pergamon, and Macedonia), and four of his companions managed to outwit their rivals and grasp a crown

---

[65] John Dryden, tr. <u>Plutarch's Lives of the Noble Grecians and Romans</u> – *Alexander*, Modern Library, New York; reprint of the 1864 edition; pg. 801.

for themselves. The remainder of Alexander's soldiers and officers had to be content with lesser rewards.

We too have been promised a share in the hopes that motivated Christ our King. Nor will they fail us, for as surely as we share in his sufferings, so shall we share in his prize. Nor do we have to contend with each other for the crown, for it is ours as the gift of God in Christ. Nor can any power in heaven or hell usurp our throne. Paul is emphatic. *Everyone* who *"loves his appearing"* will receive a crown on that day!

But notice, as we have done before, there *is* a pre-condition – the crown is for those who *"love his appearing"*. God's reward is dedicated to people who both desire it and labour for it. Those who have no desire now will have no claim then. Do you desire the coming of the Lord? Are you looking for it and waiting with eager excitement? Here is a line of demarcation. Only true Christians can have a keen expectation of the Lord's return. Only true Christians deeply desire it. Only hearts that love Christ dearly, and are yearning for him to appear in flaming fire, to burn up the dross of the world and to establish his everlasting kingdom, may claim to belong to him. On one side of this line is the church, waiting joyfully for Christ to appear. On the other, stand all who show no interest in his coming, who reject the idea of a last day, who have their eyes too firmly fixed on this world ever to *"look up"* with gladness, knowing that their redemption is drawing nigh. (Lu 21:28)

Francis Bacon (1561-1626) is generally known as the *Father of Modern Science*. He developed the experimental method upon which the entire modern scientific enterprise is based. He was also a philosopher and lawyer, and attained the summit of the legal profession when he became the Lord Chancellor of England.

Sir Francis gave his life in pursuit of science when he caught a chill, and then pneumonia, while trying out the effect of snow on preserving chicken meat. But some years before his death he quarrelled with the king (James I), and was dismissed from office and banished from the court. For a time his life was in peril, and his friends warned him to "keep looking about you", lest he be attacked unawares. He calmly replied –

> *"I do not look about me, I look above me!"*

That is what Jesus meant when he spoke about a coming time when people everywhere would be looking out upon the world with alarm and dread, because of the awful things that will happen on every side. (Lu 21:26) They will be gazing around them with terror; but not his people, who instead will be *"looking up"*, confident in the saving power of their God! (vs. 28)

THE CROWN OF LIFE

> *Blessed are they who remain steadfast under trial. When they have stood the test they will receive **the crown of life**, which God has promised to those who love him. (Ja 1:12)*

We gain this crown by loving the life that seems to be death and by hating the death that seems to be life – that is, by placing heaven before earth, eternity before time, and Christ before the world. But mark Paul's warning –

> *You surely must realise that unrighteous people cannot inherit the kingdom of God? Will you play the fool? Sexually immoral people, idolaters, adulterers, practising homosexuals, thieves, the greedy, drunkards, slanderers, swindlers – none of them has any hope of inheriting the kingdom of God. (Cl 3:5-9; Ep 5:3-6)*

James, too, the author of the text for this section, lived by those same precepts. Various accounts of him are given in the ancient documents of the church. Some of the story is probably mythological, but we are left with a clear image of an utterly godly and good man –

> This James was the brother of the Lord, (Mt 13:55; Mk 6:3) and it is said that he was so distressed by the crucifixion that he vowed to fast until the Second Coming. But Jesus kindly appeared to him, prepared a meal, blessed it, and absolved his brother from the vow.
>
> His life after the day of Pentecost was so godly that he came to be called by everyone (even his enemies) *James the Just.* He refused to drink any wine, nor would he eat flesh. No razor touched his hair or beard, and he resolved never to anoint his body with oil.
>
> He frequently went into the Temple to pray, and always knelt in the same place. So many hours did he spend there that two impressions were worn into the stones by his knees, which became hard and calloused like those of a camel. The main passion of his intercessions was a cry for God to pardon the sins of the people and to show mercy to Israel.
>
> His great piety, and his growing renown among the people, aroused anger in the hearts of the religious and civic leaders in Jerusalem, and one day, while he was preaching from the top of a high pillar, they had him thrown down upon the flagstones. As he lay there, a fuller beat him to death with his fuller's club. This murderous act was reckoned by many Jews to be the immediate cause of the destruction of Jerusalem by the Roman army, which occurred eight years later (A.D. 70). *(See Eusebius Bk. 2.23, and other early writings.)*

Thus James became an example of those *"who remain steadfast under fire, and have passed the test so that they are sure to receive **the crown of life**, which God has promised to those who love him".* (66)

THE CROWN OF JUDGMENT

Don't you know that God's people will judge the world? ... Don't you know that we will judge angels? (1 Co 6:1-3)

How long does it take to train someone to become a respected judge, renowned for integrity and fairness, deeply versed in the law, well fitted for the onerous task of administering justice? Many years! And so we should view this present life. God is preparing us for duty in the world to come. Sometimes the training is harsh, and demands from us everything we have. But the end result will be a person fit to accomplish any task required in the kingdom.

I hope you never imagined that eternity will consist of nothing more than sitting on a fleecy cloud plucking a harp? What a dreary, suffocating prospect that would be! No, the kingdom will be a place of boundless opportunity, of fascinating action, of high responsibility, of vastly creative achievement. It will have enough excitement, challenge, duties, and pleasures to keep us fulfilled across eternal ages.

Also among the tasks of the kingdom, at least for some of the saints, will be sitting in judgment on nations and angels. And if not actually sitting as judges, all the saints will possess an authority, a right to command, equal to the loftiest magistrate in heaven. In one way or another, we will all be associated with Christ in the administration of the kingdom of heaven.

---

(66)   James 1:12, paraphrased.

Opinions differ widely on how we should interpret the saying, *"we shall judge the world ... we shall judge the angels."* We cannot know how this will be done, or how large a part of the church will be involved in the actual act of judgment, or in what manner they will do so. But this much stands clear. We are given a picture of the awesome majesty, and of the royal glory that will belong to every redeemed saint in heaven. Our position will be so exalted that if it were necessary, we could compel the chiefest of the angels, and whole nations, to bow down, yielding to our command.

THE CROWN OF GLORY

When the Chief Shepherd appears, you will receive a crown of glory that will never fade away. (1 Pe 5:4)

Here the crown is based upon faithful service, which itself arises from valuing heavenly riches more than earthly.

It is sometimes said that we should serve the Lord without any thought of rewards. And of course, that is partly true. But there is no denying that in scores of places the Bible itself spells out the rewards that God is willing, even eager, to bestow upon all who serve him well and love him heartily. And among those rewards are these several crowns. Aspire to them! Catch a vision of them! They are waiting for you and me in Paradise, and will be ours on the day that we rise to meet the King, and take our seat with him at the right hand of the Majesty on high!

CONCLUSION

How can we be sure of gaining these crowns?

First, let us remember that all these crowns, thrones, and the like, must be seen as metaphors of spiritual authority. I do not imagine myself actually wearing several different crowns, or actually sitting on some golden throne. But I do accept that the royal dominion represented by those sovereign objects will assuredly belong to every overcoming saint in the kingdom of God. We are destined to rule with Christ!

The key to apprehending that promise is to trust in the Lord more than you trust in yourself. Especially, believe his word – *"This is the victory that overcomes the world, even our faith!"* (1 Jn 5:4) So, cling to faith, based upon the promise of God, and you cannot fail to win the prize!

Now let me finish this chapter with another story from Plutarch's *Life of Alexander* –

> (Alexander) went to Delphi, to consult Apollo concerning the success of the war he had undertaken, and happening to come on one of the forbidden days, when it was esteemed improper to give any answer from an oracle, he sent messengers to desire the priestess [67] to do her office; and when she refused, on the plea of a law to the contrary, he went up himself, and began to draw her by force into the temple, until, tired and overcome with his importunity, "My son," said she, "thou art invincible!" Alexander, taking hold of what she spoke, declared he had received such an answer as he wished for, and that it was needless to consult the god any further.

That is the sort of boldness the Lord wants from us. Fierce determination, unquenchable optimism, vigorous appropria-

---

(67) Known as the Pythonness, because a hissing sound, like that of a snake, emerged from a cleft in the floor of the grotto. It was deemed to be the god Apollo, but was probably no more than the sound of underground steam, or lava.

tion of the promises, a resolve to take hold of the Lord and not let go until the goal is reached – which are all commended by Christ himself. He said, *"From the time of John the Baptizer until now, the kingdom of heaven has been forcefully advancing, and forceful people have been seizing it."* (Mt 11:12, GW)

This is not physical violence, nor natural strength. It does not depend upon temperament or character. It is spiritual in nature. Even the shyest, most timid, most self-effacing people can rise up in the spirit, and in the name of Jesus decide to be all that God wants them to be, and to have all that God wants them to have.

Determine now that you, yourself, will be such a person, so that –

> *When Christ who is your life appears, then you too will appear with him in glory. (Cl 3:4)*

SIXTEEN:

FORGIVING

Be patient with each other, and pardon anyone against whom you have some complaint. <u>You must forgive each other, just as the Lord has forgiven you</u>. (Cl 3:8).

The German Army in Brussels in 1915 placed a British nurse on trial. Her name was Edith Cavell, and she had been accused of actively helping a large number of Allied soldiers to escape from Belgium to Britain. She was convicted of treason, and executed by a firing squad. On the evening before her death, she said to her chaplain, "This I would say, standing as I do in view of God and eternity, I realise that patriotism is not enough. I must have no hatred or bitterness towards anyone." [68]

And neither should we no matter how great the provocation. Indeed, scripture insists that we must end each day in a state of reconciled harmony with everyone. As Paul says elsewhere, *"Never go to bed angry. Why would you give the devil such a chance to do you harm?"* (Ep 4:26-27) And in our text, *"pardon anyone against whom you have a complaint ... for you must forgive each other!"*

Do you have a complaint against someone? Has someone angered you, or done you harm? Are you a victim of fraud or violence? Are you burning to strike back, to get even, to hurt as you were hurt? Do you yearn for revenge? Then here is the first thing you must do – forgive your enemy! Does that seem

---

[68] The full story can be found at http://en.wikipedia.org/wiki/Edith_Cavell.

too hard? Does it feel like you are being victimised all over again? As if being bruised once was not enough, now I have to be wounded even more bitterly? Now I have to repress every natural indignant response? Even worse, and even though I have a legitimate complaint, I must actually and heartily *forgive* the offender?

Why such a harsh demand? Is God altogether unfeeling and uncaring? Hardly! He insists that we must be tolerant with each other, and forgive every offence, because if we do not, then we hurt ourselves more thoroughly than any enemy can! So the Lord says, *"Just as I forgave you, so you must fully and freely forgive everyone who has done you some harm."* (Mt 6:14-15; 18:34-35) And again, from our text, *"You must forgive each other, just as the Lord has forgiven you!"* (Cl 3:8)

Furthermore, if we do heartily forgive all who have harmed us by word or action, then God himself undertakes to be our avenger, and he will inflict revenge far more effectively than we can! (Ro 12:19) [69]

So, here is a prime requisite of Christian character – we must be willing and ready to forgive everyone for everything

---

(69) I had an experience of this some years ago when an angry pastor, over his pulpit, wrongfully accused me of embezzling church funds, of watching pornography, and of using illegal drugs. A group of Christians wanted me to take him to court and sue him for slander. I rejected any kind of legal action to defend my name and character. I argued that were I to do so, I would violate scripture and make myself as guilty as he. (1 Co 6:1-8) "Besides," said I, "why should I defend myself, when the Lord can do it so much better? If God thinks I deserve defending, then he will do so. If he thinks I don't deserve it, then no action of mine can make any difference." In the end, the man who accused me was found guilty of all the offences he had falsely attributed to me, and he was dismissed, while I went merrily on under the favour of the Lord.

(especially fellow Christians). (70) In particular, before each day ends, we must be ready to –

FORGIVE GOD

How did you react to yourself this morning? Did you look in the mirror and groan at the reflected image? Were you disappointed, even repulsed by the face staring back at you? Or, did you read some story in the newspaper about a wonderfully successful person, and muse resentfully on why such good fortune was his, but not yours? Have you ever asked God why he did not give you more beauty, more skills, different gifts, more wealth – in a word, why some have so much and you have so little?

Let me go back to a text we looked at earlier, but use it now in a different way. Sirach gave this warning –

> Some people are clever enough to teach others, yet do no good for themselves. For example, here is a gifted preacher who keeps on making enemies and in the end dies in poverty. Why? Because the Lord has withheld from him grace and charm and left him destitute of wisdom.
> (37:19-21)

What a striking idea! "The Lord has withheld from him grace and charm." Does God *really* do that? Can we trust the wisdom of the old rabbi? Perhaps it is just a piece of ancient Hebrew fatalism, not agreeable with the gospel? I hardly

---

(70) Bear in mind, however, (1) that you cannot properly forgive an injury done to another person, only one done to yourself; and (2) that pardon is not the same as trust. Pardon, I owe to everyone as a man whose own sin has been forgiven by God. But trust has to be earned. I have no obligation to trust anyone until he or she has been shown worthy of that trust. And (3) although an offence has been forgiven, some kind of reparation may still be needed – say, for stolen money to be returned, or some effort made by the offender to ameliorate or remedy any harm or loss that his or her action caused.

know. Yet we do observe in life a very inequitable and unfair (in our eyes) distribution of skills and opportunities. Some do have much more than others. Is it just a product of natural causes, divine choice, or a combination of both? For some people, one answer or the other may be more correct.

In any case, because of this seeming injustice in life, many people are angry with God, resentful both of what he has done and what he has not done. They feel a pang of sympathy with Job's wife, when she cried, *"Curse God! And die!"* (Jb 2:9)

Have you trusted the Lord to answer some prayer, yet he seems to have ignored you? Have you served him faithfully, yet it seems that he has taken no notice, either of your sacrifices or of your suffering? Did you trust a divine promise, yet failed to get the expected result? Have there been times when you needed the Lord to help you out of difficulty, or to give you extra strength, or to solve a severe problem, yet you seem to have been left floundering, alone, and forsaken?

I suppose we have all been there on occasion, unhappy with our circumstances and with the Lord, because he seemed unwilling to change what we think should have been changed, or to do what we think should be done. But no happiness, as Jeremiah found, can be got by quarrelling with the Lord. Several times the prophet accused God of dealing falsely with him –

> *O Lord, why do you tell such terrible lies? You are like a dried up brook! Like a desert mirage, you promise everything, but give nothing! (Combining Je 15:18; 12:1-2; 14:19; 20:7; 4:10.)*

He went on to lament that his pain was unending and his wound seemingly incurable, and this despite serving the Lord with all his heart, enduring isolation and persecution for God's sake! (15:15-18)

Jeremiah raised a similar lament in another place –

> *God has turned my life sour. He made me eat gravel and rubbed me in the dirt. I cannot find peace or remember happiness. I tell myself, "I am finished! I can't count on the Lord to do anything for me." Just thinking of my troubles and my lonely wandering makes me miserable. That's all I ever think about, and I am depressed. (La 3:15-20, CEV)*

Do those words find resonance within your own spirit? It is likely that you too have been disappointed because the Lord has seemed powerless to meet your need, or frustrated because his promise apparently failed when you needed a miracle. Perhaps you are angry with God because of the shape life has taken, or because of what you lack, or because you are not someone else!

But such thoughts or emotions are both foolish and fruitless. God shapes this human clay one way or another as it pleases him, and our only proper response is to be pleased with what the Lord has done, and then strive to fulfil the best of what we are. Thus Paul said with some passion –

> *Perhaps you will ask me, "Since God has made us the way he wants us to be, how can he blame us for the way we are?" But, my friend, I will ask you, "Who gave you the right to question God?" Will a piece of clay dare to complain about the way a potter has shaped it? Doesn't a potter have the right to make either a lovely vase or a plain bowl out of the same lump of clay? (Ro 9:20-21)*

Some things, of course, we *can* change – either by our own action or through believing prayer and the exercise of spiritual authority in Christ – even to moving mountains! (Mk 11:22-

24). But there is much that we cannot change, and in those matters we should serenely accept our state, thank God, either for it or in it, and embrace our destiny with joy. Even that unhappy preacher described by Sirach has to accept gladly that he will never be among those who preach to a multitude. No matter what he does, he is fated to have a small congregation. Let him then be glad, thanking God for such grace and charm as he does have, and joyfully serve the people the Lord has given him!

To do otherwise – that is, to be angry with God, or to accuse him of unfair dealing, or the like – is to build a barrier beyond which the unforgiving soul will never be able to advance. It will imprison faith and bring dire impoverishment into every part of one's life. So be happy in the Lord, and in what you have and what you do not have, happily submitting to his purpose for your life.

FORGIVE LIFE

There is a scripture – which I have already mentioned – so awful, that once heard it is never forgotten. I refer to that dreadful occasion when Job's wife screamed at her suffering husband, *"Curse God, and die!"*

Yet in one way or another, we are all in that same position! –

> *Does anyone know when his time will come? Like fish that are caught in a net, or birds in a trap, any of us can be overtaken by some sudden disaster. ...*
>
> *Here is something for you to think about. If God has made a thing crooked, can you make it straight? So when everything is going your way, be happy! But when times are bad, remember this – God has made the one time as well as the other, to keep us humble and to*

> *remind us how little we really know. (Ec 9:12; 7:14).*

Good things happen. Bad things happen. Some winners lose. Some losers win. Wise men starve; intelligent women are ignored. People toil hard; yet reap scant reward from their labour. It happens to pastors, too. Many a good man, skilled, humble, hard-working, has poured himself into his ministry, yet never seen the growth for which he yearned. He may even possess in abundance the "grace and charm" Sirach spoke about, and be powerful in prayer, yet nothing avails. Time and chance are against him. (Ec 9:11)

Some preachers become so embittered, they abandon their ministry, even turning their backs on Christ, and plunging their souls into eternal darkness. But it is foolish to allow such poison to destroy happiness and fulfilment. Rather, let us determine to follow the example of Jesus –

IN HIS STEPS

His true home was an ivory palace, (Ps 45:8) but he was content to be poorer than sparrows and foxes. They have nests, but he was homeless. (Mt 8:20) He had a right to be born in the richest palace of the most powerful monarch, but his crib was a grimy manger in a foul eastern stable. As Son of God, he should have been at the centre of the empire; instead, his homeland was a minor outpost on the edge of civilisation.

He already had equality with God, but chose instead to take on human form, and to be ranked as a slave. (Ph 2:5-8) Armies of angels were his to command, but he allowed a handful of Roman soldiers to arrest and beat him. (Mt 26:53; Jn 18:12) The wind was his willing chariot to carry him to the four corners of the earth, yet he never set foot outside of tiny

Palestine. ⁽⁷¹⁾ He remained content never to go beyond the meagre knowledge of an ordinary worker of his time, although hidden in him were all the treasures of wisdom and knowledge. (Cl 2:3)

He was the King of kings and the Lord of lords, (1 Ti 6:15) but submitted to the sovereignty of Caesar. (Mk 12:14-17) He was the maker of rainbows and of glorious dawns, of the rose and every orchid; (Cl 1:16); he created the music of the spheres, and the song of every bird (Jb 38:7); yet as the Man of Galilee he painted no picture, carved no statue, wrote no song, fashioned no poem, composed no symphony. Indeed, he left behind no work of his own hand, for he depended entirely upon others to record his life, his miracles, his teaching, trusting that they would omit nothing of significance, nor include anything false.

Alexander the Great had conquered much of the known world before his 30th year, and Julius Caesar at 20 drove piracy out of the Mediterranean. Jesus too had been told that he could make the nations his heritage and the ends of the earth his possession (Ps 2:7-8); but he chose to defer that triumph. Instead, he put on a slave's apron and washed the feet of his own disciples. (Jn 13:5)

He built no organisation, established no enterprise, scorned human renown, raised no protest against the social evils of his time, never decried the barbarity of slavery, nor raised any revolt against the Roman oppressors of his people. He turned

---

(71) There is an old legend that Jesus, during his youth, visited Britain in the company of his uncle Joseph of Arimathea, who (it is said) became his guardian when his mother Mary was widowed. William Blake mentions it in his great anthem, Jerusalem – "And did those feet in ancient time. / Walk upon England's mountains green: / And was the holy Lamb of God, / On England's pleasant pastures seen!" (First stanza, first printed circa 1808.) However, it is improbable that the legend is true, for it lacks any sure historical support.

his back on the centres of power, sought no political influence, preferred the company of ordinary people to the rich and powerful, and chose his disciples without any deference to social position.

Whatever ambitions he may have had for fame, greatness, or splendid achievement, he turned them aside with the simple declaration that he had come to do only one thing, his Father's will. (Jn 6:38; 8:28; 15:10; He 10:7)

Yet how different his life could have been! Satan recognised the extraordinary greatness that was in Christ, and offered him *"all the kingdoms of the world and their splendour."* (Mt 4:8) Their conquest required only his command; their governance was within his skill; one act of obeisance could have gained him an empire that girdled the planet. Measureless riches and power were his for the asking. But Jesus scorned them all as if they were trash, and preferred to bend his knee before the Father alone. (vs. 10)

Despite all that he was, and had, and could have been, and despite an agonised plea for rescue, (Lu 22:44) he accepted without resentment the limitations imposed upon him by the Father's will. As a man, he might have been furious with God, and with life, because he was denied the freedom and opportunity to pursue all the greatness that was within him. Instead, he embraced his God-given identity and destiny, humbly yielding to shame. In place of a crown and sceptre he accepted the Roman lash. Spurning comfort, he yielded to thorns and spikes, and endured a hideous death and the cold tomb. (He 12:2)

For that reason, three days later he was able to raise himself from the grave, ascend into heaven, and is now sitting in supernal glory for ever at the right hand of God. (Jn 10:17; Ac 1:9-11; He 12:2b)

We who love him should follow his example, (1 Pe 2:21) change what we can (within the Father's will), cheerfully accept what we cannot change, maximise what we do have, and embrace life with joy!

In the end, there is nothing to forgive!

FORGIVE FRIENDS

Jesus was emphatic: *"If you forgive others for what they have done to you, then God will forgive you for what you have done to him; but if you do not with your whole heart forgive those who have harmed you, then neither will your Father in heaven forgive your offences against him!"* (Mt 6:14)

He was paraphrasing Sirach 28:2-7 –

> Forgive your neighbour for whatever harm he has caused you; then you too, when you pray, can be sure that your own sins will be forgiven. How can you seek pardon from God while you go on hating your neighbour? If you cannot show mercy to someone who is just like you, why should the Lord take any notice of you? You say, "But I'm only human!" Nonetheless, who will intercede for you so long as you hold to hatred?
> ...
>
> ... So remember what your end will be, and cast off all anger; remember that you must die, and be done with hatred; remember what the Lord has commanded, and be rid of malice toward your neighbour. Remember the covenant God has made with you, and be patient with those who don't know any better."

Are you unsure about how well you have managed to forgive everyone? Here is the test of how well you have forgiven –

> *Dear friends, never try to get even with your enemy. Instead, let God take revenge. In the Scriptures the Lord says, "You must let me be*

> *the one to avenge you and to pay back your enemies" (De 32:35)*

Scripture also says –

> *"If your enemies are hungry, give them something to eat. And if they are thirsty, give them something to drink. This will be the same as piling burning coals on their heads." (Pr 25:21-22) Don't let evil defeat you; instead, defeat evil with good. (Ro 12:19-21)*

Yet how angry we are prone to become with each other! – for any reason, for every reason, for no reason! But this is wrong. One of the dominant traits in a true Christian character is a desire to be peaceable –

> *But the wisdom from above is first pure, then peaceable, gentle, open to reason, full of mercy and good fruits, impartial and sincere. And a harvest of righteousness is sown in peace by those who make peace. (Ja 3:17-18)*

And think about the extraordinary – almost unbelievable – demand that Jesus made of his disciples –

> *Even if someone wrongs you seven times in one day and comes back to you seven times and says that he is sorry, you must keep on forgiving him! (Lu 17:4)*

So, some fellow comes up to me and knocks me down. Then tells me he is sorry, saying that doesn't know what came over him. Being a good Christian, I forgive him. An hour later he does it again. It's a bit harder this time, but still, once more I manage to pardon him. An hour later, the scene is repeated. Can I still forgive him? Perhaps, but now it's really getting hard! But then, he strikes me again, and again, and again – until he has knocked me down seven times, *all in one day!*

And still, says Jesus, I must be as willing at the end not to retaliate as I was at the beginning, and cheerfully pardon his roughness, as I did on the first occasion!

In reality, of course, after the second time, if not the first, I would be taking steps to prevent any repetition of the violence. But if I could not do so; if, in fact, I had no choice but to let him hit me seven times in one day, only to hear him tell me seven times that he repents of his violence and begs my pardon, then I must, on each occasion, pardon him with my whole heart! (Mt 18:35)

Am I equal to that? I'd rather not be put to the test! But if I were able to be so gracious, it would certainly happen only if some work of the grace of God were acting in me. Alone, I could never rise to such a demand.

Nonetheless, that is the standard Christ has set, and we have no choice but to strive to attain it. And the reason is obvious. To do otherwise is to give place to the devil, to make his rule of hate the master of our lives rather than the rule of love in Christ. May the Lord forbid that in me, and, I pray, in you too.

People can, and do, let bitterness and resentment grow into a deadly poison in their souls when they withhold pardon from those who have hurt them – but in the end, the only one hurt by the poison is the angry person! So, once again, heed the words of our text and *"pardon anyone against whom you have some complaint; for you must forgive each other, just as the Lord has forgiven you"* (Cl 3:8)

FORGIVE YOURSELF

This is perhaps the most difficult of all – yet without this, even if you forgive all others, you will still lie in a prison cell of your own making. Too many Christians, unable to forgive themselves, let their sins weigh them down. But morbid sensitivity to sin is itself ultimately the sin of selfishness. Our eyes should be fixed on Christ, not upon ourselves.

Still, I suppose that we are all prone to experience moments when suddenly the remembrance of all our follies, faults, and failures rushes upon us. We become filled with shame and self-loathing; feelings of regret strike at us; remorse burns like acid in the soul; we feel sick with disappointment and frustration. Those are times when the devil forcibly reminds us of –

- all that we have done that we should not have done; and of
- all that we have not done that we should have done; and of
- all that we are that we should not be; and of
- all that we are not that we should be!

How can we escape that thrall, forgive ourselves, and emerge to live anew in the radiant life of Christ?

I could offer you a number of biblical ways to be rid of guilt and to view yourself differently, some of which are spread across the pages of this book. But here let me quote Sirach again, with a piece of practical good sense –

> Don't indulge yourself with endless remorse, nor keep on stirring up regret. Laughter is life itself, and joy will give you many more years on earth. Live as pleasantly as you can, take whatever comfort you can get, and remove sorrow far from you. ...
>
> Unquenched remorse has destroyed many, and no advantage ever comes from it. Jealousy and anger shorten life, and anxiety brings premature old age, but people who are cheerful and merry at table will enjoy good health and many years. (30:21-25)

You would probably benefit by reading that passage two or three times. There comes a point when repentance is too prolonged, when remorse is too much indulged, when to persist in sorrow for some sin becomes itself a sin. Yes, we must repent when we have fallen short of God's demands in some way; and yes, if there is anything we can do to undo our fault, then we should do it. But then we are expected to trust in the love of God and in his pardoning grace, and stand tall again, resuming a life of praise.

Even secular writers warn against being a slave to regret –

> Make it a rule of life never to regret and never to look back. Regret is an appalling waste of energy; you can't build on it; it's only good for wallowing in. (72)
>
> It is extremely important that you show some insensitivity to your past in order to show the proper respect for the future. (73)

And then, of course, there is Paul –

> *Brothers and sisters, I can't consider myself a winner yet. This is what I do: I don't look back, I lengthen my stride, and I run straight toward the goal to win the prize that God's heavenly call offers in Christ Jesus. Whoever has a mature faith should think this way. (Ph 3:12-15; GW)*

In contrast with this, many Christians are too sensitive, too much bothered by their faults, too introverted, too self-centred; about which Esdras sternly warned –

---

(72) Katherine Mansfield: (1888-1923) New Zealand-born British short-story writer and poet.
(73) Roberto Goizueta (1931-1997), USA business executive.

> Listen, you whom I have chosen, says the Lord ... Away with your fears and doubts! For God is your Leader. Listen! You who follow my commandments and instructions, says the Lord your God. <u>You must not let your sins weigh you down</u>, nor your wicked deeds get the better of you! (2 Esdras 16:74-76, NEB)

It is a great fault, and not admirable, to become so focussed on yourself that you have scant time or energy left to devote to serving others. It is folly to become so weighed down by memory of sin that one loses capacity to rejoice in the Lord and to fulfil his purpose. "Away with your fears and doubts!" Fix your eye instead upon "God your Leader", and stand tall as a child of his love.

The antidote to being weighed down by guilt is to know –

- <u>**WHO**</u> you are in Christ – his new creation and the very righteousness of God himself.
- <u>**WHAT**</u> you have in Christ – every spiritual blessing in the heavenlies.
- <u>**WHEN**</u> you have everything in Christ – as soon as you believe the promise of God.
- <u>**WHERE**</u> you have everything in Christ – in the heavenlies, where they lie beyond the reach of the powers of darkness.
- <u>**WHY**</u> you possess everything in Christ – purely as a gift of divine grace, and solely because of what the Saviour achieved at Calvary.
- <u>**HOW**</u> you have everything in Christ – not through any work, sacrifice, pain, or prayer that you can offer, but only in response to faith in the promise of God.

CONCLUSION

God does not ask us to do what he is unwilling to do himself. So, if he commands us to pardon everyone who has offended us, (Cl 3:8) he is certainly willing to do the same. And if he says that we must never allow the sun to set on our anger, (Ep 4:26) then he too must follow the rule! This should be an assurance in your soul! If you fall asleep at peace with your neighbour, trusting in the blood of Christ to wash away all your own sin, and loving the Lord, then in the morning you will find all his mercies abundantly renewed! (La 3:23)

SEVENTEEN:

TRANSFORMATION

> I wish that there were some wonderful place
> Called the Land of Beginning Again,
> Where all our mistakes and all our heartaches,
> And all of our poor selfish grief,
> Could be dropped like a shabby old coat at the door,
> And never be put on again.

Louisa Fletcher, [74] who wrote that poem, spoke out of the depths of her own personal tragedies. Unable to endure her husband's drunkenness and wild lifestyle, she divorced him in 1911. The trouble surrounding the family break-down probably caused the schizophrenia that took the life of their only child, a daughter, Laurel, when she was but 16. One of her nephews, a noted musician, Bruz Fletcher, committed suicide in Hollywood, and Louisa's sorrows were compounded by the suicide of her sister Julia, which was followed by a bitter struggle for custody of Julia's children and of her body. Another sister, Hilda, was a lesbian, which in those days was reckoned worse than death. Louisa herself, weighed down finally by the death of her daughter, died a year later. [75]

---

(74) Louisa Fletcher, died 1923. Her full married name was Laurel Louise Tarkington, her husband being the novelist and playwright, Newton Booth Tarkington. The poem was first published in Harper's Magazine, to which she also contributed a number of short stories. The full poem has six stanzas.

(75) I gleaned the story of Louisa Fletcher from several internet sites.

Darkened by such miserable shadows, it is little wonder that she yearned for a chance to begin again, in a kinder, gentler, sunlit world!

Is there such a world? Can we find it in this life, the next, or perhaps not at all? Yes, for God himself provides a new world, based on a radical transformation –

> *Do not lie to one another. Have you not put off your old self, with all its habits? Have you not put on your new self, which, as you grow in knowledge, is being renewed in the image of its Creator? (Cl 3:9-10)*

This *"putting-off"* and *"putting-on"* is one of the most radical and extraordinary ideas in the entire Bible! Most other Christian doctrines have parallels in other writings; but not this, for nothing like it has been found in any pre-Christian literature. Here is one of those unique ideas I spoke about in my introduction, which nothing short of a divine revelation can adequately explain. It is simply not rational to suppose that Paul, in a frenzy of fictional creativity, invented the staggering concepts that occupy the first half of *Colossians*. They exist for one reason only – Paul had received them directly from God. He was simply the Lord's amanuensis.

But now, in our text, Paul solves the ancient dilemma: "How can I escape what I _am_ and become what I should _be_? How can I _begin again_?" In Christ, says he, just put off the old self, and put on the new self!

THE OLD SELF

When Paul describes the works of the "old self", he is talking about those faults and sins that are endemic in every fallen man and woman – that is, in all of us. He lists them as –

- ***five sexual sins*** – going from the outer _act_ to the inner _motivation_ (vs. 5) –

> *Put to death therefore whatever is worldly in you – sexual immorality, impurity, passion, evil desire, and greed, which is idolatry.*

- **_five verbal sins_** – going from the inner _motivation_ to the outer _act_ (vs. 8, 9).–

> *But now, put off all these things – anger, rage, malice, slander, obscene language – purge your mouth of all these. And do not lie to one another, for you have put off the old self with its practices.* (76)

In both word and deed, inwardly and outwardly, in action and in motivation, we have all been guilty of such carnality, and many still are.

But for a true Christian, such behaviour is intolerable. *"Put it off!"* cries Paul. Be done with it! Change your heart and your conduct!

Someone says, "Why?" There are two good reasons to rid yourself of all those marks of the old self –

- because the wrath of God is upon them (vs. 6) –

> *Because of these things the anger of God will fall upon everyone who refuses to obey him.*

- because the people of God must loathe them (vs. 1-3) –

> *Since you were brought back to life with Christ, set your heart on the things that are above, for that is where Christ is enthroned at the right hand of God. Keep your mind on those things,*

---

(76) I cannot remember where I first came across that analysis of the 10 works of the flesh mentioned by Paul.

> *not on worldly things, for you have died, and your life is hidden with Christ in God.*

If you have the right kind of eye, looking in the right way, you will not only catch a vision of Christ sitting on the throne beside the Father, but you will also see <u>*yourself*</u> there, in Christ, reigning with him over every principality, power, authority, ruler, and dominion of the kingdom of darkness! (2:10; Ep 1:21; 6:12) And it is from that vantage point, says Paul, we must *"put to death all the works of the old self"* (vs. 5). But some may still ask, "How shall we do that?" Must we emulate the multitudes across the ages who have struggled to kill the "flesh" by fastings, whippings, denial of all pleasure, self-inflicted pain and sacrifice? Can we gain merit with God only by violently subduing our bodies?

No, for no one has ever succeeded in that endeavour!

The ancient hermits, stylites, flagellants, and ascetics, show the folly of trying to overcome the flesh by using fleshly weapons. They crawled over broken glass, threaded their garments with thorns, flogged themselves with bone-laced whips, lived in buckets, stood for years on stone pillars, starved and beat themselves mercilessly – yet at the end, were not one whit advanced in righteousness, nor one hair nearer God.

How scornfully Paul rejected such folly –

> *These self-imposed privations look like wisdom. They seem to be disciplined and pious; they have an appearance of humility; their harsh treatment of the body seems admirable. But in the end they are worthless, for they are nothing more than another kind of fleshly indulgence! (Cl 2:23)*

So we turn back to Paul's method, which introduces the startling concept of

THE NEW SELF

Paul's method of removing the old and replacing it with the new is *faith*. And this faith is not wishful hoping, nor positive thinking. Rather, it is a deep assurance based upon a revelation of what God has done for us in Christ. Nor is it dependent upon anything more than unwavering trust in what God has spoken in the gospel through Christ. Search and see – you will find no reference to tears, pleadings, harrowing struggles, and the like! For the process of discarding the old and putting on the new is one neither of *will-power* against *sin-power*; nor of physical energy against spiritual weakness; but of *"faith"* against what Paul calls the *"flesh"*.

We may ask two vital questions –

WHAT DOES FAITH DO?

Faith *"puts off"* the old, and *"puts on"* the new. The metaphor is one of discarding old rags and donning new garments (the Greek words in Cl 3:8-10 have that particular meaning).

HOW DOES FAITH DO THIS?

FAITH RENOUNCES

Capitulation to sin must be impossible for every true Christian. We may (and do) lose some battles, but we must never finally surrender, never yield victory to the enemy, never cease to wage war against all the powers of darkness, never say that the battle is finally lost. For us, ultimate triumph must be declared inevitable. We are destined to win! We cannot ever contemplate losing, nor accept failure. This is the victory that overcomes the world, *even our faith!* (1 Jn 5:4, KJV) Cling to faith, and you cannot finally be defeated. Those who believe _prevail_! Never let go of faith! Then, no matter how many skirmishes Satan might win, you must ultimately emerge *more than a conqueror!* (Ro 8:37)

But eventual victory is not always relegated to the future. Many great conquests over corruption and sin can be had right now! You do not have to accept your weakness; you need not stay the same; you <u>can</u> be different! Declare yourself totally opposed to anything and everything spawned by Satan – even if occasionally it overcomes you – and pronounce yourself a victor in Christ. The better you can believe it, and affirm it, the more likely sin will be eradicated from your life. (77)

FAITH RESTS

Note Paul's startling assertion – *"Have you not* (already) *put off your old self? Have you not* (already) *put on your new self?"* (Cl 3:9-10)

He is saying that in the heavenlies the work is already done, but that now we must implement it in daily life; hence he adds, *"<u>put off</u> all these things ..."* (vs. 8, in which he uses the same verb as Luke uses in Acts 7:58, *"the witnesses <u>laid down</u> their coats at the feet of a young man."*) Likewise, we must cast off all the works of the old self, just as easily and just as firmly as we might toss away an old garment. And this we do in and by the name of Jesus, having all confidence in the triumph he has wrought for us in the heavenlies.

But then, not wishing to be naked, we must re-clothe ourselves in the spotless garments of righteousness that are God's gift to us in Christ. By faith (not human struggle, but simply believing) we proclaim ourselves unclothed of all

---

(77) I do not mean that we can be wholly rid of sin during this present life (except in the heavenlies in Christ). We still dwell in mortal and corruptible bodies, and this mortality will not put on immortality, nor this corruptible put on incorruptibility until after the resurrection. (1 Co 15:52-54) But that does not preclude us from growing in faith and in the knowledge of God, so that we gain ever more and ever deeper victories over the flesh and the devil.

human rags, and then reclothed in the matchless beauty of Christ.

FAITH REJOICES

All that belongs to the nature of Christ is already mine (vs. 12-14). Thus, I am not struggling to be kind, I *am* kind! Nor merciful, because I *am* merciful; nor loving, nor joyful, nor holy, nor any quality of Christ, for in him I am *already* all that he is. Hence Paul declares that we have already *"put off the old and put on the new"*. Yet he still tells us to do so! – *"As people who have been chosen by God, holy and dearly loved, clothe yourselves with compassion, kindness, humility, gentleness, and patience."* (vs. 12; and cp. Ep 4:22-24)

How can you put off what has already been put off? How can you put on what has already been put on? Here we confront one of the constant principles of scripture – what God has done for us potentially in Christ, we must seize and activate by faith. The more firmly you declare by faith the truth of what God says about you in Christ, the more brightly will the character of Christ be displayed in your life. So set yourself to speak, not what your natural eye sees, but what God says about you in Christ. *Faith* is the way to victory, not many tears and prayers; for faith releases all that Christ is and all that you are in Christ!

I remember seeing on television an evangelist who had been caught in multiple adulteries. He wept openly, complaining about how he had begged God to help him overcome his sin, but in vain. No hand reached out to him from heaven. What nonsense! What blasphemy! Subtly, he was blaming the Lord for his sin, saying it was God's fault for not helping him. But of course, all the help any sinner has ever needed has already been provided by the Father in Christ.

What that wallowing evangelist needed was not more tears, nor agonised travail against his moral weakness, nor even fasting and prayer, but *revelation* of his position in the heavenlies in Christ, and the boldness to assert his new identity. He needed to outwork the new man in his daily life by strong faith based upon a revelation of the immeasurable greatness of the power of God that is at work in all who believe! (Ep 1:18-20)

CONCLUSION

Now it is nothing to be either a Greek or a Jew, to observe some religious ritual or not to observe it, to be either civilised or uncivilised, a free person or a slave. Only Christ matters. He alone is all and he is in us all! (Cl 3:11)

EIGHTEEN:

CHOSEN

God loves you and has chosen you as his own special people. (Cl 3:12, CEV)

Why did God choose me? Was it because I am as

- Handsome as Saul?
- Rich as Croesus?
- Wise as Aristotle?
- Fearless as David?
- Strong as Samson?
- Saintly as John?
- Learned as Paul?

No! The reason why you and I were chosen to become his children is hidden in the mystery of God's will, and in the wonder of his grace. As Jesus said, *"You did not choose me, but I chose you!"* (Jn 15:16); and again, *"No one can come to me unless the Father who sent me draws him."* (Jn 6:44, 65) So we are Christians because the Father himself drew us irresistibly to Christ, for reasons that he alone knows.

But then comes another question – were we chosen aeons before our birth (as Jeremiah or Paul apparently were) [78], or was the Lord prompted to put his mark on us by something he saw only after our birth? I don't know. Or, I ask myself, "Why was I born with an intense awareness of God, whereas many people, who are in many ways better than I, seem able to ignore God altogether?" Again, I don't know. For reasons that

---

(78)   Jeremiah 1:5; Galatians 1:15.

he has not disclosed, gentle reader, the Lord chose you and me to heed his call, to love him, and to serve him, and he neither tells us the reasons for that call, nor will he ever withdraw it. (Ro 11:29)

Which leads me to consider –

AN ASTONISHING GRACE

Before you began this chapter you may have thought that all by yourself, entirely of your own volition, you made the decision to become a Christian. If so, you were wrong! You did not choose the Lord; he chose you! As one commentator puts it (commenting on *Acts 13:48*) –

> Paul says that we are "ordained to eternal life". That is a very remarkable statement, which cannot, without force, be interpreted of anything lower than this, that a divine ordination to eternal life is the cause, not the effect, of any person believing in Christ. [79]

Does this require us all to be Calvinists? [80] Well, that depends upon how such words as "chosen, elect, ordain, and pre-destined" are defined. It also depends upon how much human choice intermingles with divine election, and how far people can go in defying the will of God – that is, refusing to be *"chosen"*, or refusing to continue in faith.

This is not the place for a full discussion of those issues, but we do have to say something about our text, which plainly

---

(79) Jamieson, Robert; Fausset, A. R.; and Brown, David., <u>A Commentary on the Old and New Testaments</u>, 1871.

(80) John Calvin was a French Reformer in the 16th century. He developed a systematic theology known as Calvinism, which placed major emphasis on divine sovereignty, so that no one who was not chosen by God could hope for salvation.

declares that *"God loves you and has chosen you!"* So, did *we* make a "decision" for Christ (as some evangelists like to challenge their audiences), or did *he* first "decide" to name us as his children? Whose choice came first – mine or God's?

Some scholars escape the question by arguing that when Paul says we are *"chosen"*, he is referring to the church as a whole, not to individual Christians. That is, predestination, election, and the like, belong to the church alone, so that only if someone becomes part of the church can that person share in all that God has ordained for the church. In this view, there is no personal election until the sinner repents, surrenders to Christ as Lord, and becomes part of the church. Only then do all the blessings and promises attached to divine election belong to the new believer. Only then does the new believer join the *"chosen"*. And if he or she leaves the church, then that person will be removed at once from the number of God's elect. [81]

Others point out that while God may have elected some people to be *saved*, he does not oblige anyone to *believe*. Faith is a personal choice, and whether or not God has chosen us *we* may choose *not* to believe. In which case the election of God can be thwarted, and in the end consists of nothing more than a decision to prompt at least some people toward the gospel. If people decline to repent and to believe the good news, then the election of God is void and helpless.

Yet the sayings in the Bible about divine election are strong, and I am enough of a Calvinist to prefer placing more emphasis upon *divine* rather than *human* choice. I have more confidence in *his* call than I do in *my* faith. The love, grace, and mercy of the Lord provide a firmer foundation to stand

---

(81) The only exceptions to this rule (it is said), are those few people whom God has pre-ordained for a particular task or ministry, such as Jeremiah, Cyrus, Paul, and so on.

upon than I could ever build for myself. So I rejoice in the call of God. I find security in the knowledge that I am among those he loves, and whom he has chosen. Yet I know also that I am not just a puppet on a string. By an act of surrender to God's will, by repentance, belief, obedience, and the like, I do have a significant part to play in the great transaction.

There is undoubtedly tension between the ideas of divine election and human freedom of choice. On the one hand, I must believe that the gospel invitation is sincere – *"Whoever will may come!"* (Re 22:17); and, *"Whoever calls upon the name of the Lord will be saved!"* (Ro 10:17) Yet on the other hand, I cannot avoid feeling that I would *never* have come unless God himself had moved me! But then, no matter how strongly I may have been moved, the Lord would never have compelled me against my will to embrace Christ. I was always, and I still am, free to refuse the gospel invitation.

So then, how much of my choice to become and to remain a Christian is my own doing, and how much is God's? I truly don't know. But I do know that two things are essential both for my salvation and for its continuance – I must first repent and choose to believe; but then, at every step, I need massive help from the Lord! So my choice and God's choice are intermingled. He will not deliver me apart from my desire to be set free; and I cannot make that choice, nor continue in it, without he chooses to help me.

It seems foolish to deny that both divine sovereignty and human freedom of choice are taught in scripture. Some say that they have equal force. Some give dominance to human choice. Some give dominance to divine choice. After centuries of debate, no one has yet been able to resolve the matter. As for me, I am neither a Calvinist nor an Arminian, [82] although my instinct is to exalt God rather than man, and to give more force to his will than to my choice. Perhaps that makes me a half-way Calvinist! But I dislike labels of that sort, and prefer rather to say that I try to allow scripture alone to determine matters of doctrine.

Where the Bible is plain, then let us speak plainly. But where the Bible is unclear, then let us echo Paul's humility, acknowledging that even the best among us see only shadows. (1 Co 13:9, 12) So I shall echo the refusal of scripture to come down on one side or the other, and simply say that God chooses us to believe, and that we choose God by believing. He chose me. I chose him. Neither proposition can be wisely separated from the other.

And of this I am certain – when the Spirit of God brought me under conviction of sin and of my urgent need of a Saviour, he moved me first toward only one thing – repentant <u>faith</u>! If any person refuses to endorse the persuasion of the Spirit, refusing to accept the gospel invitation, then he or she will remain lost to the grace of God.

God does not ordain or choose or compel anyone to be *damned*. He may choose to save certain persons, and he certainly ordains that all who believe will be saved, and there may be a sense in which *every* Christian has been elected by God; *but the damned have chosen their own destiny*. Had they wished, they could have called upon the Lord, and been saved.

God won't change *his* mind, but we can change *ours*!

---

(82) Jacob Arminius was a Dutch 16th cent. Reformer. His theology insisted that human freedom of choice was paramount, and that God neither could nor would compel any person to repentance and faith.

AN AMAZING POWER

If God has chosen us to believe, it is so that we might gain from the gospel certain extraordinary blessings, all comprehended in one word – "LIFE!" –

ETERNAL LIFE

If we have been, and are, loved by God, and chosen by him to be his own *"special people"*, then we may count death as done and eternal life as won.

What is eternal life?

It is not merely *endless* life, for that would be intolerable. No matter how blissful Paradise may be, its most blessed joys must pall and become torment if they persist for millions upon billions upon trillions of years! Happily, eternal life is *not* an endless accumulation of hours. Rather, it is a different *quality* of life, outside of time, like the life of God, who himself inhabits eternity, beyond the boundaries of time. (Is 57:15)

Time came into existence only when God created the present universe, and it is inextricably linked with the physical world. If and when the physical creation finally vanishes, then time too will cease to exist; but eternity will remain. Because we are creatures of time, we cannot comprehend eternity, except to say that it is a different dimension. But the qualities of that dimension, how life is maintained within it, what are its capabilities and parameters, and similar questions, cannot presently be answered. Even the properties of the *"new"* heaven and the *"new"* earth" (2 Pe 3:13) must for now remain a mystery. People can and do speculate about these matters, but they cannot speak with any certainty. We truly know only that when Jesus comes we shall be made like him, (1 Jn 3:2) and like him, we shall escape the restraints of time and inhabit eternity. There Paradise is located. There the Kingdom of God flourishes. There the saints will experience love, laughter, and joy without measure and without end.

ABUNDANT LIFE

The lively blessings that have become ours in the gospel are summed up by the apostle in one remarkable phrase – *"We have tasted the powers* [83] *of the age to come."* (He 6:5, ESV)

Think of all the splendour of the coming Kingdom of God! In their essentials we can already, by faith, *"taste"* those "powers"!

We may summarise them as –

- The power of Healing –

    Then the angel showed me a crystal clear river, whose water gives life, flowing out from the throne of God and of the Lamb and through the middle of the City. Growing on either side of the river were trees bearing twelve kinds of life-giving fruit, which produce a new crop each month. The leaves of those trees will bring healing to the nations. (Re 22:1-2)

- The power of Prosperity –

    (The angel) showed me the holy city coming down out of heaven from God, blazing with the glory of God, brilliant as jasper, clear as crystal. The wall too was built of jasper, while the city was pure gold. The foundations of the wall of the city were adorned with every kind

---

(83) The Greek word is *dunamis*. In general, it means force, strength, power, and particularly (in scripture) supernatural power. It is the source of our words dynamic, dynamite, dynamo, and their several cousins and derivatives.

of precious jewel. The twelve gates were each made of a single pearl, and the street of the city was pure gold. (Re 21:10-21)

- The power of <u>Victory</u> –

War broke out in heaven. Michael and his angels fought against the dragon, and the dragon and his angels fought back. The dragon was defeated and I heard a loud voice in heaven, crying, "The salvation of our God has come, and the power of his kingdom, and the authority of his Christ, and his servants have conquered Satan by the blood of the Lamb and by the word of their testimony." (Re 12:7-11)

- The power of <u>Authority</u> –

"If you overcome the enemy by keeping my works to the end, I will give you the same authority over the nations that the Father has given to me, and you will rule them with a rod of iron. You will smash them into pieces as if they were clay pots. And I will give you the Morning Star." (Re 2:26-28)

- The power of <u>Fellowship</u> –

I heard a loud voice shout from the throne, "Look! God is dwelling among his people, staying with them as their God! He will wipe away every tear from their eyes, and death will be abolished. There will be no more mourning, nor crying, nor any more pain, for all those former things have passed away." (Rev 21:3-4)

Many more *"<u>powers of the coming kingdom</u>"* could be added to that list, but there is enough to encourage any believer to rise up with joy and begin *now* to grasp the inheritance that belongs to the church. We cannot in this life do more than *"taste"* those powers, for full appropriation must await the coming of Christ and the rapture of the church. But we can certainly *begin* to enjoy them now, and the more one can *believe*, the bigger the bite one can take! So, in the name of Jesus seize the *"powers"* of healing, prosperity, victory, authority, and fellowship – they are yours by right, and you may *"taste"* them as fully as you are able to believe the promise and receive the blessing.

CONCLUSION

There is nothing precarious about our salvation – it is secure in the decree of God – we are God's elect and his special people. I do not live in fear that one day I might turn my back on Christ and find myself delivered into damnation. If *my* faith is shaky, *his* is vastly sure! If *I* lack faithfulness, *he* is unshakably faithful –

> *Christ lives in me. So the life I now live in the body, I live <u>because of the faithfulness</u> of the Son of God, who loved me and gave himself for me. (Ga 2:20, NET)* [84]

My will may be faltering, my zeal sometimes cool, my obedience occasionally slack, my promises less than sure, but the Lord never resiles from his choice or his promise, and his strength never abates, nor does his love waver. He deems each of us a special child and he has chosen us to be his for ever.

---

[84] The Greek text allows either "by faith in Jesus Christ", or "because of the faith/faithfulness of Jesus Christ." The latter is the rendering followed by the NET here. As for myself, I am happy to read it every possible way – "I live in Christ because of my faith in him, and because of his faith in me, and because he is faithful to keep me living in him!"

So here is a song to sing every new day – you are a person God loves; you are ordained in Christ to *believe* and by faith to *receive* eternal and abundant *LIFE*!

NINETEEN:

PATIENCE

Since you are the elect of God, holy and dearly loved, clothe yourselves with ... humility, gentleness, and **patience***, ... You have been strengthened with all power according to his glorious might so that you might display great* **patience** *(Cl 3:12; 1:11)*

    Patience is a virtue, possess it if you can,
    Seldom found in woman; but never in a man?

Or should that be –

    Never found in woman, always in a man? *or*
    Always found in woman, seldom in a man? *or*
    Sometimes found in woman, more often in a man?

No, they are all wrong! For us Christians it should be – *"always found in woman and always in a man!"*

How do we prove that God has called us, and that his favour is with us? If we judged by the common standard we would look for wonderful miracles, extraordinary prosperity, glittering success, big crowds, answered prayer! Are they not the marks frequently looked for by both individuals and churches? But not by Paul! He urged instead things that reflect beauty of character rather than boldness of deeds, or even increase in numbers! Here I want to explore just three such virtues, mentioned in our text.

HUMILITY

Humility was not admired by the ancients (nor is it much admired in our own time), for it was associated with a cowering slave, or with cringing servitude. Thus anything that bore even an appearance of servile timidity was reckoned ignoble, mean, unworthy of any self-respecting person.

Much the same is still true today. Following the dictums of Friedrich Nietzsche, the world still says, "God is dead. He remains dead. And we have killed him!" To that bleak assertion a line from a 13th century poem is often added – "Might is right!" And nations struggle to prove their right by amassing ever greater might, ignoring any divine claim to fealty.

But against the world, the gospel insists, "Meekness is true might!" And the state of the world after twenty centuries of following its own rules shows the folly of ignoring the precepts of Christ.

Jesus came to set a different standard, and to show a different example – of gracious and cheerful service. He came, not to conquer, but to sacrifice. Yet think how differently he might have acted! He had an invincible army at his disposal, one that could have overthrown in a moment great Rome and all its legions. An army indeed so powerful that not even the combined forces of the modern world could have resisted its might! (Mt 26:53) But then, how would the scriptures have been fulfilled? And in the end, Rome crumbled, and the indestructible church of Jesus Christ rose out of its ruins!

Furthermore, Jesus was the first world religious leader (and perhaps still the only one) to present a little child as an example (Mt 18:1-5) –

> *The disciples came to Jesus and asked, "Who is greatest in the kingdom of heaven?" He called a little child and made him stand in front of them.*

> *Then he said to them, "Here is something you <u>must</u> learn – Unless you change and become like little children, <u>you will never enter the kingdom of heaven</u>. And if you would be great in the kingdom of heaven, then <u>you must become like this little child</u>!"* (85)

Suppose that question were asked of any modern church leader – *"Who is greatest in the kingdom of heaven?"* – do you think even one of them would give the answer Jesus gave? No! People would at once call to mind the pastor of a megachurch, or a world famous evangelist, or perhaps someone else in the church who has enjoyed spectacular success, or perhaps a totally self-sacrificing missionary, sparing no pain to minister to the sick, the poor, the outcasts of society.

Can you imagine *anyone* pointing to a little child as the prime example of celebrity in heaven? What a revolutionary notion! And in Bible days it was even more improbable! People then did not admire children, nor see them as unspoiled innocents, natural, loving, beautiful, for those are modern concepts. Even well into the 19th century people did not praise children, nor think they had sweet virtues that adults should copy.

---

(85) Christian legend has it that the little boy whom Jesus placed on his lap grew up to become a disciple of the apostle John, and later the bishop of the church in Antioch. His name was Ignatius. Around the year 107 he refused to obey an order of the Emperor Trajan to offer a sacrifice to an idol, and he was carried off to Rome, where he was thrown to the wild animals and torn to pieces. It is said that only his bones were left, and that they still exist as relics under the altar of the church of San Clemente. While he was being escorted in chains to Rome by a group of ten brutal soldiers, he wrote seven letters to the churches in different cities. Those letters, lively, passionate, brave, display the bishop's absolute devotion to Christ and to the church. They make great reading!

The manner in which little children were forced to toil in the factories and mines for 15 hours or more every day, in often appalling conditions, shows how little their lives were valued.

Even middle-class and upper-class children of the 19th century, who had a much easier life, were still seen as little more than small adults. Just look at a cluster of contemporary illustrations of children. You will often find a child portrayed with a childish body but quite an adult face.

Until modern times, the life of a child was cheap. Some of this was a product of the general cheapness of all life in those times; some of it was self-protection against the pain of the horrific incidence of child mortality. For example, one of the chief founders of the modern novel, Samuel Richardson (1689-1761), early lost all six children and his wife from his first marriage; and of the five children of his second marriage, only four girls survived. Such sorrow was common until less than 200 years ago. Or consider Queen Anne, the last of the Stuart monarchs in England. Despite great wealth, and access to the best possible medical care, she endured 17 pregnancies, but died without any living children to succeed her.

So people became very fatalistic about life in general and children in particular, who were deemed weak and helpless, lacking status, standing little higher than a beggar or a slave.

That is what Jesus meant by *"humble like a little child"* – not sweet, innocent, and adorable, as today his words are often taken to mean. Instead, he meant that we should be lowly, not arrogant; not proud, but vulnerable; not independent, but reckoning ourselves to be in debt to all. In the end, all other Christian virtues rest upon this foundation of *humility*. But to humility there must also be added –

GENTLENESS

Aristotle, I have read somewhere, admired this grace as *"the golden mean"*. He described it as the midpoint between being too angry and never angry. The same word was used by the Greeks to describe a tamed animal, such as an elephant – still stunningly powerful, but now under control. So never suppose that gentleness means a supine helplessness, passivity, or subservience. Rather, we should observe two things about Christian gentleness –

- ***The gentle know when to be angry***. – Think about the time when Jesus took up a whip and flogged the corrupt money changers chasing them out of the temple in Jerusalem; and his harsh words to the scribes and pharisees. (Jn 2:15; Mt 23:13, 27, 33)

- ***The gentle know when not to be angry***. They would rather *be* wronged than *do* wrong (see 1 Co 6:6-8) –

  If any of you has a dispute with another Christian, how dare you go before heathen judges instead of letting God's people settle the matter? Instead, one Christian goes to court against another and lets unbelievers judge the case! The very fact that you have legal disputes among yourselves shows that you have failed dismally. It would be better for you to be wronged! It would be better for you to be robbed! But instead, you yourselves wrong one another and rob one another, even other believers!

By all means, defend *others*, but be content to allow *God* to be *your* defence! The only really strong people in the world are those who know how to embrace true Christ-like humility and gentleness. In them, the "lion" and the "lamb" truly do lie down together and the ancient oracle is fulfilled! (Is 11:6)

PATIENCE

The old word was *"longsuffering"* – defined as "long and patient endurance of insults, injuries, and troubles."

Here is a virtue that subsumes the others within itself. It cannot exist without them; but neither can they exist without patience. Thus three old Japanese proverbs declare

> No one can succeed in life without patience . . . Patience seems bitter in the beginning, but in the end its fruit is sweet . . . With patience you can even bore through granite; those who possess patience will possess all things!

Indeed, there are people and situations that we all must bear with loving patience. To do so, reveals the beauty of Jesus –

> *If you love those who love you, do you deserve a reward? Even the tax collectors do that! Are you doing anything remarkable if you welcome only your friends? So does everyone else! That is why you must be perfect as your Father in heaven is perfect. (Mt 5:46-48)*

This is what the world is waiting to see – not more-dazzling church buildings and ever-bigger budgets, for in any case the world can far exceed the best of our achievements in such things. And even if the world still scorns us in our patience, nonetheless, godly patience is required of us as citizens of the New Jerusalem!

Remember that to reflect the beauty of Christ belongs only to us! It is an accomplishment that not the wisest or best unbeliever can ever equal. And how well that loveliness is shown by patience in an impatient world – especially when we are patient, not by necessity but by choice.

Such patience is a truly divine quality, as even the old rabbi recognised–

> For the Lord is full of compassion and mercy; he is patient, and very kind; he forgives our sin, and rescues us in times of affliction. Therefore, Woe to those whose hearts are fearful, and to faint hands, and to the sinner who tries to walk on two paths! Woe to those who are fainthearted, and who cast aside their trust! They will never be defended by God! <u>Woe to you if you have cast off all patience</u>! What will you do in the day of the Lord's visitation? (Sir 2:12-14)

So the rabbi felt that he had to warn his young disciples against losing patience. But he was equally sure that patience would bring God's reward –

> The sinner will not escape with his spoils: and the patience of the godly will not go unrequited. (16:13)

Christian patience shows itself in several forms –

- **Endurance** – *"What credit do you deserve if you endure a beating for doing something wrong? But if you endure suffering for doing something good, then God will be pleased with you."* (1 Pe 2:20) ... *Keep on rejoicing because of your hope, remain* **patient** *in trouble, and never stop praying."* (Ro 12:12)

- **Perseverance** – *"We pray that none of you will ever become slack, but that you will remain steadfastly confident until the end. Then, instead of being careless, you will imitate those who through faith and* **patience** *received God's promise."* (He 6:11,12)

- **Hope** – *"Dear friends, you must be* **patient** *until the Lord returns. See how farmers wait for their desired crops to grow. How* **patiently** *they watch for the autumn and spring rains. You, too, must be* **patient**.

Never surrender your hope. The Lord may come at any time!" (Ja 5:7, 8)

- **Tolerance** – *"We urge you, dear friends, to warn those who are not living right, encourage those who are discouraged, help those who are weak, and be **patient** with everyone."* (1Th 5:14, GW)

- **Expectancy** – *"But if you are really hoping for what you do not yet see, then you will wait for it with **patience**."* (Ro 8:25)

- **Constancy** – *"Don't lose your courage now! Confidence will bring you a great reward! But you do need **patience** so that after you have done what God wants, you can receive what he has promised."* (He 10:35)

CONCLUSION

What was Paul's great boast? His mighty deeds? No! Only one thing – <u>his chains</u>! (Cl 4:18; Ep 4:1) [86]

In the end, nothing will reach better or further into heaven than the chains of <u>humility</u>, <u>gentleness</u>, and <u>patience</u> that we gladly bear for Christ!

---

[86] For more on the chains Paul wore for Christ, see the last chapter of this book.

TWENTY:

SINGING

> *With all grace in your hearts, sing psalms, hymns, and spiritual songs to God. (Cl 3:16)*

In earlier times, every church pipe organ had to depend upon a hand-driven pump to provide its supply of air. There was a church (so I have heard), which because it owned a particularly fine organ, was often used for public concerts. On one occasion, after a remarkable performance, the guest organist went around to the back of the organ for a few minutes' rest. He found there an elderly man who had been turning the pump handle. He too was relaxing with a glass of wine, recuperating his strength for the second half. When he saw the musician, he smiled and said, "Well, we're giving them a fine concert tonight!" This seemed absurd to the brilliant organist, who replied, "What do mean 'we', old man? I'm the one who's giving the performance!"

The old man said nothing, but smiled a little more. The organist went back into the auditorium, sat down to the organ, raised both hands, and struck the keyboard with what should have been a resounding chord. But there was nothing. The organ was silent. He jumped up, rushed behind the organ again, and there was the old man, still relaxing with his glass of wine. Quickly the organist corrected his earlier remark. Said he, "You were right, my friend. *WE* are giving the people a night of wonderful music!"

We are like that, or at least we should be! Making heavenly music in the house of God is a matter of co-operation!

That is why the first word Jesus ever used in connection with his people gathering together was *sumphoneo,* (Mt 18:19-20) which means, to be in harmony, to agree, but always with a musical undertone.

That is also why Paul associates music so strongly with our collective worship, in his use of the phrase *"psalms, hymns, and spiritual songs."* (Cl 3:16; Ep 5:18-20)

WHAT MUST WE DO?

We are to *worship* God. The Greek word is *proskuneo*, which is a combination word that means literally "go towards, like a dog"! Its basic meaning is to kiss, but to kiss as an act of obeisance, hence to worship. Literally, it means to kiss like a dog licking its master's hand, hence to crouch, hence to do reverence, to adore. Such qualities of humility, dependence, joy, and eager expression, should all be inherent in Christian worship. There is also an element of boundless confidence, knowing that one is welcome, that the revered one will be equally delighted – just as my dog, when I return home after an absence, is sure to be at the door, barking, dancing around, ecstatic, optimistic, unabashed even if I pretend to growl at him!

The English word was once "worth-ship" – that is, a person is deemed so worthy as to deserve the highest honour and respect. And there are places where the word retains that original meaning. Hence magistrates and mayors are still addressed as "your worship"; and in the old wedding service the man says, "With my body I thee worship, and with all my worldly goods I thee endow."

Of course, the word is commonly reserved now for the worship of God, which can be expressed in a multitude of diverse ways and forms. Sincerity of heart, not outward fashion, is the key element needed to carry praise to the throne of God. About which I will have more to say later.

Usually, I worship in a Pentecostal environment. Now, the great *glory* of Pentecostals is their joyful freedom in the presence of God; and, the great *shame* of Pentecostals is their joyful freedom in the presence of God! Pentecostals usually manage to avoid the forms of worship that have become so stultifying in some churches, lacking spiritual life or dynamic. But that very freedom can lead Pentecostals to a worship style that is crass and clangy, which probably jars the ears of the angels as much as it does those of other auditors. Perhaps God doesn't mind the clatter, but I sometimes find it offensive. Worship should be beautiful as well as passionate; ordered as well as free; God-honouring above self-pleasing.

I think the principle expressed long ago is still valid –

> *Be careful how you behave when you enter the house of God. Some fools go there to offer empty sacrifices, not realising they are making their sin worse. It is better to go into the house of God and listen than to speak like a fool ... God is in heaven, and you are on earth, so don't mouth meaningless platitudes." (Ec 5:1-2)*

Hence Paul insists that worship should be done *"decently and orderly"*, or with grace, charm, and some dignity; and it should also be glad and joyful, passionate and spirited. (1 Co 14:40; Ep 5:19) Which leads to the question –

HOW SHOULD WE WORSHIP?

We are to worship with –

PSALMS

That is, quite literally, from the *Book of Psalms,* which some churches in the past have argued is the only valid song book for Christian worship. They reject any songs that are not part of the biblical canon. But that seems too restrictive. No doubt modern musicians, even if they cannot, like the biblical psalmists, attain canonical status, may still compose songs that honour God and are full worthy of being used in worship.

The Greek word used in our text, *psalmos*, contains the idea of a musical accompaniment, and more narrowly, a religious poem sung with musical accompaniment. Given that music is deeply embedded in the original meaning of the word, and it never lost that link, it is surprising that some churches have chosen to ban musical instruments from their worship. They argue that musical instruments are not mentioned in the apostolic letters, are nowhere authorised by an apostle, and therefore have no place in Christian practice. I do not wish to impose upon anyone something that offends them; nonetheless, when there are perhaps 150 references in the Bible to music and musical instruments, it seems a little narrow to exclude them from the church. Paul himself does mention the need for pipes, harps, and trumpets to be played clearly and melodically, although not necessarily in worship. (1 Co 14:7-8)

Psalmos certainly includes the biblical psalms, but there is nothing in the word itself, nor in the context in *Colossians*, that would limit it to the canon. Still, it is probable that Paul did have in mind, at least primarily, the songs that make up the biblical *Book of Psalms*. After all, he mentions next –

HYMNS

There was a feud between the Pastor and the Choir Director of The Backblocks Church. It seems the first hint of trouble came when the pastor preached on "Dedicating Yourselves To Service", and the choir director chose to sing, "I Shall Not Be Moved." Then there was the pastor who told his congregation one Sunday morning, "Jesus is sending me from you to another church." At once the people jumped to their feet and began singing, "What a Friend We Have in Jesus!"

Well, even if they are sometimes misused, we are still commanded to sing "hymns"! And the fact that Paul mentions "hymns" separately from "psalms" supports the idea that the latter refers to the canon, but the former to other songs. The Greek word is *hymnos,* which is obviously the source of our word. It describes a formal poem, akin to the Psalms, but not from the canon – in other words a song just like our present hymns. Another difference, too, is that a hymn may be sung with or without a musical instrument, for *hymnos* lacks the musical component of *psalmos.*

Thus a "hymn" differs from a "psalm" in two main respects – *(1)* it is not part of the canon; and *(2)* the word does not imply an accompaniment. Of course, it may and usually will be sung rather than recited, and usually will be accompanied.

Hymns have been a part of Christian worship since apostolic times. There are several selections from hymns in the NT, of which a notable example is *Philippians 2:6-11*, which may actually be an entire hymn.

SPIRITUAL SONGS

The Greek word is *ōdé,* from which also comes our word "ode". It means any kind of short song, about any theme – such as a battle song, a harvest or love song, or some other theme. By contrast, a *psalm* or a *hymn* was always focussed on God. Hence Paul adds the adjective *"spiritual"* to *"ode"* (*"spiritual songs"*), but not to the other two terms. We make the same distinction. "Hymns" and "Psalms" mean to us what they did to Paul; that is, songs addressed to God, or about sacred things. But an "ode" can be about anything, unless some distinguishing term is attached to it – hence we talk about "religious" or "sacred" odes or poems. Paul used "spiritual" songs.

Another adjective, "new" is also associated with "ode" (Re 5:9; 14:3), suggesting that such songs were short-lived, just as they tend to be with us. The psalms are manifestly for ever; and good hymns, too, tend to be sung for many decades, even centuries. But our "odes", that is, our "choruses" or short songs of one or two verses, drop off the "hit" list very quickly. In many churches there is a restless quest for "new" songs to replace those that have been sung almost to death over a few weeks or months.

But perhaps "new" does not mean "recently created" so much as "new" because they are about the gospel, the "new" covenant that replaces the old, and the "new" company of believers who alone can truly sing them in "newness" of life in the "new" heavens and earth that will follow the return of Christ.

SINGING IN THE SPIRIT

Paul talks about *"spiritual songs"* (Cl 3:16; and cp. *Jude* vs. 20). Since the word *pneumatica* ("spiritual") is linked also with the charismata (1 Co 12:1 ff.; etc.), then we may see here a reference to "singing in the spirit", for "spiritual songs" could mean "songs of the spirit." (cp. 1 Co 14:15, *"I will sing with my spirit"*)

What does that mean?

Several *Psalms* use the word *"glory"* as a description of that which most reflects in us humans the likeness of God, namely, our power of speech. This is true especially when our voices are uplifted in praise and worship of God. (Ps 3:3; 16:9; 30:12; 57:8; 108:1) In particular, the phrase *"awake my glory"* carries a feeling that David understood the high place praise and worship occupies in a godly life.

It suggests also that there is a dimension or experience of worship the psalmist had not yet fully discovered. It seems that he felt within himself a power of worship, of thanksgiving, that he had not yet been able truly to release. Hence his cry, *"Awake! Awake!"* (57:8) This dimension, in my opinion, has been opened to us by Holy Spirit baptism and glossolalia. Our tongues have been set free to praise God in a way that was not possible for saints of former dispensations.

This opens another possibility. The word *"glory"* may refer to Old Testament glossolalia, which David wished to arouse within himself. However, that was then more difficult and rare than it is today, occurring apparently only in a more or less ecstatic setting. (cp. 1 Sa 10:5-6, 10-13)

Several New Testament passages indicate that one of the highest expressions of this *"glory"* is *"singing in the spirit"* (1 Co 14:15; Ep 5:19; Cl 3:16; Ju 20). In response to which, Paul asks a question: *"What shall I do?"* –

MIND AND SPIRIT

He asks that question in a setting of worship, that is, *"What shall I do in worship; how shall I conduct myself?"* Then he explains how worship should be structured, what the people should do when they gather for worship, and he lists many things; but the *first* thing he stresses is this: *"I will **pray** and **sing**!"*

This crystallises what was in Paul's mind; it is a kind of summary of the worship experience, the essence of worship. What is that essence? Worship consists of

- "praying and singing" – with one's **mind**; and
- "praying and singing" – with one's **spirit.**

All else in worship either springs out of those actions or is an application of them.

Another way to look at it is to say that there are two dimensions in Spirit-filled worship – the **natural** and the **supernatural.** One arises from the human **mind**, moved by the Holy Spirit; and the other arises from the human **spirit**, moved by the Holy Spirit.

Those two dimensions could also be expressed as the **rational** and the **irrational**. That is, worship needs input from an informed **reason**; but it also needs input from that godlike attribute that we call the human **spirit**. This spirit is the mark of God in us, separating us from the beasts. They are bodies that have life; but we are spirits that have bodies; therefore the spirit should be the pre-eminent part in our makeup. Unhappily, sin has so stifled our spirits that the physical and material have gained a sorry ascendancy; therefore we are condemned to labour with much toil and tears, depending mostly upon physical powers. By contrast, the human spirit acts solely by the *spoken word;* in fact we were intended to be spiritual creatures, acting on the same basis as God acts, which is, *the principle of authority expressed through the spoken word*. Thus, the human spirit always acts through the spoken word; only the flesh has to operate through physical toil.

EDEN RESTORED

In worship, therefore, we are seeking to escape those trammels of the flesh, to come back to true spiritual fellowship with God, to capture Eden again, even if only fleetingly. And in worship the human spirit reasserts its ascendancy; that is, we demonstrate our recognition that we are primarily *spiritual beings*, and for a time we cast aside the earth-bound identity the flesh has imposed upon us.

So when we come to worship, and our spirits are reaching out to God, we should do so in the way that the human spirit most deeply wishes to express itself, not primarily through *actions*, but through *words*, awaking within us, as the psalmist cried, our *"glory"*!

In this we are emulating God, who always expresses himself through the Word: whether the Word spoken, or the Word written, or the Word made flesh. The Holy Spirit too manifests his presence by words; hence the usual first sign of Holy Spirit baptism is that we *speak* (in other tongues).

It is in the very nature of each true spirit to express itself through words, especially words of worship, which is exemplified in the never-ceasing songs and acclamations of the heavenly host around the throne of God. (Re 4:10-11; 5:11-13; 7:9-11; 11:16-17; etc) So then, if worship is a **spiritual** activity, if it is the placing again of the believer's human spirit upon the throne of life, the re-assertion of our true identity as spiritual beings (rather than mostly physical or material), then worship will inescapably be a thing of words. And those words, as we have seen, should arise from both the human *mind* and from the human *spirit*, giving both a rational and an irrational, a natural and a supernatural dimension to worship.

Let us look again at the use of glossolalia in worship, especially what scripture means when it speaks about *"singing in the spirit"* -

"AWAKE, MY GLORY!"

The phenomenon of entire congregations singing together in other tongues is now widespread in the charismatic/pentecostal movement. Many feel that such *"singing in the spirit"* should always be spontaneous, unstructured, unplanned, uncoordinated – that it should be the result of an invasion from heaven irresistibly carrying the people along.

But scripture shows otherwise, because glossolalic song arises

FROM THE HUMAN SPIRIT

Notice that "spirit" in *1 Corinthians 14:15* has a small 's'. It is not the Holy Spirit but the human spirit that sings in other tongues. Once a person has been baptised in the Holy Spirit and has spoken in other tongues, it becomes just as natural for the spirit to express itself in glossolalia as it is for the mind to express itself in a vernacular tongue.

That is why Paul is able to say, *"What am I to do? I will pray with the spirit* (in glossolalia) *and I will pray with the mind* (in the vernacular); *I will sing with the spirit, and I will sing with the mind."*

UNDER CONTROL

Notice that the choice either to sing or speak in tongues is entirely at his own volition, for he says, *"I will...."* So whether or not a glossolalist exercises the gift is a matter for that person to decide; the use of glossolalia is not governed by the Holy Spirit, but by the human will. So it is clear that glossolalic song occurs because the people have chosen at that moment to sing in the spirit instead of with understanding. For that reason, the length of time they sing, and the manner, are also at their discretion. Despite what is sometimes claimed, they truly can start or stop at will; they can sing softly or loudly, sorrowfully or cheerfully, discordantly or harmoniously.

PROMPTED BY THE HOLY SPIRIT

I hasten to allow that the Holy Spirit may prompt the Spirit-filled church to praise God in other tongues. Indeed, let us fervently hope that our worship will always be guided by the Spirit! Nonetheless, the maintenance of order, beauty, dignity, and harmony in the church are not the responsibility of the Spirit, but of the worship leader, and of the congregation. No matter how strongly the Holy Spirit may be moving in the church, Paul's instructions make it clear that singing in tongues remains just as firmly within our control as does singing in English. The Holy Spirit never robs the church of its freeborn prerogative to select which form of song to employ in worship, and we always have liberty to determine the time, manner, and place of our song, whether glossolalic or vernacular.

MELODIC FORM

Singing in the spirit should therefore have form. It is no more unspiritual to require that the people harmonise with each other in *glossolalic* song than to do so for *vernacular* song. It does not restrain the Holy Spirit to impose a chordal structure on glossolalic song. Worship leaders should not abandon their office just because the people are singing in tongues; they should not hesitate to give direction, to keep sweetness and grace in the worship, to restrain those who become too boisterous, or to exhort those who are too lax, or irritatingly discordant.

Paul is clear that glossolalic singing is not an arbitrary miracle wrought unexpectedly by the Holy Spirit. Rather, it is (or should be) beautiful praise that the Spirit-filled church itself lifts up to the glory of God. Being filled with the Holy Spirit, and having now an ability to praise or sing in other tongues, the church should seize that ability and *"strive to excel"* as it offers back to God a sacrifice of glossolalic praise. (1 Co 14:12; He 13:15)

SPIRITUAL EXCELLENCE

Achieving a goal of excellence in worship will require –

- that the people be truly filled with the Holy Spirit;
- that the worship leader gives wise and sensitive direction, neither intruding too much nor abandoning his or her role; and
- that the people maintain a balance, concentrating their adoration upon God while remaining aware of each other and blending with each other in song.

It is no doubt wonderful in private "to get lost in the glory", and to worship God in any way one pleases; but such liberty is not appropriate in a public service. When the people are gathered together is not the time (as a familiar chorus unfortunately says) to "forget about yourself and concentrate on him, and worship him". Rather, hearts, hands, and voices should be raised in unison to bless the Almighty with conscious harmony and beauty.

WHY MUST WE WORSHIP?

CALVARY

For what greater reason should we worship than because Jesus died and rose again that we might live for ever! Can there be any higher incentive? Can you contemplate the cross and not be profoundly moved, first to deepest repentance and then to highest joy?

Hence our text says that we should be marked as people who are continually *"singing and making melody in our hearts to the Lord!"* (Cl 3:16) How can it be otherwise? For who can measure the joy of sins forgiven? Who can tell the delights of fellowship with the King? No wonder the Psalmist cried, *"in thy presence there is fullness of joy; at thy right hand there are pleasures for evermore."* (Ps 16:11) All worldly pleasure is ephemeral – life cannot last; friends depart; illness prevails; loss happens; but divine pleasures begin now and can but increase beyond the grave, onward and upward for ever.

TWENTY-ONE:

HEARTILY

With all grace in your hearts, sing psalms, hymns, and spiritual songs to God. (Cl 3:16)

In the year 1727 Johann Sebastian Bach wrote his magnificent oratorio, the *St Matthew Passion*. He thought it would be performed only once, at the Lutheran Church in Leipzig, on Good Friday afternoon. He would probably be astonished to find it still being presented annually around the world, and acclaimed everywhere as "the greatest work of its kind ever written."

The members of the original congregation were given copies of portions of the music, and they were expected at the appropriate times to sing along with the choir, which they did [87] with great devotion and joy. The whole performance must have occupied at least three hours, for the oratorio was interspersed with the regular parts of the church service – prayers, scripture reading, oblations, a homily, and the like.

That was the worship style, and experience, of a Lutheran congregation nearly 300 years ago.

Have we advanced since then? Or have we gone backward? Is our worship more glorious or less? Do we have anything at all to boast about in the way we worship God, the kind of music we use, the practices we follow?

---

(87) They must also have been vastly more musically literate than most modern congregations are.

More importantly: why *do* we do the things we do? Are we following *culture* or *Christ*? Is there any *biblical* underpinning for our worship style? What is our *theological* justification, our prime motivation, our ultimate goal, for the way we worship? Does *God* approve or disapprove the way we structure our church services? Does anyone in our churches even *ask* such questions, let alone know the answers?

I am not suggesting that we must revert to the 18th century for the only correct way to worship God. But I do say that we should not glibly assume that we are following the best path. Perhaps our way is good; perhaps it is poor. But at least let someone in the church ask the right questions! The answers may leave us exactly where we are. Or they may take us into a new dimension. Best of all, they may give us a renewed sense that our worship is indeed fully pleasing to the Lord.

A DIVINE GIFT

God has given three special gifts to the church, within which its worship should be framed –

- the **_Word_** – which must always remain supreme
- the **_Eucharist_** – which is next in value
- **_Music_** – especially when it is associated with words.

Of music in the church, we can say that it has

AN EXALTED POSITION

Some say that music has a place second only to the word. Thus Martin Luther –

> I am not satisfied with him who despises music, as all fanatics do; for music is an endowment and gift of God, not a gift of men. It also drives away the devil and makes people cheerful; one forgets all anger, unchasteness, pride, and other vices. I place music next to theology and give it

the highest praise. And we see how David and all saints put their pious thoughts into verse, rhyme, and songs, because music reigns in times of peace. .... Music I have always loved. He who knows music has a good nature. Necessity demands that music be kept in the schools. A schoolmaster must know how to sing: otherwise I do not look at him. And before a youth is ordained into the ministry, he should practise music in school. I firmly believe, nor am I ashamed to assert, that next to theology no art is equal to music; for it is the only one, except theology, which is able to give a quiet and happy mind. [88]

But Luther was long preceded by Plato, who twenty centuries earlier had argued that music not only stirred the emotions but had power to influence character. He insisted therefore that great care should be taken to choose the best kind of music, and that the young could not achieve full virtue without a thorough training in music. [89]

Likewise, Aristotle believed that music profoundly influenced the soul, and therefore only the noblest kinds of music should be employed in education and religion. [90] Many other philosophers in the ancient world, and also in modern times, have echoed those ideas. The Church Fathers, too, with few exceptions, honoured the noble role music has in worship, from which flowed several necessary consequences –

---

(88) What Luther Says, compiled by Ewald M. Plass, Concordia Publishing House, Missouri, 1959; Vol II, Selections # 3091, 3092, 3104.
(89) Respublica, 398c-399d; Laws, 653d-673a; 795a-812e.
(90) Politics 8.1339-1342.

- They insisted that nothing but the best of which we are capable should be offered to God.

- They insisted that worship cannot be mainly for "moral uplift, nor ecstatic feeling, nor aesthetic pleasure; on the contrary, worship means giving to God (Ps 29:2; cp. 96:9) that of which he is worthy (the root word means 'worth-ship'), that which is his due." [91]

- They insisted that the point of worship is neither to amuse nor please people (although good worship will certainly bring joy to the human heart), but rather to delight the Lord.

- They insisted that while the music must be meaningful to the people, mere popularity was never in itself sufficient reason for adopting a particular style. [92]

In agreement with the Fathers, Christian leaders across the centuries have consistently denounced the use of music that pulls attention to itself rather than pointing toward God. They have demanded good music, that is, music possessing form, harmony, melody, beauty, balance – in fact, all the qualities that are needed to identify a piece of music and its performance as "good". [93] But they have equally demanded

---

(91) Baker's Dictionary of Practical Theology, article, "Worship - Aids to Worship."

(92) Those affirmations have been culled from my reading of the Fathers, although I regret that I did not annotate the sources.

(93) It is probably fair to say that the best music is pleasing to the ear of all cultures and all generations, although some measure of "training the ear" may be necessary before one can enjoy an unfamiliar style of music.

that both music and performance must always be kept within a framework of glorifying God. (94)

Church leaders across the centuries have also been wary about music that seems too sensual or emotional in its character, stirring the passions of the soul rather than arousing pure spiritual worship.

So long, then, as worship is focussed on God, music that helps to achieve that aim may rightly be given an exalted position in the liturgies of the church.

AN EXTRAORDINARY WITNESS

Music celebrates the victory of Christ. Those who have entered into the Saviour's triumph cannot help but make merry, expressing their joy, triumph, and adoration in song. Will victors weep? I would hope not.

Such worship is an excellent tool of evangelism, for it is not uncommon for visitors to a church to find in a hymn or song the best sermon, and to be drawn by it to repentance and faith. (95) For that reason, Paul commends the saving power of a good worship service, but denounces the contrary effect of a bad one (1 Co 14:23-26). He reckons that a properly

---

(94) I once preached in a church where the pastor was very unhappy with the quality of its spiritual life. After I had been there a few days, he asked me what he could do to lift the people to a higher level. I replied that first, I would sack the pianist. The astonished pastor asked why? I said, "He plays for his own glory, not the glory of God." But the church was proud of its brilliant pianist, who constantly performed the most amazing keyboard pyrotechnics, and my advice went unheeded. They continued in the doldrums.

(95) From an article in the Sydney *Sun Herald* (14/03/99), just after the death of the renowned violinist, Yehudi Menuhin – "George Bernard Shaw wrote: 'Listening to an artist like Yehudi makes even an atheist believe in God.' ... At (Menuhin's) first concert in Berlin a few days before his 13th birthday, a man followed him backstage, hugged him, and declared, 'Now I know there is a God in heaven!' The man was Albert Einstein."

functioning congregation will attract to itself a kind of prophetic mantle (*"everybody is prophesying"*), so that every part of the worship service will echo with the voice of God and be redolent of his presence. (96)

Further, people are unconsciously yet forcibly taught doctrine when they repeatedly sing a hymn or chorus. Hence attention must be given to the theological message of our hymns and choruses (1 Ti 4:16); we should not tolerate constant singing, over and over again, of error. How can God be glorified or spiritual life strengthened by repetitiously singing heresy?

Music will bear its best witness when words and melody are in symmetry with each other, and with scripture, creating a harmony not only of melody but of truth. Give attention then not only to the *sound* of the words, but their *meaning*. The doctrine they teach, the kind of praise they offer, should blend readily with the music, its melody, tempo, rhythm, and mood.

AN ELEGANT VICTORY

Martin Luther (as we saw above) had no doubt that music can drive the devil away as surely as does sound theology. (97) On another occasion he said –

> The devil is a spirit of sadness and cannot stay where a heart is spiritually joyful . . . (and) that is why he stays far away from music."

---

(96) In ancient Israel, too, a prophetic unction rested upon their worship – "Chenaniah, a Levite leader, instructed others how to sing prophetic songs because he was skilled at it. ... David was dressed in a fine linen robe, as were all the Levites who carried the ark, the Levites who were singers, and Chenaniah, the leader of the musicians' prophetic songs." (1 Ch 15:22, GW) See also 1 Chr 25:1, 3, "Jeduthun prophesied with the lyre."

(97) In this he echoed scripture. (1 Sa 16:23)

Of course, Luther meant only godly music, from a heart joyful in Christ. Still, he probably would have agreed with the 18th-century preacher Rowland Hill, who once said in a sermon that "he did not see why the devil should have all the good tunes."

Does our music attract or repel the Evil One? It is a question worth pondering. Scripture suggests that suitable music may indeed drive the devil away! (1 Sa 16:16, 23)

Does the Lord open his ears to it, or turn aside in grief, or even anger? Probably there is no particular musical form that is offensive to God, or need be offensive to us, except that lack of excellence, discordant harmonies, shoddy performance (below what the musicians are capable of achieving), poorly matched words, and the like, may strip the glory from any kind of music.

The point is, music used properly in the church can be a great enhancement of Christian victory, helping to break the strength of sin, to uplift the soul, to drive away darkness, to enliven the mind, to stir faith, hope, and love. But the contrary is also true. So it is our responsibility to ensure that rich blessings are in fact the product of our worship, and in particular, of music in worship.

AN ETERNAL PRESENCE

MUSIC CAN WITNESS TO THE PRESENCE OF GOD IN THE CHURCH

Music cannot *create* that presence, which depends solely upon God's promise, and not upon any effort of ours. (He 13:5b-6; etc.) Nor can we *"break through"* to God, simply by singing louder, faster, or more passionately. (98). But music may help us to fulfil better the injunction to come *"boldly into the holiest by the blood of Jesus."* (He 10:19-23) Music may make us more receptive to the word of God, more able to hear his voice and to respond to it. Elisha, when he could not catch any word from God, called for a minstrel to play to him. Very soon, the hand of the Lord fell upon him, and he received an extraordinary vision. The result was a great triumph for Israel. (2 Kg 3:15)

MUSIC CAN WITNESS TO THE PRESENCE OF GOD IN THE CREATION

Music heralded the majestic work of creation, (Jb 38:4-7) and still has power to carry us behind the veil into the mystical origins of the universe, hence into converse with the Lord of Creation. (99) The God of Creation can be and has been discovered by many through the agency of music, and music often expresses a yearning desire for that very discovery –

> Music is the art of the prophets, the only art that can calm the agitations of the soul; it is one of the most magnificent and delightful presents God has given us. (100)

---

(98) "Breaking through" is the prerogative of *"the Lord of the break-through"* – that is *"Baal-Perazim"* – a name God is given in Ex 19:22,24; 2 Sa 5:17-21; Is 28:20-22; Mi 2:13.

(99) Many of the greatest musical compositions embody this idea, as, for example, Beethoven's Sixth Symphony (The Pastoral), or his Ninth (The Choral), or Vivaldi's "The Four Seasons".

(100) Martin Luther. Quoted in A Treasury of Christian Wisdom, ed. Tony Castle; Hodder & Stoughton, London, 2001; pg. 166.

> Bach opens a vista to the universe. After experiencing him, people feel there is meaning to life after all. (101)

The ancient Greeks captured that yearning in their myths about Aeolus (the god of the wind) and the magical instrument that was named after him, the Aeolian harp. They sensed an awesome mystery in the strange humming harmonies of the wind-swept chords, for the soft melodies seemed to promise an anthem inspired by the gods, transcending any sound that human fingers could entice from the taut strings.

But we are dealing with the true heavenly wind, the eternal Spirit of God, (Ac 2:2) who is flowing across the strings of our hearts, and in the divine melodies he produces there is a haunting beauty, a sound of limitless freedom, a miracle of love, a splendid glory of inspired worship.

AN EXTENSIVE GRACE

Music has a sacramental value. That is, divine grace can be communicated to the devout worshipper through the channel of music, (Ep 5:18-20; Cl 3:16) for it can bring the worshipper into a closer communion with Christ. (cp. 2 Kg 3:15)

Music can unleash the glory of God. (2 Ch 5:12-14) But note that the temple choirs and musicians had been preparing for some ***ten years*** (102)for the great day of dedication. (1 Ch 6:31-32) They were highly skilled, dedicated artists. And the result of that disciplined and beautiful performance? –

---

(101) Helmut Walcha, *ibid.*

(102) 1 Kg 9:10. Solomon took 20 years to build temple and palace – 13 years for the palace (1 Kg 7:1), hence 7 years on the temple. From the time David began to make preparations, then, the whole was at least 10 years.

> *The house of the Lord was filled with a cloud, so that the priests could not stand to minister because of the cloud, for the glory of the Lord filled the house of God!*

I am not saying, of course, that the glory of God fell upon them merely because their music and song were flawless. Rather, by offering to God the finest gift of praise they were able to present, in conjunction with fervent devotion, strong faith, and sincere prayer, they moved God to a greater manifestation of his presence and power than a careless performance would have attracted.

CONCLUSION

Not all music achieves these goals. Hence the Church Fathers long ago discovered that the more music was highly valued the more potential it had for peril; the very thing that can most enhance *worship* can most easily be turned into *idolatry*. Thus Augustine, who in several places in his writings expresses his great love of music, nonetheless saw three problem areas –

- a stifling legalism that seeks to ban all music, just as it frowns also upon painting and other expressions of the fine arts, deeming them "worldly"; and

- music becoming so gorgeous, or sensual, or appealing to the ear that it ultimately fixes attention upon itself rather than upon God; and

- music of such poor quality or style that it degrades worship, diminishes the glory of God for the hearers, and offends good aesthetics.

Augustine confessed that he had been guilty of all three errors, and then he says –

> In this life, the whole of which is termed a trial, no man should be sure whether one who can pass from worse to better might not also pass from better to worse ... (So it is with) the delights of the ear, (which) had more firmly entangled and subdued me, but you broke them and set me free ... Thus do I waver between the danger of sensual pleasure and wholesome experience. I am inclined rather to approve the practice of singing in church ... so that through the pleasure of the ears the weaker mind may rise to feelings of devotion. However, when it so happens that I am moved more by the singing than by what is sung, I confess that I have sinned, in such wise as to deserve punishment, and at such times I should prefer not to listen to a singer. [103]

In reaction against those perils, the church has tended to adopt several extremes –

- ban all music from worship, restricting music to secular play and pleasure alone, which seems too extreme and lacks any true biblical warrant.

- ban all use of music outside the church, restricting its use solely to worship and the glory of God; but that is an impossible, and indeed, unnatural demand.

- ban the use of all musical instruments and sing only *a cappella*; but that generally results in lacklustre and ineffective singing.

- ban the use of all musical forms except those approved for worship; but the world will not be denied its music,

---

[103] The Confessions of St Augustine; tr. by John K Ryan; Image Books, New York, 1960; Book 10, Chapters 32, 33; pg. 261-263.

and the church should be free to use whatever musical forms can be employed to glorify God.

- ban all lyrics except those that come directly from scripture; but that deprives modern poets from using their talent to glorify God.

None of those extremes seem reasonable or biblical. Israel's ancient example surely shows that music and lyrics can be composed and professionally performed with musical instruments, along with choirs and dancers, for the highest glory of God and the greatest benefit of the church. Our aim should be simply to achieve the same, so that we do indeed

> *sing psalms, hymns, and spiritual songs to God, with all grace in our hearts. (Cl 3:16)* [104]

---

[104] Also see the addendum at the end of this book, John Wesley on Congregational Singing.

TWENTY-TWO:

BLISSFUL

Wives, submit to your husbands, for this is fitting in the Lord. Husbands, love your wives and do not treat them harshly. (Cl 3:18-19)

> Fair Genevieve, my early love!
> The years but make thee dearer far.
> My heart shall never, never rove;
> Thou art my only guiding star.
> O Genevieve, sweet Genevieve,
> The days may come, the days may go,
> But still the hands of memory weave
> <u>The blissful dreams of long ago</u>. (105)

Many old songs, like *Sweet Genevieve,* describe the reflections of a couple who have been long married and are reminiscing about the days of their young love. Here are a few that I remember from my boyhood (which too was long ago!) –

> Darling, I am growing old,
> Silver threads among the gold
> Shine upon my brow today.
> Life is fading fast away,
> But my darling, you will be
> Always young and fair to me. (106)

---

(105) *Sweet Genevieve,* by George Cooper (1869).

(106) *Silver Threads Among the* Gold, by Eben Rexford (1848-1916). This song I remember well, because it was popular at the great community sing-alongs that my Mother used to take me to, back in the early 1940s. They were held

> My darling I am dreaming of the days gone by,
> When you and I were sweethearts,
> Beneath the summer sky;
> Your hair has turned to silver,
> The gold has faded too;
> But still I will remember, where I first met you. (107)
>
> You are the same sweet girl I knew
> In happy days of old,
> Your hair is silver, but your heart is gold.
> Time has not changed your loveliness . . .
> You're just as sweet to me
> As in the days that used to be,
> When you wore a tulip, a sweet yellow tulip,
> And I wore a big red rose. (108)
>
> Just a song at twilight, when the lights are low;
> And the flick'ring shadows softly come and go.
> Tho' the heart be weary, sad the day, and long,
> Still to us at twilight comes love's old song,
> Comes love's old, sweet song,
> Love's old, sweet song. (109)

When I was a boy, some of those songs were already more than 50 years old, but they were all still well known, and they were often heard on the radio, or sung around the piano at family gatherings, or at community sing-alongs. But such

---

in the old Tivoli Theatre in Adelaide. The song was written in 1873 by Eben Rexford when he was only 18! It was one of a collection of poems by him, called *Growing Old*. In later life, Rexford gained fame as a writer of articles and books on gardening.

(107) *Down by the Old Mill Stream*, by Tell Taylor (1908).
(108) *When You Wore a Tulip*, by Jack Mahoney (1914).
(109) *Love's Old Sweet Song*, by J. Clifton Bingham (1884).

songs do not seem to be written anymore! Rather, themes of adultery, treachery, deceit, infidelity, seem far more common.

Is there a reason for this? Do people no longer expect longevity in marriage? What has happened to those "blissful dreams of long ago"? How did "love's old sweet song" turn so sour? Has love become impossible once "silver threads appear among the gold"? Is an aging wife now to be told that she is not "as sweet to me as in the days that used to be"? Should we now scorn the fervent avowal of Shakespeare's sonnet? –

> Let me not to the marriage of true minds
> Admit impediments! Love is not love
> Which alters when it alteration finds,
> Or bends with the remover to remove:
> Ah! No! It is an ever fixed mark
> That looks on tempests and is never shaken! [110]

Perhaps moderns are fearful of the seeming confinement of a loving marriage, or of its curtailment of their precious "liberty"? Yet in a true marriage there is enlargement and enrichment, as each partner helps the other to discover and to fulfil their full potential. They grow together. They mature together. They discover ever finer treasures in each other. They remain lovely in each other's eyes.

I do not mean that single people cannot know such things, for they can; but they have to discover them in different and often more difficult ways.

MORE THAN 60 BLISSFUL YEARS

Across the more than six decades of our life together, my wife Alison and I have never had any reason even to think about divorce; but in any case, divorce was never an option. I do not

---

[110] The first 6 lines of *Sonnet 116*.

belittle anyone who has been obliged to suffer the anguish of divorce, nor that divorce was impossible for us, but only that we truly meant it when we vowed before God to live together in love until death alone should part us.

There are certainly things that might have forced a divorce – if either of us had run off with someone else; if either of us had been abusive to the other, physically or verbally; or if either of us had turned to violent drunkenness, drug addiction, child abuse, and the like. In such circumstances, divorce is not only permissible, but almost an obligation (1 Co 7:15). [111]

But divorce, merely because one of us found someone else more attractive, or to suit some other selfish goal, or for anything less than an extreme and unendurable cause, was for us unthinkable.

From the beginning, in March 1954, we were, <u>*both of us together*</u>, resolved to remain wedded for life, and to make the marriage work happily for us and for our children.

We are a bit like the late British actress Dame Sybil Thorndike who was married for 61 years to the writer Sir Lewis Casson. Toward the end of their life-long union she was asked if she had ever considered divorcing him? She replied, "Divorce? Never! But murder? Often!"

I hasten to say that never even jokingly have I wished to murder Alison! But she and I have been as emphatic as Dame

---

[111] "But if the unbeliever wants a divorce, let it take place. In these circumstances the brother or sister is not bound. God has called you in peace." (CEV) I understand "unbeliever" here to include any person who either has no faith in Christ, or has abandoned faith, choosing to behave unspeakably. For an extensive discussion on matters of divorce and remarriage, see my book Corinthians – the First Letter in the series Treasures from Paul, Vision Publishing, Ramona CA; 2014.

Sybil – divorce has simply never been on our list of allowable things to do.

So, if one is resolved on the permanency of marriage, how can it be achieved? Here are a few ingredients of a long and happy marriage – yet not just of marriage, but also of any true relationship. They apply, too, to our relationship with God.

FRIENDSHIP

Many marriages founder because the couple never became true friends. No doubt they once felt a strong physical attraction for each other, but they lacked any deep sense of goodwill. There needs to be an element of brother/sister in the relationship as well as being lovers –

> *This is my beloved and this is my <u>friend</u>, O daughters of Jerusalem!" (Ca 5:16) ...You have ravished my heart, my <u>sister</u>, my bride!" (4:9, 10, 12; 5:1)*

She calls him *"friend"*; he calls her *"sister"*. Indeed, four times he calls her his *"sister"* <u>before</u> he calls her his *"bride"*. Here then is an essential but often forgotten reality. Marriage cannot survive on sexual attraction alone. As well as passionate lovers, the couple must also be simply friends, with a very large measure of goodwill toward each other. From the day I began to court her, in 1953, Alison has not only been (and still is, 2014) my sweetheart, but also my *best friend*. I always prefer her company to that of anyone else. Of course, I have sometimes been obliged to travel away from home, and I have many wonderful friends around the world, but I am never so happy as when I get home again, and Alison is there.

After all, this is true love, the love of God, who showers benevolence upon all, good and bad alike (Mt 5:45). The Greek word is *"agape"*, which not only describes the kindly love of God, but is often enjoined upon every Christian, and especially upon wedded couples. (Ep 5:25, 28, 33; Cl 3:19; 1 Jn 4:7-8)

Think about this. We are the Bride of Christ, and he calls us *"friends"*. (Jn 15:15) So should we call each other. It is important, then, for any two people contemplating marriage to ask, not, "are we *lovers*?" but, "are we *friends*?" For if they cannot establish between them a fond, warm, committed friendship, it is unlikely that romantic love will long survive.

GOODWILL

> The COMMITTEE promoting the EMIGRATION of SINGLE WOMEN to AUSTRALIA hereby give Notice that a fine SHIP of about 500 tons burden carrying an experienced surgeon, and a respectable person as superintendent to secure the comfort and protection of the Emigrants during the voyage, will sail from GRAVESEND on Thursday 1st of May (1834) next, (beyond which day she will on no account be detained) direct for HOBART TOWN, VAN DIEMEN'S LAND. Single Women and Widows of good character, from 15 to 30 years of age, desirous of bettering their condition by Emigration to that healthy and highly prosperous Colony, where the number of Females compared with the entire population is greatly deficient . . . may obtain a passage on payment of Five Pounds only.

The above advertisement appeared in several London journals during the early part of the year 1834. The vessel was the *Strathfieldsaye*, and she sailed on the stated date with a complement of 286 emigrant women and one cabin passenger, a Miss Baker. Four months later, on August 19th, the *Colonial Times* in Hobart Town reported her safe arrival, but added an indignant editorial about the way the ladies had been mobbed by an enthusiastic crowd of some two thousand men. With much difficulty the emigrants were safely brought to their hostel, and within a few days, as the London committee had promised, they all found employment. For most of them, marriage soon followed, and according to an early historian, John West, few of the unions proved unsatisfactory.

In addition to free emigrants some 25000 female convicts were transported from the United Kingdom to Tasmania during the first half of the 19th century. Concerning them, Coultman Smith writes,

> Their transportation was more for the benefit of the new colony than for the relief of the United Kingdom, for the discharged convict and the adventurous pioneer must have the means to bring him consolation and children if Tasmania was to grow from a liability to an asset. On landing, the women were placed in hiring depots to be assigned to settlers. . . . (Many) became diligent servants, or tolerable wives or consorts to settlers and discharged convicts. . . . The authorities encouraged marriage, and many unions proved highly successful." (112)

Similarly, but 40 years earlier, in June 1790, the *Lady Juliana* arrived at Sydney Town with 222 female transportees, plus a number of babies that had been born on the year-long journey. The ladies were obliged to wash themselves thoroughly, dress in their finest gowns, which during the voyage had been put aside for this purpose, and then disembarked to be met at the wharf by a crowd of men. Hence

---

(112) The History of Tasmania; published in 1852; Part Three, Sec. 12. The advertisement and the report of the Strathfieldsaye's arrival I copied direct from the *Colonial Times*, which can be read in the Tasmanian State Library.

they were called "wharf women". Within a short time most of the ladies had been matched with a man, and many of those couples were eventually wedded, apparently, in the main, with good success.

Sian Rees reports that –

> a marine arriving in 1792 on another female transport said that his ship was overrun by male colonists thrusting each other out of the way to claim their prize. (113)

As may be imagined, the strongest seized the prettiest, and the remainder took the rest. Not all the couples married, but most of them did, and most of those unions proved to be satisfactory. As suggested above, in the story of the *Strathfieldsay*, this practice continued for several decades until growing public morality forced the authorities to protect the women, restrain the men, and strive to effect a more regular meeting and marrying of the sexes. Much pressure was put upon suitable couples by the authorities to wed, with little time or thought allowed for loving courtship. Yet a survey taken toward the end of the century by a Hobart newspaper reporter (114) showed that only a tiny number of those marriages had failed (115)

For a more modern, albeit fictitious, example, consider the story in the 1951 Western film, *Westward the Women*, (116) which tells how 140 women were recruited in Chicago in 1851, to travel by river boat and then wagon train to California,

---

(113) The Floating Brothel, Hodder, 2001; pg. 214-218.

(114) Many years ago I read an account of this but I have since been unable to track down the source.

(115) See the *Addendum* below on "Happy Marriages".

(116) Starring Robert Taylor and Denise Darcel. Based on a story by Frank Kapra, and released by MGM, to excellent reviews.

where a hundred bachelors on a cattle ranch were waiting for them. After an incredibly arduous journey, overcoming nearly insuperable perils and hardships, most of the ladies arrive at the ranch and are hurriedly wedded to the eager men. Any kind of courtship was singularly lacking. The presumption, however, is that the unions were successful and helped to make the valley richly prosperous.

What was the key? Simply, _goodwill_. (117) Since no other spouses were available, the only way to find a happy marriage was to make the existing one work! So, with goodwill toward each other, they did whatever they had to do to achieve harmony, joy, and even abiding love.

To us, the success of those hasty marriages seems astonishing. But they show that while romantic love is important, and couples should do all they can to sustain it (think about *The Song of Solomon*), goodwill is even more important! This is because "goodwill" is a particular quality of the love of God – it is the essence of the Greek word *"agapé"*, which is used in the NT to describe divine love. It is, once again, the loving goodwill the Father showers upon all mankind –

> *God causes the sun to rise on both evil people and good, and he sends rain upon the righteous and the unrighteous." (Mt 5:45)*

And it is the quality of love the apostle enjoins upon every believer –

---

(117) For example, see 1 Ch 23:22, which tells about Mahli, who had two sons, Eleazar and Kish. The first of them left behind him at his death only daughters, who were married to the sons of Kish (their cousins), in accordance with the rule laid down by Moses (Nu 26:6-9). Similar examples can be found in the OT. The young people were not asked if they "loved" each other. Their duty was to marry, and make the marriage work, which they did.

> *Dear friends, let us <u>love</u> (agape) one another, because <u>love</u> (agape) comes from God. Whoever <u>loves</u> (agape) is a child of God and knows God. (1 Jn 4:7, GNB)*

I began by saying that "friendship" is a major key to success in marriage. But sometimes friendly feelings can be strained, or even temporarily annihilated. It is then that "goodwill" comes particularly to the fore, carrying the marriage along, until the couple have tossed aside ill feeling, and are again friends and companions, serving God in harmony together.

PATIENCE

In the late 4th cent., a Roman civil servant, Prudentius, wrote a dramatic epic poem, *The Psychomachia* (The Struggle for the Soul), which describes the fierce battles of a war between a cluster of Vices and the Seven Heavenly Virtues. [118]

In one of the battles, Wrath savagely attacks Patience, thrusting a spear at her, striking her with sword, club, and other weapons, and beating at her violently. Prudentius describes the battle vividly, and the violence of Wrath's attack –

> From a distance swelling Wrath, showing her teeth with rage and foaming at the mouth, darts her eyes at Patience, all shot with blood and gall, and challenges her with weapon and with speech.

---

(118) The "Seven Heavenly Virtues" are *Purity - Self Control - Love - Diligence - Patience - Kindness - Humility*. "Psychomachia" can be found on the internet, translated into English. It consists of about 1000 lines. The translation I have used is adapted from Prudentius, by H. J. Thomson; pub. William Heinemann Ltd, London, 1949.

Wrath falls upon Patience in wild ferocity, trying to kill the unarmed Virtue. But the strong armour worn by Patience protects her from every fiery dart until Wrath, in mad despair, finally capitulates. Weakened, weaponless, and defeated, the Vice picks up the shattered remains of her useless spear, pushes it into the ground, throws herself onto it, and perishes.

After her triumph (says Prudentius), Patience declared that,

> Fury is its own enemy; fiery Wrath in her frenzy slays herself and dies by her own weapons.

Then the poet adds this —

> Patience presses through the massed legions and clashing columns, stepping unhurt amid the deadly showers. To all the Virtues, Patience alone joins herself in company and bravely adds her help; for no Virtue enters on the hazard of the struggle without this Virtue's aid, for she has nought to lean upon, whose strength Patience does not uphold.

Thus, what seemed weakest to the carnal mind (gentle Patience), was in fact, as scripture also affirms, the strongest and the best ally of all the other Virtues! Yet many of us are prone to be like the boy who pleaded with God to give him patience, waited for a few moments, then cried, "Hurry up!"

Patience is a difficult virtue to cultivate. Yet we must grow into it, for no relationship can flourish in an atmosphere of impatience. Hence the apostle says, in the quirky translation of the CEV, that we must —

> *Patiently put up with each other, and love each other. (Ep 4:2)*

Also Rabbi Sirach, at the very beginning of his wise book stresses the importance of patience, and admonishes his readers –

> Wild rage is always inexcusable. Anger will be the ruin of anyone who surrenders to its passion. But those who restrain themselves, who are <u>patient</u> all day long, will soon be cheerful again. <u>Patient</u> people fetter their thoughts and feelings, so that later everyone will praise their good sense. (1:22-24)

And Paul, too, adds his own admonition –

> *I, Paul, a prisoner in the Lord, urge you to live the kind of life that <u>proves God has called you</u>. Be <u>humble</u> and <u>gentle</u> in every way, and be <u>patient</u> with each other." (Ep 4:1-2; see also Cl 1:11; 3:12)*

Indeed, there are people and situations that we all must bear with loving patience. Even God, when he chooses to make us wait, and wait, for some desired good! But doing so reveals the beauty of Jesus, and never more than when a couple are humble, gentle, and patient toward each other in a godly marriage. How patient my wife Alison has been with me over the years! And I, too, have striven for the same quality. Patience is a virtue that truly is an essential component of a happy and lasting marriage.

ROMANCE

Keep the courtship alive! When did you last have a romantic dinner together? Just the two of you? When did you last say, *"I love you!"*? When did you last give each other a special gift, or even a simple hug, apart from birthdays and anniversaries? Courtship is lifelong! Pleasant surprises are a wondrous stimulus to amatory feelings – roses when they are unexpected; a dreamy night out, when the only reason for it is love; an occasional act of extravagance. Out of such things lasting romance is fashioned.

So many marriages grow dreary because the couple take each other for granted; they settle into a humdrum relationship from which all the zing seems to have drifted away. But as in any garden, the blossom of marital bliss needs to be constantly nurtured; it demands watering with loving words, and fertilising with loving deeds. It needs pruning to rid it of weeds of discontent and strife. It needs the bright sunshine of God's love, and the sweet refreshing rain of his inflowing grace. Happy marriage doesn't happen by itself. It must be made to happen. It is a matter of choice. Two people *choose* to be happy together, and they continually do what needs to be done to build and sustain that happiness, whether prosaic or romantic.

The same is true of our relationship with God, as his Bride. Many poets and hymn writers have recognised that we have to make an effort to keep our divine "romance" flourishing –

> Jesus, the very thought of Thee
> With sweetness fills my breast;
> But sweeter far Thy face to see,
> And in Thy presence rest. [119]

> O royal bride, give heed,
> And to my words attend;
> For Christ the King forsake the world
> And every former friend.
> Thy beauty and thy grace
> Shall then delight the King;
> He only is thy rightful Lord,
> To him thy worship bring. [120]

---

[119] Bernard of Clairvaux, 12th century.
[120] Anonymous.

So we should never weary of worship nor of sharing joyfully in the Table of the Lord. True believers will maintain their "romance" with Christ until the day they finally join with him at the marriage festival in heaven. (Re 19:7-9)

DEMONSTRATION

A kiss a day keeps the lawyer away.

Flowers are the best divorce insurance!

Words are better than silence, and actions are better than words! **And both together are perfect!** It is said that women need, or at least desire, to hear often the words, *"I love you!"* And men, it is said, complain, "She should *know* that I love her, because of all the things I do for her!"

The real truth, for both men and women, is that no words sound sweeter than, *"I love you,"* whether spoken by spouse, child, relative, or friend. But they do become empty if they are not accompanied by action. For true love is always both *word* and *deed*.

So, every day, let us follow the example of Christ, who so loved that he gave his life for us, and ....

- TELL someone that you love him or her.
- SHOW your love by acting lovingly.

SUBMISSION

Wives, submit to your husbands. (Cl 3:18)

That is a much misquoted passage of scripture. Too often, it is applied only to a wife, ignoring the further injunction that husbands must love their wives, and never treat them harshly. (vs. 19)

Paul actually says elsewhere that we must *all* be in submission to each other. (Ep 5:21) He means that there is a quality of submission that each of us owes to each other, especially in the church. Thus –

- wives must submit to their husbands (vs. 24; Cl 3:18)
- husbands must submit to their wives (vs. 25; Cl 3:19);
- children must submit to their parents (6:1; Cl 3:20);
- parents must submit to their children (vs. 4; Cl 3:21);
- slaves must submit to their masters (vs. 5; Cl 3:22);
- masters must submit to their slaves (vs. 9; Cl 4:1).

So in a truly happy relationship, and in a happy family, there will be a pervasive deference that each member freely offers to the other. The manner in which that duty is expressed will differ in *kind*, but never in degree or *quality*, for Paul is emphatic, *"submit yourselves to each other out of reverence for Christ."* (Ep 5:21)

Christ himself, of course, is our example in this truly lovely virtue. "Submission" is a particular expression of the love of Christ that each of us is called upon to show to everyone. He demonstrated this himself when he washed his disciples' feet. (Jn 13:4-9) He then applied the lesson –

> *"Do you understand what I have done for you? You call me 'Teacher' and 'Lord', and you are right, because that is what I am. But if I, your Lord and Teacher, have washed your feet, then you too should wash each other's feet. I have set you an example, and you should do just as I have done for you. ... If you know what these things mean, and do them, you will be truly blessed!"*

Does that mean we must literally wash each other's feet, and if so, how often, and in what manner? Some churches *do* take the command quite literally, and foot washing is part of their liturgy. There is nothing wrong with that, but I doubt that it captures the intention of either Christ or Paul. (1 Ti 5:10) The idea is not a ritual to be followed, but a need to be met. That is, when most people went barefoot, or wore only light sandals, foot-washing was a courteous and necessary service, almost always done by a slave, as the people reclined at table.

We wear socks and shoes, we no longer recline, we have no slaves, and our circumstances are vastly different. So we need to find ways to "wash each other's feet" (that is, to behave courteously, respectfully, and lovingly) that suit our present conditions.

Married couples "wash each other's feet" when they cheerfully submit to each other's needs, and, in their daily care and concern for each other, unselfishly strive to bring happiness to the other. Happiness cannot be found by grasping for it, but rather by giving it.

As Jesus said, *"If you know what these things mean, and do them, <u>you will be truly blessed</u>!"*

TWENTY-THREE:

PARTNERS

I love the words of the song quoted at the beginning of the previous chapter –

> Still to us at twilight comes love's old song,
> Comes love's old, sweet song,
> Love's old, sweet song.

Alison and I, after 60 years of marriage to each other (in 2014), have, I suppose, reached the twilight of our life together. It cannot be long now before one of us is taken from the other. But "still to us at twilight comes love's old, sweet song," ringing pure and clear in our hearts. Its refrain has not changed across the years, its sweetness has not diminished, nor have its joys become lethargic. We love each other as deeply as ever, our friendship is unimpaired, and we face the future with hopeful excitement.

I have already shared several reasons for this marital longevity, and why the "blissful dreams of long ago" remain untarnished, and as sweet as ever. Let me add to them –

PARTNERSHIP

> *You have been clothed with the new person who is being renewed in knowledge, to take on the image of the one who created it. Here there is neither Greek nor Jew, circumcised or uncircumcised, barbarian, Scythian, slave or free, but Christ is all and in all. (Cl 3:10-11)*

Any Christian couple should recognise that before the throne of God there is neither man nor woman, but simply believers, who in God's sight are all equal to each other in value and in salvation. Certain things should follow from this recognition –

THEY NOTICE EACH OTHER

A feeling of being neglected is the bane of many homes. Hence a wife once said that she would be happy if her husband would only give her the attention he gave to the family dog – a *look*, a *word*, and a *touch*! But then, perhaps she should have greeted him in the same manner as the dog did – all enthusiasm, and ecstatic joy!

A good time to start noticing each other is early in the day, by saying *"Good morning!"* – with perhaps an added kiss!

But that "dog" story does suggest three key secrets to sustained love – [121]

- **_talk_**! – both speaking and *listening* to each other.
- **_look_**! – notice each other, for there is more treasure in your spouse than you can unearth in two lifetimes.
- **_touch_**! – with love and compassion, for words without feeling are empty.

Just those three rules alone would be enough to rescue many a troubled relationship!

THEY COMMUNICATE WITH EACH OTHER

Human relationships can suffer from either too little or too much communication –

---

[121] I acknowledge that the "dog" story is well-known, along with the three lessons drawn from it; however, I have no idea as to its origin. I hope, however, that it will be new to at least some readers.

TOO LITTLE

In a marriage, two different people are involved, with different views, desires, methods, perceptions. Yet, in all matters of importance to their happiness, they must now become one in their goals, decisions, actions, and values. That won't happen of its own accord.

In mutual respect, begin by discovering each other's "positions" on various matters. Recognise which things that are too important for your spouse to surrender or change. Be willing to compromise – you can't have it all your own way. Compromise is cool! As a general rule, if Alison feels more deeply about a matter than I do, then I'll yield to her, and vice versa. We are willing to submit to each other if it is right that we should. If we both feel too deeply about a matter to yield, then we take ourselves to prayer, and put the matter aside until the Lord shows us his will.

Work then toward a common mind on significant family issues, but still allow each other liberty in matters of personal preference. It is not obligatory to enjoy the same books, like the same music, pursue the same hobbies, have only the same friends, eat only the same food. The couple may be "one flesh" but there should still be plenty of room for diversity, they each need some space of their own around them.

In doing these things, families should set their own patterns, conformable to their own needs. Have the courage of your convictions! Do respect the opinions of other people, but also have the strength to do it your own way! Thus, some families do well opening their table to all comers, but others will be destroyed by it. Some enjoy a daily time of devotion; others find it restrictive, even suffocating. Some enjoy an outing together to the movies, others deem it too worldly. Each family must serve God and its own needs in ways that bring the highest level of happiness and well-being to all the members.

So don't bind yourself to some outside rule of conduct, nor be governed by the opinions or style of other people. You are obliged to heed only such rules as must be obeyed by all upright citizens, or good Christians. For the rest, you and your family have freedom to choose for yourself how you will live and flourish.

Then the opposite of *too little* communication is the foolish compulsion toward

TOO MUCH

Beware of the urge to tell everyone everything about everything! People are often moved to this folly by two misunderstood rules –

"LIVE IN THE LIGHT"

That is undoubtedly a useful principle, (cp. 1 Jn 1:5-7) and we should certainly shun a life of darkness. But being open and honest with everybody needs to be tempered by common sense –

> *When people talk too much they keep digging pits for themselves to fall into. If you are sensible you will keep your mouth shut (Pr 10:19) ... Those who are wise keep their thoughts hidden; but silly people open their mouths and ruin themselves (10:14)*
>
> *If you are prudent, you will keep what you know to yourself, unlike those fools who cannot help blurting out whatever comes into their heads (12:23) ... So you call yourself a person of discernment? Then you will keep a cool head and a close mouth! Even a fool, if he knows how to keep quiet, may be thought wise; so show*

> *good sense, and keep your mouth shut! (17:27-28)*
>
> *Have you met people who must tell everything they know? There is more hope for a fool than there is for them. (29:20)*
>
> *Have you learned a secret? Keep it to yourself, it will not make you burst! Don't be the kind of fool who suffers agony from a secret, like a woman giving birth. A secret locked in the heart is more painful to some people than an arrow through the leg. (Sir 19:10-12) ... Here is a man who maintains silence, and he is thought wise. Here is another who indulges in endless chatter, and he is loathed. (20:5)*

There are another two-score similar sayings in *Proverbs* and *Sirach*, which can be summarised as –

> Silly people tell everything that is in their head; but those who are prudent know when to keep their mouth shut!

Someone may protest, "Surely we should be totally honest with each other, and is not 'confession good for the soul'?" [122]

But confession that brings pain to others while it eases the penitent is nothing but self-indulgence. Often, "discretion is the better part of valour:" [123] and "silence is golden"! [124] So there are times when by far the best policy is to keep your counsel to yourself; or at least to share your secret only with someone who cannot be harmed by it, or who will not harm

---

[122] A Scottish proverb.
[123] *Henry IV, Part I, V, iv, 120.* William Shakespeare.
[124] An English proverb.

others. Have you and a partner sinned? By all means, repent and confess your own sin. But think carefully before you reveal your partner's complicity. How much harm will be done if you drag him or her down with you? Would silence be more honourable, more Christian, or bring better healing?

Perhaps someone has sinned alone, and then feels compelled to make a public confession. Strangle that urge! Think carefully before you speak. Perhaps a public confession is the proper thing to do; but perhaps not. What will result from openly disclosing everything? Benefit or grief? A repentant sinner who seeks only personal relief from guilt, but cares nothing for how much a public confession might hurt other people, is still lost in a fog of self-importance.

Then, second, people often mistake the meaning of

"BE RECONCILED TO EACH OTHER"

Jesus was adamant –

> *If you are offering a gift at the altar and you remember that another believer has something against you, then leave your gift right there, go away, and make peace with your neighbour. Only then should you come back and offer your gift. (Mt 5:23-24)*

People often get that passage back-to-front. They think, if they have a grudge against someone, they have a right to challenge the offender. Rather, read the passage this way –

1. If you are the <u>offended</u> one, then simply forgive the offender, as in *Mark 11:25* –

   Whenever you pray, forgive whatever grudge you may have against another person. Then your Father in heaven will forgive your failures.

2. If you are the <u>offending</u> one, then go to the person you have hurt, and try to restore friendship, as Jesus instructed.

If the offended party refuses to be reconciled, then you can do no more, and at least your own prayers will no longer be hindered. A married couple may have to go a little further and talk about why one of them has been offended; but not always. Sometimes it is enough simply to forgive, and forget. Further discussion may be nothing more than a cause of further hurt.

And never forget the power of prayer to effect change, even in a husband or a wife!

THEY AGREE ON PRIORITIES

Generally speaking, the proper order is *God, Spouse, Children, Job, Church*. But to everything there is a proper season! (Ec 3:1) Which means that sometimes the church may have to come before all other loves and duties. Usually, that will not be true, and the normal order should prevail. Some people, of course, can use this as an excuse to neglect the church too much. But no reasonable Christian who truly loves the Lord and loves the people of God, will be so dense.

Married couples, at the very beginning of their union, and preferably during their courtship, should thoroughly discuss this matter of priorities, and agree on them, for dissension here can uproot the very foundations of a marriage.

THEY DON'T EXPECT TOO MUCH

Anyone who expects another person to bring happiness will be disappointed. Happiness is not something you <u>get</u>, but rather something you <u>give</u>, and which you then <u>receive</u>. The man had already doomed his marriage to misery, who said to his wife, on the day after their wedding, "Here I am. I married you. Now start making me happy!" Life doesn't work like that!

The highest quest in any relationship must be the happiness of the other person. The rule, *"it is more blessed to give than to receive,"* (Ac 20:35) is just as true in marital bliss as it is anywhere.

Couples must also allow each other a fault or two! No one can fully live up to your expectations. Indeed, only when you yourself are perfect can you demand perfection from another.

BEDROOM SECRETS!

Nowhere is the need for tolerance more apparent than in the area of sex. Let me mention three things –

LIKE AN ICE-CREAM ON A HOT DAY!

The experience of sex will never equal the anticipation of it; it is always better in imagination than in performance. So ignore the text books, the romantic novels, and popular movies. Let us instead be wise, and temper the unrealistic expectations of rapture that are encouraged by many writers of modern romances. Young people who approach marriage expecting their union to agree with some absurdly ecstatic story will be sadly disappointed! Beyond question, sex is a lot of fun, and it can be deeply spiritual, intensely euphoric, and wonderfully rapturous. It will even have moments that soar to the dizzy delights described by novelists. But perhaps not often. For sex can also be earthy, awkward, and disappointing for either or both of the partners. The romantic effusions in some novels are irresponsible in their exaggerated idea of what a newly wedded couple may reasonably expect from their union.

In reality, it takes several years of patient endeavour for a married couple to achieve true congruence, to their fullest mutual fulfilment. And even then, their couplings will seldom reach the heights of voluptuous ecstasy.

Since abiding joy and divine benediction in a union cannot usually be attained in a few days or even weeks, the idea of a pre-marital "trial", to see if a couple are compatible, is absurd. No brief session of illicit heated intercourse will ever be enough to show whether or not a couple can reach the highest level of joy and intimacy in coitus. How then *can* this be discovered? Simply by two people who deeply love each other, and yearn to make the other happy, devoting themselves to a patient, tender, and tolerant pursuit of the goal of reciprocal pleasure and delight in their union.

KNOW WHEN TO LAUGH!

Here is a very good rule – don't get too serious about sex. People make love behind locked doors, not because sex is somehow unclean, but because it is *private, holy*, and most of all (aside from true love) *ridiculous*! As Sir Thomas Browne long ago wrote –

> I could be content that we might procreate like trees, without conjunction, or that there were any way to perpetuate the world without this trivial and vulgar way of coition: it is the foolishest act a wise man commits in all his life, nor is there anything that will more deject his cooled imagination, when he shall consider what an odd and unworthy piece of folly he hath committed. [125]

Admittedly, Sir Thomas was a little chauvinistic in his views, [126] and somewhat prejudiced. But looking at the

---

(125) Religio Medici, Part Two, Sec. 9. Published in 1643, and never since out of print.

(126) For example, he says in the same passage, "Man is the whole world, and the breath of God; woman the rib and crooked piece of man."

matter objectively, it is hard not to agree that only deep love can introduce beauty or divinity into the act of human congress. Two naked bodies, writhing, sweating, groaning on a bed, are hardly a picture of poetic beauty or of divine grace. No doubt the couple are having a wonderful, and even a deeply spiritual time; but any unwilling observer would find it hard not to break out laughing.

So it behoves even the sweetest lovers to keep a good humour about their love-making. It will often go wrong. The body sometimes betrays the finest intentions of the soul. Mutual delight or satisfaction is not always achievable. One or both parties may be left frustrated, disappointed, embarrassed, or unfulfilled. But a good laugh can heal even the worst wounds of coital meltdown.

It is a good rule of life never to take anything *too* seriously –

Then let us mock with ancient mirth this comic, cosmic plan;
The stars are laughing at the earth;
God's greatest joke is man.
For laughter is a buckler bright, and scorn a shining spear;
So let us laugh with all our might at folly, fraud, and fear.
Yet on our sorry selves be spent our most sardonic glee;
Oh don't pay life the compliment to take it *seriously*.
For he who can himself despise, be surgeon to the bone,
May win to worth in other's eyes, to wisdom in his own! (127)

THEY KNOW HOW TO FORGET

Some things, of course, MUST be remembered –

- Birthdays
- Anniversaries

---

(127) Robert Service, <u>Laughter</u>, Stanza Three.

- And the like.

But a capacity to laugh at, or altogether to forget the bad days, while rejoicing in the good days, is a key element in extended happiness in marriage.

THEY ARE RESOLVED TO LOVE

In scripture, love is not something you feel, but something you do! Love is a command to be obeyed, whether or not we feel loving. Love is not merely an impulse, but a choice that you make. It is not just a surge of emotion, or some sort of physical chemistry, it is more a matter of firm decision. At the altar of marriage, I *vowed* to love my wife, and love her I will, despite the waning and waxing of emotional sensations.

Here is the truth – if you *behave* lovingly, it is nearly certain that you will soon once again *feel* loving!

CALVARY

The quality that most needs to be brought into and kept in a marriage, and all relationships, is *the sacrificial and unquenchable love of Christ*. He remains our example, especially in his love for the church. Indeed, says Paul, he loved the church, not only when she was lovely, but when she was deformed, blemished, and rebellious. Yet he gave himself for her, and has promised to redeem her by his blood and bring her into his uttermost glory! (Ep 5:25-27) To which Paul adds –

> *Let each one of you love his wife as himself, and let the wife see that she respects her husband. (vs. 33)*

CONCLUSION

One of the minor mysteries of life is that no one seems to know the origin of the popular wall hanging; *Christ is the Head of this House.* (128) During the years our children were growing up, we had two or three different versions of it hanging in our house, usually near where we shared our meals.

Some people have denounced it as heresy, saying that the husband is, or should be, the head of each Christian home. But that seems a bit specious, since scripture clearly declares that Christ is the Head of every man, whether those men want it so or not. In any case, any home that is built around the lordship of Christ, and where both husband and wife display his love, grace, and kindness to each other and to their children, can hardly fail in happiness, and will end, not with acrimony and division, but with "blissful dreams of long ago"!

And now, let Sirach have the last word on this matter –

> Three things are pleasant to see, for they delight both the eyes of God and of everyone around – children playing happily together; friendship among neighbours; and a *husband and wife who love each other*. (25:1)

---

(128) Christ is the Head of this House,/ The Unseen Guest at every meal, / The Silent Listener to every conversation.

TWENTY-FOUR:

PRAISE

> *We give **thanks** to God and the Father of our Lord Jesus Christ, praying always for you. (Cl 1:3)*
>
> *Always give **thanks** to the Father, who has made us fit to share in the inheritance of the saints in light. (vs. 12)*
>
> *Stay rooted in the faith, and built up in Christ, steadfast, as you have been taught, abounding every day in **thanksgiving**. (2:7)*
>
> *Be **thankful**! Let the word of Christ dwell in you richly, teaching and admonishing one another in all wisdom, singing psalms and hymns and spiritual songs, with **thankfulness** in your hearts to God. (Cl 3:15, 16)*
>
> *And whatever you do in word or deed, do it in the name of the Lord Jesus, giving **thanks** to God and the Father by him. (3:17)*
>
> *Continue in prayer, and watch in the same with **thanksgiving**. (4:2)*

Do you get the message? We are supposed to be _thankful_! Why? Is God a narcissist who cannot be happy unless we are endlessly stroking his ego? Hardly! The reason lies in a powerful spiritual principle, of which praise is just one part. What is that principle? Simply this – God's favour, God's blessing, where we stand in the presence of the Lord, and the things God does for us, all largely hinge upon *what we say and the way we say it.* Hence, says Hosea, the most acceptable sacrifice we can offer God is our praise –

> *Come to the Lord and <u>bring words</u> with you, making him an offering of the calves of your lips. (Ho 14:2)*

What a strange expression! Bring God the bulls, the oxen, the calves, the animal sacrifices of your lips, and come to him with *words*. It sounds weird, yet it is a wonderful idea! The best thing God wants us to bring into his presence is *words*! Come to the Lord and bring *words* and let those *words* become a sacrifice of praise, an offering of thanksgiving. This becomes the most acceptable sacrifice we can offer God.

But that raises a question – <u>*when is praise a sacrifice*</u>? We should recognise the importance of the words we speak and the way we speak them when we come into the presence of God to praise and worship him, but when does that offering of our lips become a sacrifice to God?

WHEN PRAISE IS OFFERED CONTINUALLY

Hebrews 13:15 is a passage in the New Testament based on the verse from Hosea. The apostle words it a bit differently. He puts it this way –

> *Through Jesus, let us continually offer to God a sacrifice of praise – that is, the fruit of lips that confess his name.*

Mark the adverb '*continually*'. Praise becomes a sacrifice when we set ourselves to praise God continually, which countermands a pernicious idea that is floating around the church. I mean, the idea that worship and praise must always spring out of a heart full of laughter and song; that true praise will always bring with it an experience of pleasure. Some claim that when we are praising God and worshipping the Lord we will *always* have some sort of divine encounter, enlivening, energising, filling us with joy, dance, and rapture. That really is a foolish notion.

Worship can be, and very often is, the most enjoyable and sweet experience in human life. But if the only time we worship God is when we feel like it we are not worshippers at all. Indeed, the best time to praise God is when you least feel like it! Praise gains its greatest power when it hurts; when the last thing on earth you want to do is to praise God. That is the very best time to praise him! When it seems as if heaven is like brass above your head and the earth iron underneath your feet (Le 26:19); when it seems that God has never been so far away; when all divine consolations have been withdrawn from you; when there's no sense of God's presence; when you cannot feel anything of the touch of his hand upon you; when your mind is dull; when your heart is barren; when your spirit is dry; when, as the prophet said, you feel yourself standing in the midst of a dry and barren land; when it seems as if God had never touched you, or you had never encountered him; as if he'd never blessed your life; when it seems that heaven's ear is deaf and heaven's hand is still – that is the time when we most need to praise God!

That is what turns praise into a sacrifice. When God sees that we are willing to praise him, not only when we feel like it but when we don't feel like it; not only when good things are happening, but also when nothing is happening; not only when our praise brings us joy and laughter and a wonderful exhilaration and happiness, but when every word of praise seems to compound our burden, and to draw out of our souls what little life is left in them, *then* praise is a sacrifice indeed!

When also, the more we praise God, the further away he seems; when the more we set ourselves to offer him thanksgiving and worship, the more heaven seems to withdraw from us – that is when praise truly touches the heart of God, for he has found in you a man or woman who is willing to praise him _continually_, in the good times and the bad times alike.

That helps us to make a very important distinction – to mark the difference between praising God *in* all things and praising God *for* all things.

PRAISING GOD _IN_ ALL THINGS

There is a pestilent doctrine attached to praise in our time – the idea that we should praise God _for_ everything – that no matter what happens, we should thank God for it. Is your child killed in a highway accident? Praise God for its violent death. Do you hit your thumb with a hammer? Praise God for the fierce pain. In the midst of death, in the face of brutality, sin, wickedness, and corruption, in your own shame and despair, in the presence of human decadence and failure, suffering the worst the devil can do, lift up your voice (it is said) and heartily thank God for them all!

What? Is there no proper emotion in human life except laughter, no proper response to pain, except joy? Hardly! The wise man said in *Ecclesiastes 3:4*, there is *"a time to weep and a time to laugh, a time to mourn and a time to dance."*

Paul has much the same idea in his letter to the *Romans 12:15* where he says that we should *"mourn with those who mourn as well as rejoice with those who rejoice."*

The Bible is a very human book and allows us to express the entire range of human emotions from the high peaks of rapture to the deepest abyss of despair. No, it is folly to suppose that we should praise God _for_ all things, which comes perilously close to blasphemy. What then should we do? We should praise God _IN_ all things. In every situation if you look for it, you can find some cause to thank God.

For example, we might praise him for the opportunity to experience a miracle of answered prayer. We can at least determine this much from our need – the mere fact that we are needy offers God an opportunity to stretch out his hand and meet that need in a staggering way.

We might praise God for the unchanged reality of the victory that is ours in Christ, the recognition that in the end we Christians never can be defeated. Let me illustrate it this way. In my more than 65 years of Christian life, (129) I've heard many hundreds of sermons; but out of that great mass of preaching there are probably only four or five so memorable and powerful that I will never forget them. One was a sermon by the American healing evangelist, Jack Coe, about Absalom burning Joab's barley fields to get the general's attention. (2 Sa 14:29-30) Mr Coe preached the forceful idea that there are times when God will burn *our* "barley fields" to get *our* attention.

I also heard Billy Graham preach in Melbourne on the third commandment – *"Thou shalt not take the name of the Lord thy God in vain"*. I have forgotten all his other sermons, but that one I won't forget till the day I die!

Likewise, I heard Leo Harris (130) preach scores of times, but there were two messages that are still burned in my memory. One was a Christmas message, *The Miracle of Christ Reborn in the Human Heart* – a staggeringly powerful sermon on the new birth. The other was a sermon on the theme, *A Christian Can Never Be Defeated*. The idea had never occurred to me before, that *we Christians cannot be defeated*. We are made to win! We cannot lose! We might fail a skirmish here or there.

---

(129) I surrendered to Christ as Lord and Saviour when I was 16.

(130) Leo Harris (1904-1990), was the founder in Adelaide, South Australia, in 1945, of the group of churches now known as *CRC Churches International*, which in 2014 had about 200 congregations in Australia and 600 overseas.

We might even lose a battle occasionally; but, if we cling to Christ, we cannot lose the *war*!

We are like the British, during the dark depths of the Second World War. The Allies were being defeated on every front, in the air, at sea, on land and it seemed that their cause was lost. In the midst of the crisis, Sir Winston Churchill made the declaration, "The British are prone to lose every battle except the last. And that one" said he, "I promise you, we will win." [131]

Well, we Christians are like that. We may lose a tussle here and there, but in the end it will be Satan in the Lake of Fire while we enjoy the Throne! That is why we can praise God in the midst of the most terrifying and awful circumstances. Further, we actually settle our victory when we praise God for the unchanged reality of all that belongs to us in Jesus Christ. So never stop saying to yourself, "I cannot be defeated. I cannot lose. I am made by my God only to win."

PRAISING GOD FOR HIS GLORY

We can praise God for his unwavering love which we know will not, cannot ever fail us in our time of need. We may not feel that love. We may have lost all sense and awareness of it, but the certainty of it gloriously remains.

We can praise God for the knowledge that we are still indwelt by Christ, the hope of glory. How hard the devil strives to rob us of Christ. But he cannot do it. I opened my Bible yesterday and behold, it was written there, *"Christ is in me, the hope of glory."* I opened my Bible today and it is still there, *"Christ is in me, the hope of glory."* I will turn to the sacred volume

---

[131] He was actually quoting a statement made earlier by a Greek politician, Eleutherios Venizelos, "In all her wars, England always wins one battle, the last." Churchill corrected "England" to "Britain".

tomorrow, and it will still be written there, *"Christ is in me, the hope of glory."* I turn to that Scripture in times of victory and triumph and it says, *"Christ is in you, the hope of glory."* I've turned to that Scripture in times of sin, of defeat, of failure, when I've let myself down, my neighbour down, my family down, my church down, and it still says, *"Christ is in me, the hope of glory!"* (Cl 1:27b)

Thank God he doesn't re-write the Book every hour on the hour, to make it match my experience down here on earth. What a changeable Bible that would be! I'm changing all the time, from better to worse, from worse to better. But the Word stays the same. I'm indwelt by Christ, the hope of glory. So I thank God in every situation for the certainty that I can rise up in the power of the Holy Spirit and crush my enemy underfoot. He may seem to have the victory for the moment, but I know somewhere, somehow, I will find the strength to stand tall again, and to overcome him.

PRAISING GOD FOR RIGHTEOUSNESS

We can praise God in the worst of circumstances for the assurance that our defeat or failure on earth does not affect the righteousness and authority that remain ours in the heavenlies in Christ. How I love the Scripture that says, *"God has blessed me with every spiritual blessing in the heavenlies, in Christ."* (Ep 1:3)

The beauty of that is, I can't get my hand on those treasures, except in faith and by faith. Satan can't get his hand on them at all. Those multiplied blessings are secure in the heavenlies in Christ, beyond the marauding hand of either man or devil. They can only be tapped into by faith based upon confidence in the promise of God. Nothing negative, nothing destructive, nothing sinful, nothing wicked can touch those blessings. And in the worst of my defeat and failure I can look up through the dark tunnel and still see that radiant light shining at the end.

The blessings, the authority, the righteousness, all that belongs to me in the heavenlies remains perfectly safe, waiting until I come back to spiritual reality, get on track with God once more, and resume my walk with him in fellowship and victory.

While I cannot praise God *for* many things that happen, because they are wicked, terrible, and ruinous to me, I can always find cause, despite them, to praise the Lord *in* them. There is always something to grasp from God – some miracle, some grace, some promise, some goodness that the believer can seize even in the midst of the worst of circumstances. For that we can and should praise God continually.

Second, praise becomes a sacrifice:

WHEN IT IS OFFERED BROKENLY

Ha! my enemy, you rejoice too soon. I may have fallen, but I will stand up again. I may seem to be surrounded by darkness, but the Lord is still my life. I will bear with the anger of the Lord, and he will bring me out into the light and once again show me his righteous-ness. (Mi 7:8-10)

I suppose that this is one of the hardest circumstances in which to praise God – in the face of our own defeat! We've all been there – overcome by some work of the devil, by some opposition of hell. Pulled down by sin, wracked by sickness, broken by personal failure, succumbing to some temptation, hurt by some force that is undermining our fruitfulness and happiness – whatever it is, we see ourselves defeated. That must be one of the most difficult times of all in which to set ourselves still to praise God, to offer him the sacrifice of thanksgiving.

Think about the following illustrations.

Many years ago a man (call him John) in our church was stunningly healed by the Lord of multiple sclerosis, for which medical science had no cure. He was marvellously delivered by the laying on of hands and prayer in Jesus' name. From lying bedfast in a darkened room, he was able within a few days to go back to work and to resume a normal life. Twelve months later, I asked him to give a testimony in church at a special Sunday night healing service, which he did, with much joy.

On Monday morning, the telephone rang. It was John [132] in despair! He had woken up that morning with his body on fire, his limbs beginning to stiffen again, unable to move properly. His body had already begun to twist over as he lost the strength to support himself. "What has happened? What's gone wrong? I've got MS again! What should I do?" he cried.

I said, "Hold everything! Do nothing! Just stay where you are and wait. I'm coming over." I got in my car and drove over to his house and there he was with his wife, sitting on the bed in a darkened room, arms wrapped around each other, both of them sobbing bitterly.

I said, "I'm not going to pray for you. You were healed 12 months ago. You're still healed. We'll do only one thing. We're going to get you up on your feet. Your wife and I will prop you up, and we're going to hold hands and start praising God, speaking in other tongues, rejoicing, and worshipping in the Lord until you've got the victory again."

And, all credit to John and Helen, they had the courage to do that. He struggled to his feet, still in his darkened bedroom. We held hands together in a kind of small circle and began to speak in other tongues, to praise the Lord and worship. We kept that up without pausing for at least an hour, or maybe

---

[132] The names in this story are fictitious, but the miracle was real.

longer. By the time we were done every trace of that disease had left his body, and he was soon back at work.

It's not easy to praise God when you've lost your miracle. I suppose that without my encouragement and insistence, John and Helen would not have done it, could not perhaps have found the courage to do it. I don't know. I do know it is very hard when some precious prize has just been snatched from you to set yourself to offer enthusiastic praise to the Lord! Yet that is what we need to do.

Or, another example, perhaps against your expectation you are dismissed from your job. Or, your business is declared bankrupt, your hopes of promotion are taken away from you, the plans you had for your enterprise turns into ruin. You may find your world collapsing around you, leaving you no income, only debts and chaos. How are you going to meet them? How will you cope with this disaster? How hard it is to praise God in the midst of financial defeat!

Or, perhaps some cherished goal eludes you, some sweet dream you had, maybe even a dream you felt God had planted in your spirit, a goal you were sure was born in heaven. You set yourself to achieve it, never thinking for a moment that God will seemingly abandon you, that the dream will not be fulfilled. You can hardly even imagine that happening. And yet it does. Against all your expectations, all that you anticipated receiving from the hand of the Lord, against all your hopes and aspirations, the castle collapses, and you find yourself shattered and broken. How can you cope with that? How can you find a heart to praise God in the midst of tears?

Or, against your own loathing of it, sin has overwhelmed you. How hard it is to praise God in the face of our own sin. It almost seems blasphemous. Here you are in sin. Yet still you're expected to praise the Lord, to come to him with words, and offer him the *"calves of your lips"*? Yes, you are! That's what it means, to offer him the sacrifice of praise continually.

It means, no matter what condition you find yourself in, no matter what circumstances surround you, no matter what pains or hurts or problems you may be suffering, still you set yourself to praise God. Not *because* of the circumstances, but *despite* them.

That, of course, is exactly what the prophet Micah did. He refused to capitulate to failure, *"Ha! My enemy! You rejoice too soon. I may have fallen, but I will stand up again."* The poor broken man is stuck on his face in the muck of this world, and the devil is stomping all over him laughing, "I've got this prophet, this so-called man of God! Look at him! Lying there in the mire of sin! How he has fallen! Oh, down, down! How he has fallen!"

But, lying there in the spew, with the devil trampling all over him, somehow the prophet finds a way to turn his head and begin the pathway back to victory. He cries, "Yes, I know I'm bearing the anger of God. I know the Lord is furious with me. But I also know this. *You* might leave me here devil, but *he* won't. You might enjoy seeing me humiliated, but God doesn't. So I will bear with the anger of the Lord, knowing that he will bring me out into the light and once again show me his righteousness."

Or think of the striking example of Habakkuk –

> *Even if my fig trees have no fruit and no grapes grow on my vines; even if my olive crop fails and my fields produce no grain; even if all my sheep die and my cattle stalls are empty, still I will be glad, and I will rejoice because the Lord God is my saviour. (Ha 3:17-18)*

Likewise, even in the midst of our sin, our fallenness, even in the presence of evil and pain, we can still, out of our brokenness offer God a glad sacrifice of praise.

The spiritual principle is this. Do you believe what God says about you in Christ, or what you say about yourself in defeat? I know what I *could* say about myself. If you have some bad things to toss at me, I assure you they are a polite compliment compared to what I can say about myself. But the only opinion I'm really concerned about is God's, "What do YOU think about me God, what do YOU say about me, how do YOU look at me, what is the manner in which YOU will treat me?"

As soon as I ask the question I get the answer from the gospel. God has already made this resolution, "I will see my people only as they are reflected through the prism of Christ." He sees us clothed in the righteousness of Jesus Christ. He sees us garbed in the beauty of the Bright and Morning Star. He sees us carrying the image of the Fairest of Ten Thousand. The Father declines to look at you in any other way than haloed by the glory and splendour of the Saviour. Reject every other viewpoint. Resolve to see yourself only as God sees you in Christ, and thank him for it without ceasing!

When I look at you, if you are truly born again, I say, "There is a man, there is a woman, whom God says is beautiful, righteous, glorious, splendid, wonderful, and marvellous. There is a man, there is a woman who is everything that Jesus is in the Father's eyes." Knowing that is what God says about us in Christ what can any other opinion in heaven, earth or hell possibly matter?

The third way in which praise is a sacrifice is –

WHEN IT IS OFFERED CONFIDENTLY

Praise is never so hard as when it seems that God himself has failed.

I've just said that praise is hard when it seems that *I* have failed, and truly it is hard to praise God when you see yourself at fault or defeated. But when you look to heaven and it seems that *God* has failed – that's when it really gets hard! Yet there are times when it does seem as if God is like a desert mirage, promising much yet giving nothing.

We sometimes do find ourselves, like a thirsty traveller, trudging through the wilderness. He sees a green and beautiful oasis in the distance, which promises a bubbling spring, sweet nourishment, and the saving of life. He drags himself across the hot burning sands and reaches the oasis, to find only more sand. Or perhaps an oasis is actually there, with a brook. But he finds it dry as the surrounding desert. Yes, there's a well there, too, but it's empty. The promise becomes a hollow mockery!

Who has not been there some time? Who has not claimed some promise of God, only to have it unrealised? Who has not known the grief of hope decaying, of prayers turned back, seemingly unheeded? The weary sufferer feels that no sound can be heard except the jeering and scorn coming from the ramparts of hell.

No one can walk the Christian pilgrimage for too many years without reaching such a dark place.

Do you remember, from an earlier chapter, the story of Jeremiah, and his anguished protest? –

> *Why is my pain unceasing, my wound incurable? ... O Lord, why do you tell such terrible lies? You are like a dried up brook! Like a desert mirage, you promise everything, but give nothing! (Combining Je 15:18; 12:1-2; 14:19; 20:7; 4:10.)*

Why did the prophet have to suffer such misery? If you know something of his book, you'll know that Jeremiah was called while still a young man. But he had not the slightest desire to be a prophet. In fact, he kept on refusing the call of God, until the word of God became like molten fire in his very veins. He was tortured by it, tormented by it, wrung with the sheer agonising driving pain of it until he finally cried, "I surrender. I'll go! Get this pain out of me."

So God spoke to him, and said that he would make Jeremiah like a mighty army, stronger than nations, kingdoms, and empires. He said that what men had built the prophet would pull down, and what men tried to pull down the prophet would build again –

> *Get yourself ready! Stand up and say to them whatever I command you. Do not be terrified by them, or I will terrify you before them. Today I have made you a fortified city, an iron pillar and a bronze wall to stand against the whole land – against the kings of Judah, its officials, its priests and the people of the land. They will fight against you but will not overcome you for I am with you and will rescue you, declares the Lord. (Je 1:17-19)*

Mightily encouraged, out went young Jeremiah, no doubt thinking, "I'll show these backslidden scoundrels, I'll show these miserable rascals, what it is to be a man of God and a prophet of the Almighty!"

But what happened? Instead of invincible triumphs, he was flogged, stoned, imprisoned, thrown into a dry well and left to die there of hunger and thirst. He suffered mockery, scorn, and rejection. Everybody turned against him. Nobody turned toward him. The whole world opposed him – prince, priest, prophet, and almost everybody else as well, until in the midst of his despair Jeremiah cried, "God, you are a terrible liar! You promised so many great things, yet none of them has happened the way you said they would."

That is a hard place to be in. What does God do when you call him a liar? Does a lightning bolt sizzle down and burn you to a pile of smouldering ashes? Does the earth open its gaping jaws and swallow you down to the deepest, darkest, damnable abyss?

What does God do?

I'll tell you what he does. Not a lightning bolt, but nonetheless a stern reply. The Lord came back to the prophet, reminded Jeremiah of his former promises, and added a rebuke! –

> *If you repent, I will restore you that you may serve me; <u>if you utter worthy, not worthless words</u>, you will be my spokesman. Let this people turn to you, but you must not turn to them. I will make you a wall to this people, a fortified wall of bronze; they will fight against you but will not overcome you, for I am with you to rescue and save you, declares the Lord. I will save you from the hands of the wicked and redeem you from the grasp of the cruel. (Je 15:19-21)*

How remarkable! The Lord sternly repeated the promises he had made earlier to Jeremiah, only adding to them a sharp warning. The prophet had allowed his foes to turn him around, but God said, "Now, Jeremiah, you had better repent. Stop turning yourself, and instead compel the people to turn back to me!" And he was to do that, not by force, but by declaring the word of the Lord. "No longer speak those worthless, defeatist words of complaint," said God, "but start again speaking worthy words – my words, my promises."

As Hosea said, *"Come to the Lord and bring with you words."* And although we can, for a time, get away with words of complaint, even of accusation, anger, frustration, or despair (as God allowed Jeremiah to do for a time), eventually the Lord requires us to stir up faith and courage, and to speak his own great word.

Praise becomes a sacrifice when we offer it with unwavering confidence, even when it seems that God has failed, that his promises have failed. Even then, we must set ourselves and say, "Lord I will praise you, I do trust you, I can never accuse you of lying or cheating or deceiving me. I know that your word is true. I know that victory will come!"

Jeremiah did that, as you will know from his book, and nations did rise and fall at his word, and the people, prince, priest, and prophet, did turn to him and say to him, "What is the word of the Lord?"

So we can conclude! Paul said, *"Be thankful! Never stop giving thanks to the Lord!"* In that injunction to offer continual praise to God, we find a major key to ongoing victory in Christ.

And once again, why should we praise God? Is it because of what he does? Well, yes, of course, but vastly more because of who he is. Our praise should not rest upon what the Lord does or does not do; our praise should rest upon the Lord himself. He is God. I am man. I can do no less than offer to him the sacrifice of thanksgiving continually, the fruit of my lips, to his eternal glory for ever in Jesus' name. (133)

---

(133) For a passionate and stirring exhortation to praise God at all times, and the reasons for doing so, see the addendum at the end of this book, "Chrysostom."

TWENTY-FIVE:

BLAME

> *Please keep on praying for us, for God to open to us a door for the word, and to declare the mystery of Christ, on account of which <u>I am in prison</u>. (Cl 4:3)*

Paul was in prison, and would be executed, for no other reason than he was a Christian. Is this fair? Is this just? Why didn't God intervene, to rescue him as he had rescued Peter? (Ac 5:18-20; 12:5-11) Why was one man favoured, and not the other? Or why didn't the Lord repeat for Paul the miracle he had enjoyed in Philippi? (Ac 16:25-26) Why was Peter rescued by an angel, but James had his head cut off? We don't know. But we do find ourselves living in a world where such questions are constantly being raised.

When a wall fell down in Jerusalem, killing eighteen people, the bystanders wondered if those who died were being punished for their sins. Jesus rejected that idea. Nor did he offer any other explanation for the disaster. He simply warned his hearers that they too would perish if they refused to repent of their sins. (Lu 13:1-5)

In a land (Australia) that is sometimes ravaged by floods greater in area than Germany and France combined, Jesus' response so long ago remains informative. He refuses the suggestion that sundry disasters must be God's judgment upon sin, but also warns that we should take them as a call to repentance.

IS IT GOD'S FAULT?

In a world fraught with many perils, natural and social, where droughts, floods, fires, pestilence, famine, injustice and cruelty abound, we must resist those who try to blame God. It's just life. We live on a wild and untamed planet, which has been racked and torn by far worse natural catastrophes countless times across the millennia, and will continue to be torn by them in the future. Our society too, despite its veneer of civilisation, has an untamed and wild underbelly, in which all sorts of barbarities remain common. But in this study, I want to focus more on natural disasters, using Paul's imprisonment as a kind of metaphor for all the dismal things that happen in life.

On natural disasters, we may observe that when people choose to build homes on land that is subject to flood, fire, or earthquakes, they can hardly blame God when the inevitable happens. Take San Francisco. Only one thing is more predictable than the earthquake that will sooner or later tear it apart again – thousands of people will howl a protest against God and demand to know why he caused, or at least allowed, such misery! What folly! They know it must happen. Yet they live there, hoping it won't happen in their lifetime.

Similarly, the city of Brisbane sits on a flood plain, which has been inundated countless times in the past, and will be flooded again in the future. There is not much sense in blaming God for an inevitable natural event, nor asking him to stop it from happening, nor expecting him to protect one from it. If people choose to live there, then they must put up with being washed away.

Or, think about Lake Taupo, near the centre of the North Island of New Zealand. It is the largest lake in the country, with a perimeter of nearly 200 kilometres. It also sits in the caldera of a dormant volcano, which erupted some 26500 years ago, and has done so on average every one thousand years since. The last major eruption occurred early in the Christian era, and it devastated much of the island. While the Taupo volcano is currently sleeping, it will probably erupt again, shredding the northern half of New Zealand, and probably causing vast damage throughout the south as well. The loss of life will be enormous. The nation will be all but destroyed. Will that be God's fault? Hardly! The two islands (with all their volcanoes) have been in place for several million years, whereas the first humans arrived from Polynesia less than 800 years ago. If people choose to go there, then they must wear the consequences of the inevitable volcanic eruptions.

Not that I can claim to be any better. I live in Sydney, which will be flattened by a huge tsunami if Taupo does erupt. This has happened in the past, and will happen again. But of course, like most people, I hope it will not happen yet! But if it does, I cannot blame God when the ocean starts lapping at my front door. I alone must bear the blame for purchasing a house that sits in a danger zone.

Nonetheless, some do accuse God in anger, calling him vindictive or unjust or even helpless, because he either causes or allows manifold tragedies to happen. Others piously declare that such events are acts of divine providence from which we should learn humility. Others go even further, and say they are a judgment by God upon human iniquity. But pious, angry, or righteously indignant, such people are all saying more than they can possibly know.

THINK ABOUT JOB

The issues today are the same as those raised in *Job* at least 3,000 years ago. After listening to several hours of debate, God was finally roused to anger against all the characters in the story – against Job's three friends, because they kept on insisting that the patriarch's tragedies must be caused by sin; and against Job, because he was righteous in his own sight.

Nonetheless, the Lord refused to give any reason for Job's sufferings, nor for the horrible deaths of his sons and daughters, nor for the violent murder of his servants, shepherds, and gardeners, nor for the loss of his stock. He offered no justification for allowing such awful things to happen. God did not reveal whether or not they came from his hand. [134] The Lord declined to explain either his activity or inactivity – he simply showed his glory to Job and to his companions. They were struck silent. They got no answers from God; but they lost their questions!

NO EXPLANATIONS OFFERED

Today, heaven will not tell us whether or not a divine hand is stirring up the elements, nor if certain floods are wholly natural events, nor why they happen to some and not to others, nor why, in the middle of horror, some are incredibly rescued while others miserably perish.

To all human *"whys"* heaven will remain as silent as it did to the agonised cry of Jesus at Calvary, *"Why have you forsaken me?"* (Mt 27:46) The only word we will hear is a call to repentance for those who are strangers to the Lord, and a call for trust to those who love him. In the end, no matter what is happening, every believer must emulate the dying Christ, *"Father, into your hands I commit my spirit!"* (Lu 23:46)

But on natural disasters in general, here is a summary of my opinion –

- To say that God did or did not have a hand in them is beyond the purview of any mortal currently alive. We are not Hebrew prophets, and the prophetic gift in the church differs significantly from that of Israel. It is true

---

(134) Some later editor probably added the prelude to the story, detailing Satan's part in the ruin of Job's life.

that Agabus predicted a famine, (Ac 11:28) but he made no attempt to define it as an act of God or of Satan. He simply said it would happen; and it did.

- When Jesus was asked who should be blamed for a terrible accident, he declined to satisfy idle curiosity, but bade his hearers to repent lest something worse happen to them. (Lu 13:1-4)

- Floods, fires, earthquakes, famines, wars, pestilences all happen. They are neither signs of the end of the world, (Mt 24:4-7, *"the end is not yet"*) nor necessarily acts of God, although they may be. It is impossible for us to say. Only one thing is sure – such things happen and are part of the ordinary course of events on this turbulent planet. They have happened before, they are happening now, and they will happen again in the future. Our part is to be ready for them and do whatever we can to mitigate them, without blaming God.

- If people choose to build their homes and cities in places that are known to be flood plains, or prone to earthquakes, or in the middle of a flammable forest, they can hardly complain when the unavoidable happens. They do complain, of course, but it is irrational. Brisbane will be flooded again as surely as San Francisco will be wrecked again by an earthquake, and Los Angeles will one day be next to Seattle. New Zealand will be torn apart by a volcanic explosion and the resulting tsunami will sweep away most of Sydney. Everyone knows that these tragedies are inevitable, so how can they be God's fault? It's just life on Earth.

- The issue of pain and human tragedy is dealt with in *Job*. God finally intervenes in the debate to express annoyance at all the participants – the friends, because they insist that Job's sufferings must be the consequence of sin; Job, because he was righteous in his own eyes. Yet the Lord himself offered no explanation or justification for what happened to the patriarch. Nor did he give a reason for the savage deaths that fell upon his children, shepherds, workers, and orchardists, none of whom deserved such a fate. But they died anyway. God simply showed the patriarch his glory – not even his heavenly splendour, just his work in creation – and it was enough to silence the debate. Once again, they got no answers, but they lost their questions.

- God is no more inclined to explain himself to us when we raise a clamorous "why?" than he did for the Saviour at Calvary. He simply demands repentance and trust, no matter what the circumstances.

- For a quaint but comprehensive theodicy, read 2 Esdras 3:1-8:3. [135] It contains all the major questions and the usual responses to them. Nothing ever written on theodicy since then has ever said any more. In the end, they all say little of value, because the ways of God ultimately lie beyond our scrutiny.

- Further, no matter what pious justification for pain is raised, eventually a level of suffering, of human torment, of measureless loss and anguish is reached that no explanation can soften or excuse, and we are left with inexplicable mystery. At that point, like Jesus himself, we have to silence our "why" and say simply, *"Father, into thy hands I commend my spirit."*

---

(135) If you don't have the book in your library, you can find it on the internet.

So no theodicy ⁽¹³⁶⁾ can fully satisfy our demands, or remove the pain of horrible disaster, or explain the anguish of injustice, or justify God's silence while people are torn to piece in the hideous torment of a torture dungeon, or why he watches, seeming uncaring, while the Titanic rushes to its dreadful encounter with an iceberg. But some defence is possible, which maintains the wisdom and goodness of God.

GOD KNOWS ALL ABOUT IT

No earthquake, flood, famine, pestilence or fire ever takes God by surprise. So, why doesn't he prevent them, or at least give adequate warning? Even our own law requires this of a good citizen! Failure to take whatever action one can to prevent a crime or an accident is a violation of the duty the law expects from everyone.

So why doesn't God intervene whenever he sees something awful about to happen? How can he sit silent in heaven while the Titanic surges towards its icy doom? Why doesn't he warn the people when a terrifying earthquake is about to shake the city apart? How can he remain apparently unmoved when men and women, even young people and children, are shrieking their lives away under a torturer's pitiless hand?

We don't know, for many things are hidden from our eyes. But remember that Jesus predicted such things, and was able to accept them without condemning the Father –

> *You will hear of wars and rumours of wars. Don't be alarmed! These things must happen, but they don't mean that the end has come. Nation will fight against nation and kingdom*

---

(136) "Theodicy" is "the branch of theology that defends God's goodness and justice in the face of the existence of evil". (WordWeb.info)

against kingdom. There will be famines and earthquakes in various places. (Mt 24:6-7, GW)

There has never been a greater moral philosopher or ethicist than Jesus of Nazareth. If he could live with the problem of horrendous and undeserved pain, then we too must accept the inevitability of suffering in this world.

We live on a violent and savage planet, with a raging inferno at its core, and a turbulent surface. Its vast energies are released without respect of person or place. It is a fact of life that we must simply endure.

The same is true of the universe as a whole. The seemingly serene sky above us is an immense holocaust of surging nuclear activity. Old stars are dying; new stars are endlessly being created. Some dying stars come to their end in an awesome explosion of unimaginable power that astronomers call a *supernova*. The destruction is staggering in its ruinous force, yet such events also spread across the universe the heavy metals and essential elements upon which life itself depends. So too, the fertility of the planet depends upon thunderstorms, lightning, earthquakes, even floods. That is, if the skies above us and the earth beneath us were less violent than they are, we would simply not exist. We have to accept the good with the bad.

MAN IS BORN TO TROUBLE

As surely as sparks fly upward, so all who live in this world will know trouble! (Jb 5:7)

Ever since the Fall, suffering has been an inescapable part of the human condition. Thus the earth produces thorns and is subject to decay and death. Likewise, beginning with the Flood, the earth has known many disasters worse than any current event. To give just one example: in China, in 1556, an earthquake caused by the same kind of tectonic plate movement that created the tsunamis of recent years, killed no less than 820,000 people.

Those tragedies did not impugn the integrity of the Almighty any more than a contemporary crisis can.

Remember too, that we have never been promised immunity from trouble. We are part of human society, and must accept ill fortune along with good. Note *Jeremiah 45:1-5* —

> *This is what the Lord says to Baruch, "I am tearing down what I have built, and I am uprooting what I have planted throughout the earth. <u>Why then do you look for some great thing for yourself</u>? No! You can't expect any special favours, for I intend to bring disaster everywhere," says the Lord!*

We are part of our society and must share its woes as well as its welfare. Just because we are Christians, we cannot expect some great thing that will spare us the pains suffered by our neighbours in times of war, or of natural disaster, and the like.

That is why Jesus himself gave several warnings about locating your treasure on earth instead of in heaven. (Mt 16:19-20) Nothing in this world is permanent or free from all overshadowing peril.

THE MYSTERY OF JOY

There are three special things we can say about the mystery of human suffering –

1. Like Job, we will lose our questions when we finally see the glory of God. (Jb 40:1-5; 42:1-6)

2. The mystery of joy is even greater than the mystery of pain.

Sir Thomas Browne declared that he would not bother to try to fathom the mystery of *pain* until someone could explain to him the mystery of *happiness*. Neither of them is deserved by mortals, but we experience them anyway, and mostly, such is the grace of God, more of the latter than of the former –

> While many are obsessed with the problem of evil, and of pain, we should rather explore the equally complex problem of the existence of goodness, and of joy. (137)

The fact is both pain and pleasure are equally inexplicable and equally undeserved. If we are happy to accept the one, we cannot escape the other.

3. God himself has shared this valley of tears through the sufferings and terrible death of Christ, so he is not indifferent to human need, but has himself known the worst anguish of pain and death.

NIMBY

Everybody wants God to do something, but only if his intervention is confined to some other place! It is the typical n.i.m.b.y syndrome! Interfere, O Lord, as much as you please over there, but stay out of my backyard!

How loudly people would shriek and complain if the Lord decided to take control of *their* lives! How they would resist him if he asserted mastery over *their* homes, or insisted upon sitting in *their* board rooms, or demanded that *their* government should acknowledge his sovereignty in everything!

---

(137) Op. cit. The quote above comes from the *Introduction* by C. A. Patrides to the edition of Browne's works published by Penguin Books, London, in 1977.

Do you doubt that people would furiously oppose him? Then look at how they treated Jesus when he tried to introduce the government of God! The Jews hated him, the Greeks laughed at him, and Romans killed him! Do you really suppose that overt divine intervention would be any more welcome now than then?

How about if the Lord decided to curtail their pleasures because of their sin? No! They want God to stave off disaster, pain, or loss, but they reject any accounting of their misdeeds.

WE TRASH OUR OWN PLANET

When we ourselves are busily wrecking the environment, annihilating scores of animal species, and killing each other with zeal, it ill behoves us to blame God for nature's fury! By self-inflicted wars, pestilence, famine, global warming, and the like, we slaughter millions of people. Why then should the Lord suppress natural cause and effect whenever it threatens our contentment? We are, after all, happy to receive the *benefits* of natural law, so we cannot honestly complain when that same law works to our disadvantage.

Yet, having said that, we must also observe that a measure of struggle seems to be an inescapable part of God's plan at this time. There are several reasons for this, among them the following –

- The restless energy of fallen humanity, especially while we are confined to this planet, needs some kind of release, which often finds its outlet in war.

- Crisis forces people to search for and find creative solutions (consider the many wonderful inventions that were wrought last century out of the two World Wars).

- Suffering stirs up compassion and benevolence.

- Tragedy compels people toward dependence upon God.
- One disaster may well prevent an even worse horror – for example, by stopping a war; forcing preventive action against disease, the ravages of natural forces, and the like.

The idea is this – unbroken peace and prosperity, health and happiness, would leave the human race enervated, dull, empty of dynamic vitality. By contrast, the present conditions drive us ever onward to higher achievement.

There is an undoubted mystery here, and we remain, as Paul says, at best like people *"looking through a piece of smoky glass"*. Yet we can be sure that –

- God knows what he is doing! And that –
- The most awful ***disaster*** of all, and the most glorious ***triumph*** ever, still lie ahead of us – see *2 Peter 3:8-18* –

THE WARNING

My dear friends, here is something that you should never forget – in the sight of God one day is like a thousand years, and a thousand years are like one day! So the Lord is not tardy in fulfilling his promise, as some have said. Rather, he is patient with you, because he does not want anyone to be destroyed. Instead, he is giving time for everyone to abandon their sins.

THE DISASTER

Nonetheless, the Day of the Lord, like a thief, will come without warning. On that Day the very galaxies will vanish with an awful clamour, and the earth and everything on it will be destroyed. Yes, the heavens will be aflame, they will burn with fire, and the stars above will melt away in the heat.

THE LESSON

Since we know that all these things are destined for destruction, what kind of people should we be? Surely, as we wait for the Day of God, and do all that we can to hasten its coming, we should strive to be holy and we should dedicate ourselves to the service of God. ... In the meantime, we are waiting for what God has promised: new heavens and a new earth, where only righteousness can flourish.

THE TRIUMPH

Therefore, my friends, as you wait for that Day, do your best to be pure and faultless in God's sight and to be at peace with him. ... Be on your guard, so that lawless people will not be able to entice you to folly, and cause you to lose your security in Christ. Rather, continue to grow in the grace and knowledge of our Lord and Saviour Jesus Christ, to whom be the glory, now and forever! Amen.

TWENTY-SIX:

ARCHIPPUS

> *Pass this instruction on to Archippus, "See that you complete the task that you have received in the Lord." (Cl 4:17)*

During the reign of the Roman emperor Nero, a fierce persecution broke out against the churches in Colossae. Among the many martyrs were a man, his wife, their son, and a slave, who were all put to death with great cruelty.

Who were they?

<u>Philemon</u> — a wealthy citizen of Colossae, with a large house where a small church gathered.

<u>Apphia</u> — his wife and partner.

<u>Archippus</u> — their son, who was probably also pastor of the house church, whom Paul urged to fulfil his ministry. (Cl 4:17)

<u>Onesimus</u> — their slave, who had run away, but was sent back home by Paul.

They are all mentioned in Paul's *Letter to Philemon*, which begins —

> *Paul, a prisoner of Christ Jesus, and Timothy our brother, to Philemon our dear friend and fellow worker, to Apphia our dear sister, to Archippus our fellow soldier, and to the church that meets in your home." (vs. 1-2)*

Notice how Paul included the house church in his greeting. Indeed most churches in those days met in a house or a small hired hall. Paul, for example, taught daily for two years in a rented lecture hall. (Ac 19:9) Not until well into the 3rd century do we read of any dedicated church buildings.

Mark this – Paul has forever honoured the small group by treating them as real churches! By all means let us build the church as large as we can, but always remember that the Lord is not impressed by mere size! I cannot forget the words of the gospel –

> *When Jesus saw the crowd, he went up a mountain! (Mt 5:1)*

He was not excited by a large crowd. He knew how easily they could be turned against him. Instead of rushing toward the mob, he beat a hasty retreat to the mountain. He made the crowd come to him. So too Paul, commending a house church, showed that he did not *"despise the day of small things."* (Zc 4:10)

But back to our text. Philemon was a man wealthy enough to own slaves, and had a house large enough to host a local church. Apphia was his wife, and Archippus probably their son.

So here is a picture of a Christian family, with high honour given to all its members.

Paul mentions Onesimus and Archippus in his letter to the *Colossians*. (4:9, 17) To them, let me add Apphia, who was co-owner of one and mother of the other, as an example of the status the gospel has given to women.

Which brings us to our first idea —

EQUALITY

The reason for supposing that Apphia was Philemon's wife, is because of the way the letter is addressed –

- Paul groups the people together before he mentions their home, (Phm 1) which suggests that they all lived together in that home.

- *Philemon*, too, is the only letter Paul addressed to an individual, or to a single family (apart from the letters to Timothy and Titus).

- The letter deals with a family matter (the return of the slave, Onesimus), and unless Apphia and Archippus were related to Philemon there was no reason for their names to be included.

Notice too how Paul names them — Philemon is a *"co-labourer"*; Archippus is a *"fellow-soldier"*; but Apphia is *"dear sister"*! Paul's use of that expression shows how highly he valued the lady and her position in the family and in the church.

Further, Apphia was one of the addressees of the letter, coming right after her husband, and even before her son, though Archippus was probably pastor of the church that met in their home. (Cl 4:17)

It is hard for us to imagine how radical all this was in the Greek and Roman world of those days! Paul's greeting broke down barriers of class, gender, and status. This is one of the chief glories of the gospel — it brought equality to all people. Husbands, wives, children, slaves, rich and poor, single and married — they were all equal members of the mixed congregation that met in Philemon's house. And even on such an important matter as the treatment of a runaway slave, Paul reckoned that Apphia's voice was as important as her husband's. He addressed his appeal just as much to her as to him. Apphia, then, was seen by Paul as the partner of her husband, having a right with him to determine how the family should run, and what decisions should be made.

On the other side, Paul and Onesimus had to trust in the power of the gospel to overwhelm social custom. The normal penalty for a recaptured slave was at least a severe flogging, which was usually followed by execution, and often by crucifixion. Paul appealed not just to Philemon, but also to Apphia his wife, and to Archippus their son and pastor of the church, to forgive Onesimus. In Christ, they all had a right to speak and to decide to scorn ancient custom, and to live instead by the gospel.

The same should be true of Christian congregations today.

AUTHORITY

Philemon is mentioned in the writings of the church fathers as being a bishop, or pastor, which is probably the reason why this personal letter has been preserved, when many others that Paul must have written were allowed to perish. In any case, it is a literary gem, which provides us with many fine lessons, including Apphia's high status in the family. She must have endorsed her husband's decision to accept Paul's request for mercy, because it seems that Onesimus was freed and later became active himself in Christian ministry. [138] He is mentioned in *Colossians* as *"a faithful and dear brother, who belongs to your church."* (4:9)

In recognising Apphia's authority as a woman and wife, the apostle was echoing a biblical rule that had been long established, but somehow forgotten, especially in the Greek and Roman world –

---

(138) Ignatius of Antioch mentions a bishop in Ephesus by the name of Onesimus, whom some scholars think is the former slave of Philemon. Several denominations recognise him as a saint, and there are various traditions associated with his life and ministry. If Philemon's slave did in fact become the bishop of Ephesus, then he was martyred in the Trajan persecution, not the one launched by Nero.

> *If you curse your mother, you will be left in pitch darkness, like a snuffed-out lamp. ... Do not despise your mother because she is old. ... The eye of one who mocks a mother and refuses to obey her, will be plucked out by ravens in the valley and eaten by young vultures. (Pr 20:20; 23:22; 30:17)*

The last reference refers to parent-despisers being denied proper burial. They will be tossed into the valley where trash is dumped, there to feed the carrion birds. Since a lack of proper burial was considered a deep disgrace by the Jews, the proverb means that people who despise their mothers are behaving scandalously.

Sadly, the church itself has sometimes forgotten this rule, and has tried to subjugate Christian women under male tyranny; but the gospel has always prevailed, and the rule of equality has been re-instated, as in our own time.

There is a peculiar illustration of this fault in the letter itself. Did Paul call Apphia a lady dearly loved, a sister, or a dearly loved sister? The KJV has "beloved"; the NIV has "sister"; some MSS have both! It seems that Paul actually wrote "beloved", to match his address to Philemon. But some later copyist, not liking this level of equality, or perhaps offended by its intimacy, changed it to "sister". Others, not knowing which to write, included both!

Whatever Paul actually wrote, his general teaching on the status of women could not be denied. Thus by the time of Justinian (circa 500 A.D.), women had a status much the same as they enjoy in the western world today. The collapse of the Roman Empire led to a decline, but as Europe re-built, so did the lot of women improve, until by the middle ages they once again stood nearly equal with men.

Thus the cycle has been repeated, until the present time, when male and female equality, at least in western society, is taken for granted. One hopes it will never be lost again!

INHERITANCE

Apphia received the same benediction as her husband — *"Grace and peace come to you from God our Father and from the Lord Jesus Christ"* (vs. 3, "you" is plural).

As Jesus said, in heaven there is neither male nor female, for we are all united in Christ –

> *In this present world, people marry and are given in marriage. But those who are considered worthy of taking part in the world to come and in the resurrection from the dead will not marry, for they will be like the angels. Neither will they ever die. Since they are children of the resurrection, they will be God's children for ever!" (Lu 20:34-36)*

Apphia and her family lived, loved, laughed, worshipped, served God, and were martyred together in the joy of Christ.

When Paul wrote to Philemon, neither he nor they knew the awful fate that would befall them. But it would have made no difference. They would have continued to love the Lord and to serve him with all their heart. Their eyes were fixed, not on earth but in heaven, where Christ sits enthroned on the right hand of God. They were not enamoured of earthly things, but of heavenly. They were waiting for Christ to appear, so that they might appear with him in glory, (Cl 3:1-4) which hope, dear reader, I trust beats just as firmly in your heart.

CONCLUSION

Let me return here to Archippus, and to the admonition Paul gave him –

Make sure to complete the task you were given as a servant of the Lord!" (Cl 4:17)

There is no need to suppose that Archippus was somehow failing in his duties, perhaps as pastor of the church in Colossae. After all, Paul cheerfully describes him as a *"fellow soldier"* (Phm vs. 2). Rather, the apostle was encouraging the young man to be faithful in fulfilling all that lay in the Father's purpose for his life. It is a goal toward which we should all aspire, summed up perhaps best of all in Paul's last words to the elders of the Ephesian church –

> *I did not allow anything to make me shrink back from declaring to you the whole purpose of God. So now, watch out for yourselves and for the whole flock which the Holy Spirit has placed under your care. Be faithful shepherds of the church of God, which he has purchased with the blood of his own Son. (Ac 20:27-28)*

TWENTY-SEVEN:

CHAINS

Remember my chains! (Cl 4:18)

Why should we remember Paul's chains? Was he trying to elicit sympathy? Was he complaining about his fate? Did he expect the Colossian church to secure his release from prison? Or rather, was he hoping to challenge them (and us) to make sure that they too bore the chains of Christ?

What are these chains?

THE CHAINS OF GRACE

Christian wives should yield authority to their husbands, because this is what Christ wants you to do. In turn, Christian husbands should love their wives, and never treat them harshly. And you children should always obey your parents. How pleased the Lord will be when he sees you all behaving like this!

Fathers, don't be too stern with your children. Why would you want to rob them of all spirit?

Christian slaves should set a good example in their service. Don't obey your masters only while you're being watched – like a bunch of people-pleasers – but provide good service always. Your motives should always be sincere – remember who is your true Master!

You slave-owners must treat your slaves fairly, and with justice, because you too have one true Master in heaven.

> *All of you, be wise in the way you act toward those who are outside the church, continually looking for an opportunity to bring them to Christ. In fact, you should always speak kindly and thoughtfully, in a way that will be appealing to everyone who hears you. (Cl 3:18-4:1, 5, 6)*

What a dramatic passage!

I have already mentioned the extraordinary impact such ideas must have had upon the first readers of *Colossians;* but I want to add a little more.

The apostle takes four groups of people (wives, children, slaves, strangers) who were all deemed proper victims of exploitation, and insists instead upon fair dealing between all of them. There is to be no violence, no harsh exploitation, no crushing blows by word or fist, but only kindness, fairness, justice, and mutual respect.

By contrast, think about the Roman law of *Patria Potestas*; and the low status of women and slaves. A Roman father, the head of a family, had nearly total power over every person in the house.

All the members and property of a household were subject to the authority of its head male. He even had a power of life and death over every person under his roof, whether related or not, slave or free.

In addition, the law stated that

- an obviously deformed child must be put to death
- the father could sell his children into slavery
- he had the power to approve or reject the marriages of his sons and daughters
- while he lived, all the property owned by his children, young or old, married or single, remained under his

authority, and he had a complete right to sell it or dispose of it in any way he pleased.

Those Roman laws were largely echoed in the laws of ancient Israel. For example, note Laban's claim that he owned everything that belonged to Jacob –

> *These young women (Jacob's wives) are my daughters; their children are my children. The flocks are all my flocks. Everything you have belongs to me!" (Ge 31:43)*

Rabbi Sirach echoed the same ideas in his instructions to his students –

> A man who loves his son will whip him often so that when he grows up he may be a joy to him. An unbroken horse turns out stubborn, and an unchecked son turns out headstrong. Pamper a boy and he will shock you; play with him and he will grieve you. Do not share his laughter, for fear of sharing his pain; you will only end by grinding your teeth. ...
>
> Do not give him freedom while he is young or overlook his errors. Break him in while he is young, beat him soundly while he is still a child, or he may grow stubborn and disobey you and cause you vexation. Thrash your son often and take pains with him or he may offend you by some disgraceful act. ...
>
> Never be ashamed of frequently disciplining your children, or of drawing blood from the back of a worthless servant. (Sir 30:1-13; 42:5-6, NEB)

But long before Sirach, Solomon wrote several proverbs to the same effect –

> *Don't be timid about disciplining your child; strike him hard – it won't kill him! If you beat him, and harden your heart against his tears, you will keep him from destroying himself. (Pr 23:13-14; 13:24; 19:18)*

And mark the violence (which no-one in the church today would sanction) in *Proverbs 10:13; 17:10; 19:29; 20:30; 26:3; etc.* Those texts talk about flogging someone merely for being a "fool", and brutally beating various other miscreants. To the list of gruesome punishments sanctioned in old Israel, we could add such barbarities as stoning to death a rebellious son; burning an immoral daughter at the stake; mutilation of offenders; branding them with a hot iron; hanging them from a tree, to be torn to pieces by carrion birds; imprisoned in stocks to be beaten or tormented by any bystander; and so on. [139]

The gospel has changed all that. The question is no longer, *"What rights can I demand?"* but rather, *"What service can I*

---

[139] Some Christian parents quote the passages that speak about taking a rod to a child to justify the use of corporal punishment in raising their children. It is capricious to quote the Bible in that context unless one gives equal weight to the references about beating fools, slaves, and others, until their blood runs. Apart from such cruelty being currently illegal, I doubt that any modern Christian congregation would sanction erecting a flogging triangle in its courtyard! I mean, whether or not corporal punishment should be inflicted on children (I am personally opposed to it) must be determined, not by quoting some Old Testament texts, but on social, philosophical, cultural, and legal grounds, which may or may not sanction beating a child. But in today's world, the biblical passages cannot be construed as meaning any more than the need to maintain well-ordered homes, in which the love and grace of Christ prevails. For us, discipline in our homes must be achieved by means far less savage than *Proverbs* suggests. Yet we find the anomaly, in many churches, of people saying, "I am a Christian – therefore I would never flog an adult. I am a Christian – therefore I will certainly flog a child!" That is, of course, absurd, and any biblical argument for physical violence against a child can be maintained only by a very selective, and arbitrary, use of the Bible.

give?" The focus is no longer on me but on you; not upon what you can do for me, but upon what I can do for you.

All those notions were revolutionary in the ancient world. People who read Paul's letters for the first time were stunned. They wondered if society could possibly survive such radical changes in attitude and action.

Women and wives in particular, became beneficiaries of this gospel mandate of love –

- **_In Christ_** – women have full equality with men before the throne of God and in heaven. (Mt 22:29-30
- **_In the Church_** – women are full members with men of the Body of Christ. (Ro 12:4-5; 1 Co 12:12-14)
- **_In the Family_** – women, as wives and mothers, are especially honoured –
    - Their **_husbands_** are to love them more than life itself; (Ep 5:25-28)
    - Their **_children_** are to obey and revere them; (Ex 20:12; Ep 6:1-3; Cl 3:20) and
    - Their **_brothers_** in Christ are to protect and care for them –

    You men should treat the women in your church with sympathy and understanding, remembering that they are not as strong as you are. You should honour them, because they have received from God the very same gift of life that God has given you. If you don't do this, you may find that God will turn his ear away from your prayers. (1 Pe 3:7-12, paraphrased)

Sadly, at times in the past the church has dismally failed to live up to those demands of the gospel. At least among us I hope that both men and women, married and unmarried, those who are childless and those with families, young and old, and whatever nationality, will all be equally loved and honoured. As Peter says –

> *So that your prayers may not be rejected, you should treat each other with sympathy and understanding, for you are all heirs together of the gift of eternal life. Keep unity in the church, along with compassion, brotherly love, tender hearts, and humble minds. For scripture says, "If you want to love life and enjoy good times, then turn away from evil and do good; seek peace and pursue it. For the eyes of the Lord are on the righteous, and his ears are open to their prayer." (Based on 1 Pe 3:7-12)*

Thus the chains of selfishness are broken, and replaced by chains of love, which cause us to deal graciously with all, (Cl 4:5-6), (140) knowing that every believer has an equal value in the sight of God, for we are all -

- *IN* the Lord (Cl 3:18), and

- *UNDER* the Lord (3:23), and

- *FROM* the Lord (3:24).

---

(140) Notice, too, how Paul instructs us to speak graciously at all times, not just to Christians, but also to unbelievers. There are of course exceptions, as Jesus showed when he took up a whip and drove the money-changers out of the temple, (Jn 2:15) and when he castigated the Scribes and the Pharisees. (Mt 23) On those occasions, Jesus had just cause to speak and act roughly; otherwise, he was equally gracious to all people, no matter their learning, social status, or wealth.

THE CHAINS OF PRAYER

Steadily persist in prayer, staying alert, and always thankful. Remember too to pray for us, so that God will open to us a door to preach the word, declaring the mystery of Christ. It is on account of that word that I am now in prison. And I pray that my preaching will always be what it should be – easy to understand. ... Your fellow church member, Epaphras, who is, like you, a servant of Christ Jesus, sends you greetings. He never stops struggling on your behalf in his prayers, desiring that you might grow to maturity, remaining strong in faith, and obedient to the will of God. I bear him witness that he has worked hard for you and for the Christians in Laodicea and in Hierapolis. (4:2-4, 12-13)

The KJV translates vs. 2 as, *"Continue in prayer, and watch in the same with thanksgiving."* The key words in that verse summarise the entire passage –

PERSEVERANCE

Perseverance in prayer may seem at times like a heavy chain upon the soul, especially when prayer appears to be ignored. In years long gone, people had some strange ways of dealing with unanswered prayer –

> When the ancient Chinese storm god Lung Wang failed to stop an incessant downpour from heaven, the priests threw his image into prison, telling him that he would stay there until he behaved himself and stopped the rain. Or, in Japan, when the rain god failed to deliver any refreshing showers, the priests carried his image into the parched fields, saying that he would

stay there, baking in the heat, until he acted to end the drought. Or, when Alexander the Great was besieging Tyre, one of its citizens had a dream that their god Apollo was about to leave them and go over to the enemy. At once the people rose up, hastened to the temple, bound the image with ropes, and nailed it to the pedestal. Later, when the siege conditions worsened, they took him out to the public square, where they flogged him zealously! [141]

Modern Christians may not be as petulant as the ancients, but I have often seen disappointed Christians, albeit in more subtle ways, emulate the angry people of Tyre, or wishing, like the Chinese and Japanese, to take some kind of petty revenge against the Lord.

But learn this – the very demand for perseverance *presupposes* delay, struggle, disappointment! Scripture would not tell us to *persist* in prayer unless there is an assumption that prayer is not always answered quickly or easily. Those who pray must not only expect that the Lord will hear and answer them, but also that there may not be any immediate sign that heaven has taken even slight notice.

Perhaps you have prayed, seemingly in vain? Do not despair, but fall upon your knees again, boldly, believingly! *Persist*, and in time the Spirit will either show that you are asking for the wrong thing, or that an answer is on the way, even if it is not the response for which you had hoped.

---

[141] Culled from various sources, mostly the now defunct *History* magazine.

WATCHFULNESS

The Greek verb is *gregoreuo* ("I am awake!"), from which the early Christians coined the name *Gregory*. We could see here two things –

PRAY WISELY

That is, condition your prayer to the word and will of God. Notice how Paul, though he was in prison, facing trial and a possible death sentence, did not pray for his own peace, comfort, release, riches, happiness, or any such thing, but only that his work and witness might prosper! (vs. 3, 4)

Someone might say, "But why didn't he claim any number of promises of divine protection, prosperity, deliverance, and the like, and seek a miracle of rescue, such as he himself had experienced in Philippi, or as Peter had in Jerusalem?" (Ac 5:19; 16:26)

Answer: while there are indeed times when the Lord will intervene supernaturally in human affairs, he does not usually do so, and mostly allows things to take their natural course and reach their natural outcome. Also, while there are some circumstances when God does urge us to "prove" him by trusting a promise, and by receiving a miracle, they are few. For example, we are certainly encouraged to give generously and to expect prosperity (Ma 3:10; 2 Co 9:8-11) – yet the promise is tempered by the reality of persecution (He 10:34); or perhaps by a divine command to give away everything one possesses. (Mt 19:21) Usually, too, we have to share the fortunes of the community in which we live. Thus, in times of war, the righteous will suffer along with the unrighteous, and a tumultuous flood or a ravaging fire will destroy the homes of the godly as quickly as those of the ungodly. We cannot usually expect God to do some *"great thing"* just for us. (Je 45:1-5)

Then, too, it is futile to expect a miracle of divine healing while one is behaving in a manner conducive to sickness – perhaps by poor diet, lack of exercise, excessive consumption of alcohol, smoking, a failure to *"discern the Lord's body,"* (1 Co 11:30) and the like.

Common sense tells us that we are expected to do what we can to help ourselves. The Lord seldom does for us what lies within the skill of our own hands. So several maxims instruct us –

> *"God helps those who help themselves."*
>
> *"Praise the Lord, and pass the ammunition."*
>
> *"Put your trust in God, my boys,*
> *and keep your powder dry."*
>
> *"Ask God for as much as you like,*
> *but keep your spade in your hand."*
>
> *"God does not bargain, and God does not change."*
>
> *"God gives birds their food, but they must fly for it."* (142)

And in harmony with that last proverb, consider these from scripture –

> *Every living thing depends upon you to provide them with their food. And you provide it. But they must gather it up. (Ps 104:27-28)*
>
> *I give you this rule – if you won't work, then neither shall you eat. ... We command and*

---

(142) (1) From Aesop's fable, "Hercules and the Wagonner." (2) From a supposed saying by American naval chaplain, Howell Forgy, who helped man the guns when the Japanese attacked pearl harbour in 1941. (3) Supposedly spoken by Oliver Cromwell, during the 17th century English civil war. (4) An Armenian proverb. (5) A Yiddish proverb. (6) From Holland.

> *urge you in the Lord Jesus Christ to work patiently and to provide your own food to eat.*
> *(2 Th 3:10, 12)*

Many other places throughout the Bible urge the necessity of daily toil, of doing what you can to provide for yourself and your family, to solve your own problems, to meet your own needs. Don't depend upon God to put out a fire when there's a fire extinguisher on the wall, or a hose in your hand! Don't expect God to stop the pond from freezing because you were too slow in drawing water from it.

The spiritual principle is the need to strike a balance between believing the promise of God while avoiding *"putting the Lord to the test"*. This is a rule that Jesus himself understood well, and applied to Satan when the devil tried to tempt him to throw himself down from the pinnacle of the temple. Christ quoted Moses, (De 6:16) and sternly rebuked Satan, *"You must not put the Lord your God to the test."* (Mt 4:7) Which is to say, God cannot be coerced, bullied, or pressured into answering some prayer. Nor is it wise to try to bargain with God, as if to say, "Lord, if you do this thing for me, then I will do that for you!"

Hence I said above, that praying wisely means praying according to the *word* and the *will* of God. That is, first, discover his promise from his Word; but then, set that promise within a sensible understanding of the will of God – that is, what is his purpose for your life; what other circumstances may modify the promise; what is he saying to you personally about the time and manner in which he will respond to your petition?

There is a right way and a wrong way to test God. We may certainly "prove" him by joyful trust in his promise, and by responding to that promise with keen anticipation of its fulfilment. But we may not "test" him by deliberately trying to provoke him to action, forcing him into a corner, striking a bargain, supposing that we can do something that will leave the Almighty no choice except to grant our demand. Hence, for example, I know several former churches that were ruined by taking on expenditure that was beyond both their resources and their income. They believed they had a mandate from God, say, to erect a new building, so they began to build, expecting the Lord to supply the needed finance. He didn't. And they were bankrupted, and in a couple of cases, completely destroyed. The Lord is under no obligation to rescue us from our own folly. Read the many verses about "fools" in *Proverbs*!

Jesus spoke about this in his remarks on the man who began to build a tower, but when it was only half finished, ran out of money. Because of his folly, he became a mockery to all. (Lu 14:28-29)

The rule is, pray in the money *before* you spend it! Don't think you can put the Lord under pressure to rescue you if you go ahead unwisely with insufficient resources. Don't expect the Lord to keep you well, if you are constantly undermining your own health. If you choose to run down the freeway, the Lord will not prevent you from being run over. Stand on a rifle range, and it cannot be a surprise if you are shot.

Don't play the fool, and so reap a fool's reward. Don't put God to the test. Pray wisely, and you will pray well.

PRAY WATCHFULLY

When I was a child in primary school, more than 70 years ago, we used to have a one-hour lesson each week, known as "Religious Instruction". Clergy from several different Christian denominations presented the lessons, which undoubtedly had an influence on my later life. But out of all those scores of lessons across six years, I remember only four of them –

- on the perils of consuming alcohol, replete with gruesome charts and pictures. Most of us children signed the pledge at the end of the lesson, although I assume that in adult life, most of us then broke it!

- on the declaration of Christ that he would make his disciples *"fishers of men."* (Mt 4:19; Mk 1:17) Somehow that lesson impacted me, and I resolved, despite my youth, that I would become such a fisherman.

- on using wisdom in determining the will of God, which the pastor illustrated by recounting his experiences as a chaplain to the Australian Army during its Second World War campaigns in the jungles of New Guinea. He told us how the greatest threat to the soldiers came from Japanese snipers hiding in the jungle canopy. He himself was an excellent shot, so, despite being a chaplain, he carried a gun and successfully eliminated several of the snipers. His argument: either he died or the sniper died, and he thought he was more useful to God than they, so he chose to shoot them rather than be shot by them. I decided that I would follow the same policy. Not that I would go around with a bloodthirsty hunger to kill someone, but that I would be guided more by informed pragmatism than ignorant piety. (143)

- on the second Coming of Christ, which the pastor (who I remember was a Methodist minister) described with such vivid passion that ever after I have frequently been driven to search the sky, alert to the possibility that Jesus may come, not tomorrow, but today!

---

(143) I do not mean that I am not pious, for I most certainly am, but that I do not emulate those super-pious people who scorn the use of natural means and try to depend entirely upon the supernatural.

Indeed, since we do not and cannot know the day nor the hour of the Lord's return, (Mt 24:36) we should certainly, by continual wakeful prayer, be making ready to meet him!

Before leaving this discussion about praying "wisely" and "watchfully", let me share with you a story from the great 15th century work by Sir Thomas Malory, *Le Morte D'Arthur*, which is known as "the greatest of the prose medieval romances" in the English language [(144).] The story tells how a fair maiden came to the court of King Arthur, with a strange tale –

> When she came before King Arthur, she told from whom she came and how she was sent as a messenger unto him for a certain cause. Then she let fall her mantle that was richly furred, and she was girt with a noble sword. Whereof the king had marvel and said, "Damosel, for what cause are you girt with that sword? It beseemeth you not."
>
> "Now I shall tell you," said the damosel. "This sword that I am girt with doth me great sorrow and encumbrance, for I may not be delivered of this sword except by a knight who must be a passing good man of his hands and of his deeds, and without villainy or treachery or treason. If I may find such a knight who hath all these virtues, he may draw this sword from the sheath."

King Arthur assayed first to draw out the sword, but was unable to do so. Then all the assembled knights endeavoured to do so, but with equal lack of success. In the midst of these

---

(144) The Cambridge Guide to English Literature, ed. Ian Ousby; Cambridge University Press, Cambridge; 2002; article, Sir Thomas Malory.

fruitless activities, a poor knight, Sir Balin, clad in garments that were little better than rags, came in and besought the maiden for permission to take hold of the sword. With some reluctance, the maiden agreed, and to the astonishment of all, Sir Balin withdrew the sword easily from its scabbard.

The maiden warmly commended him, and then said, "Now, gentle and courteous knight, give me the sword again." But Sir Balin liked it too well to yield it to her, and vowed that he would keep the sword "unless it be taken from me with force!"

The maiden remonstrated with him, but he refused all her demands, insisting that the sword must be his to keep for ever. Whereupon she warned him,

> "You are not wise to keep that sword from me, for you will slay with that sword the best friend you have and the man you most love in the world; that sword shall be your destruct-tion." (145)

Sir Balin ignored her cautions and girding himself with armour and the sword went out adventuring. On his way he met a full-armoured knight whose horse was garbed in red. They challenged each other and fell into combat, smiting each other furiously, to such effect that they were both mortally wounded. Only as they lay dying and had removed their helms did they discover that each had slain his own brother.

When King Arthur heard how those two brothers, Balin and Balan, had unwittingly fought each other to death, he lamented, "Alas, this is the greatest pity that I have ever heard

---

(145) <u>Le Morte D'Arthur</u>, by Sir Thomas Malory (died 1471); ed. R. M. Lumiansky; Collier MacMillan Publishers, London; 1986 edition; Part One, Ch. II, sec. 1 & 2.

about two knights. For in this world I know not two such other knights." (146)

It is of course merely legend, but the moral is true. Be careful what you insist upon having, especially in prayer. You may end up getting your own way, to your own ruin. Long before Malory, the Israelites learned the same lesson. God gave them what they demanded, but it led to their destruction. (Ps 78:29-31; 81:12; 106:14-15)

THANKSGIVING

I have heard it said that all the joys of yachting can be more comfortably experienced by standing in a cold shower tearing up $50 notes.

Well, that may be true of many earthly pleasures, but nothing can ever equal or quench the joy that all true believers have in Christ. As Peter said, in the words of the old version, to believe in Christ is *"joy unspeakable and full of glory!"* (1 Pe 1:8) Hence, although Paul is in chains as he writes this letter, yet it is full of optimism, laughter, gratitude, and praise!

Here is a quality of prayer that should never be absent. Always, in everything and in every situation, let your requests reach God garbed with thanksgiving. (Ph 4:6)

THE CHAINS OF FELLOWSHIP

> One of the ancestors of Chinggis (Genghis) Khan was a woman named Alan-q'oa. She had five sons whom she one day found quarrelling. So "she boiled some mutton and sat all five boys down in a row. Then she gave each an arrow,

---

(146) Ibid. sections 18 & 19.

> saying: 'Break it!' They all broke the arrows easily and tossed them aside. Then she took five arrows and bound them together. She gave the arrows to each boy in turn, saying: 'Break them!' But however hard they tried, the clutch of arrows would not break. ... Then (she) went on to instruct her five sons with the following words: 'You boys were all born of my flesh. If you stand alone you can easily be broken, just as those five arrow shafts were broken. But if you stand together, like this bundle of shafts, no one can ever overcome you!'" (147)

The Bible, of course, long ago taught the same wisdom – *"a three-stranded cord is not quickly broken."* (Ec 4:12) Aesop, too, told a fable about it –

> A Lion used to prowl about a field in which Four Oxen dwelt. Many a time he tried to attack them; but whenever he came near they turned their tails to one another, so that whichever way he approached them he was met by the horns of one of them. At last, however, they fell a-quarrelling among themselves, and each went off to pasture alone in a separate corner of the field. Then the Lion attacked them one by one and soon made an end of all four. <u>Moral</u> – *united we stand; divided we fall.*

The last lines of *Colossians* (4:7-18) exemplify the same principle. Notice the chain of friends and companions Paul mentions: Tychicus, Aristarchus, Mark, Barnabas, Justus,

---

(147) <u>Chinggis Khan: the Golden History of the Mongols</u>; tr. Urgunge Onon; rev. by Sue Bradbury; the Folio Society, London, 1993; pg. 4. The Khan (died 1227) built the greatest land empire in world history, spanning 8000 km from west to east.

Epaphras, Luke, Demas, Archippus, Nympha (a lady house-church leader), and the brothers and sisters in Laodicea.

Observe the qualities of all those people, and the benefits Paul gratefully gained from them – *"a beloved brother, a faithful minister, a fellow servant in the Lord ... encourage your hearts ... faithful and beloved brother ... fellow prisoner in Christ ... co-workers for the kingdom of God ... a comfort to me ... a servant of Christ Jesus ... always wrestling in prayer ... so that you may stand mature and fully assured in everything that God wills ... he has worked hard for you."*

No servant of God, standing in such a bond of fellowship with other believers can ever be broken away from faith or from the kingdom. Such treasures, Paul is unconsciously telling us, do not exist apart from the fellowship of the local church, for all those people were actively joined to a church. Away then with the toxic idea that belonging to a church is an optional extra in Christian life. On the contrary, union with a local church is imperative for your very soul's salvation. Only where attendance at church, and participation in its life, work, and witness, is impossible can a Christian be excused from being part of a local church.

The Body of Christ is comprised of the company of local churches, and the only way to be in true union with Christ the Head is to be a living part of his Body. Cut yourself off from the church, and you are cut off from Christ. [148]

---

[148] Those remarks are based on the idea that the Body of Christ is not composed of some ethereal, diffuse, group of believers scattered across time and space. Rather, the Body is represented by the organised company of local congregations, gathered together under their God-appointed leaders, to worship and serve the Lord in the unity of the Spirit. The Body is visible, not invisible; on earth not in heaven. Thus Paul talks about the church at Cenchrea (Ro 16:1), and at Corinth (1 Co 1:2; 2 Co 1:1), in the house of Nymphas, (Cl 4:15) at Laodicea, (vs. 16) at Thessalonica, (1 Th

THE CHAINS OF FAITHFULNESS

And tell Archippus, "See to it that you fulfil the ministry you received from the Lord." (Cl 4:17)

Who is Paul rebuking: the church; or Archippus? The wording is strange. Why did Paul himself not admonish Archippus? Why does he tell the church to do so? Perhaps Archippus was giving up because the people were; or perhaps the reverse. Yet Paul elsewhere calls Archippus his *"fellow soldier,"* (Phm vs. 2) so it seems unlikely that the weight of Paul's rebuke falls upon him.

It seems likely, then, that Paul, rather than entreat Archippus personally, instructed the church to do so. Pastor and people must provoke each other to faithfulness; neither can succeed without the other. Nor, does the entirety of that task fall upon the leaders of the church only. Paul includes the whole congregation, whether ordained or lay. The people as a whole have a duty to encourage their leaders, even instruct them, as well as the leaders have toward the people.

Two things are suggested by the Greek word translated *"complete"* –

- the task was not yet ***fully*** done: either Archippus or the people were giving up too soon; or
- the task was not being ***properly*** done: either Archippus or the people were doing too little.

1:1) plus the church of the Cretans, (Ti 3:15) and the church in the house of Philemon. (Phm 1) Also, the church at Babylon, (1 Pe 5:13) and at Ephesus, Smyrna, Pergamos, Thyatira, Sardis, and Philadelphia. (Re 2:1, 8, 12, 18; 3:1, 7, 14) They are very visible, tangible, real congregations, on earth, not wafting around in heaven.

The injunction reaches to us all – *"complete the task that you have received from the Lord"*. This is how we can emulate the martyrs, these are the chains that we can wear for Christ, this should be our only boast on the day we meet the Lord, that we have run the race well and done all that he asked.

One of the renowned generals of Chinggis Khan, Boro'ul, was killed in battle. After his death, the great Khan praised him in song, saying –

> When the arrows rained on us
> you were my shield;
> At the time of the whistling arrows
> you were my shelter.
> When you were wounded
> you stayed in the saddle –
> Boro'ul, my man amongst men. [149]

Is that how our General feels about you and me?

CONCLUSION

In his closing remarks, Paul mentions a letter he had written to the church at Laodicea. (4:16) Such a letter still exists, which purports to come from Paul, and was for several hundred years included in many editions of the Bible. It is unlikely that Paul was truly its author, although it uses his wording in many places. Probably, it was compiled by an unknown hand to fill a gap left by the loss of the letter Paul did write to the Laodiceans. The extant letter dates back at least to the 4th century and perhaps much earlier. In the past, it was

---

[149] Ibid. pg. 171.

often quoted in church as scripture, because it certainly reflects the true heart of the great apostle – (150)

> *I will not hide the chains of suffering that I bear for Christ, for they are my chief joy, and because of them I am glad. I know that my salvation is secure for ever, especially when I am upheld by your prayers and by the power of the Holy Spirit. Can it matter if I live or die? For if I live, it will be a life in and for Christ; and if I die, it will be all joy!*
>
> *I am confident that the Lord in his mercy will grant you the kind of love for each other that will bind you together in unity of mind and service. Therefore dearly beloved, remember how I told you about the coming of the Lord and hold fast to your faith, working in the fear of God, knowing that your goal is eternal life. And remember that it is God himself who is working in you. ...*
>
> *The grace of the Lord Jesus be with your spirit. Amen! (vs. 6-11, 18)*

"Remember my chains!" cried Paul, meaning that we should emulate him and value nothing beyond the chains we gladly wear for Christ. (Cl 4:18)

---

(150) My version, given above, is compiled from several sources. See also the eponymous article in Wikipedia.

ADDENDA:

HAPPY MARRIAGES

1. The *Sydney Morning Herald* (Wednesday, Jan 31st, 2007) contained the following report, based on a letter that Captain Arthur Phillip (1738-1814), wrote to his superiors in London, announcing the safe arrival in Port Jackson of the First Fleet. Among other matters, Captain Phillip expressed concern about the imbalance of the sexes among the convicts, and suggests that an example set by the French might be followed –

   > Captain Phillip appears hugely concerned about the shortage of women for the new colony, and fancies himself a matchmaker. He suggests an increase in the number of "frail fair ones" on the First Fleet to lift the ratio of one woman to five or six men.
   >
   > "Without women, no colony can thrive - and a deficient number will certainly occasion … at length bloodshed, not to mention more odious consequences," he writes.
   >
   > This sounds progressive. But the tale turns dark as Captain Phillip reveals his chauvinistic leanings.
   >
   > "There can be no objection (except the expense of their transportation) to supplying the colonists with plenty of mates – each convict, if encouraged, might easily find himself a companion … The method used by the Regent of France, when he colonised New Orleans, might be adopted … The men were forced to draw lots

and were married to the women, pointed out by correspondent marks, before they were permitted to have any liberty on shore. Their eagerness for a commerce from which they had long been restrained made them take their destined spouse with readiness, and we do not find that these predetermined weddings turned out worse than the run of marriages commonly do." (151)

2. The following report, from the Hobart Mercury, January 2, 1861, adds some sarcastic colour to the shipping of convict brides –

> A good deal of anxiety is felt as to the probable continuance of the system under which our female population is at present being recruited. Whilst (earlier female) migrants continue to parade the streets of Hobart Town, ... we are daily expecting a new consignment of this interesting class of goods. Where will it end? To all appearances the thing is going on prosperously, and the public money will be spent with a liberal hand in transplanting the "social evil" of London and the other great towns of England to the Boil of Tasmania, so destitute of women that it is glad to get them of any kind!

---

(151) First Fleet Letters Lament Surplus of Sydney Coves; "Signposts from London," by Julia May; pg. 16. A more detailed report of French practices at a somewhat later date can be found at the National Library of Australia web site, under Trove. Go to – http://trove.nla.gov.au/ and search for "Convict Brides". You will observe in all the reports of similar events in the mid- to late 19th century, that the marriages so contracted were generally successful, primarily, I presume, because the couple had no choice except to look upon each other with good will and to strive to make their unions happy.

> If we cannot obtain any information as to how long this system of immigration is likely to last, there are one or two minor points, explanatory of its working, on which we may probably not be going too far if we venture to put a question. We have heard – will Government be good enough to tell us whether it be true or not? – that amongst the female immigrants lately imported at the cost of the Colony, to assist in laying the foundations of our future society, have been several English ticket-of-leave women? Not actual convicts undergoing sentence, it may be, but women who have been convicted of crime and having undergone their punishment have become the objects of charity, and been powerfully recommended to the benevolent sympathies of the gentleman charged with the selection of young females for Tasmanian wives. We do not know that female convicts from England are a worse consign-ment of domestic goods than the occupants of the Reformatories and Magdalene asylums, from which it is becoming notorious that many of our immigrants are taken. But the case furnishes a further illustration of the system, under which we are paying a heavy price for the importation of honest and virtuous young women, and under which we get something slightly different.

3. The Hobart Mercury, April 25, 1930, published a review of a book by Beatrice Grimshaw, *A Star in the Dust*, which said in part –

   > If Beatrice Grimshaw's investigations into conditions at Noumea some thirty years or so ago have yielded reliable information, it is plain that the French penal island in the Pacific was

even so short a time ago a veritable Port Arthur, or Norfolk Island. ... There are many vivid scenes of convict life in Noumea, including the religious travesty of the convict weddings, where male and female convicts were married by the score, all shouting names and responses in chorus, [152] and then liberated on ticket-of-leave to till the soil and produce children.

JOHN WESLEY ON CONGREGATIONAL SINGING

The great 18th century evangelist gave this advice to congregations, in his *Select Hymns*, published in 1761 –

> That this part of divine worship (singing a hymn) may be more acceptable to God, as well as more profitable to yourself and others, be careful to observe the following directions: —
>
> 1. Sing *all*. See that you join with the congregation as frequently as you can. Let not a slight degree of weakness or weariness hinder you. If it is a cross to you, take it up, and you will find a blessing.
>
> 2. Sing *lustily*, and with a good courage. Beware of singing as if you were half dead, or half asleep; but lift up your voice with strength. Be no more afraid of your voice now, nor

---

(152) That is, they were married *en masse*, the crowd of men and women being treated as one person, and giving their responses all together. Similar scenes occurred, as the author notes, in Tasmania. Indications generally are that the unions, if not deliriously happy, were at least satisfactory and lasting.

more ashamed of its being, heard, than when you sang the songs of Satan.

3. Sing *modestly*. Do not bawl, so as to be heard above, or distinct from, the rest of the congregation, that you may not destroy the harmony; but strive to unite your voices together, so as to make one clear melodious sound.

4. Sing *in time*. Whatever time is sung, be sure to keep with it. Do not run before, nor stay behind it; but attend closely to the leading voices, and move therewith as exactly as you can. And take care you sing not too slow. This drawling way naturally steals on all who are lazy; and it is high time to drive it out from among us, and sing all our tunes just as quick as we did at first.

5. Above all, sing *spiritually*. Have an eye to God in every word you sing. Aim at pleasing him more than yourself, or any other creature. In order to this, attend strictly to the sense of what you sing; and see that your heart is not carried away with the sound, but offered to God continually; so shall your singing be such as the Lord will approve of here, and reward when he cometh in the clouds of heaven.

CHRYSOSTOM

St John Chrysostom (circa 347-407), in a splendid sermon on giving thanks to God, used as his text, *"giving thanks always and for everything to God the Father in the name of our Lord Jesus Christ,* (Ep 5:20) and said –

What then? Are we to give thanks for everything that befalls us? Yes; be it even disease, be it even penury. For if a certain wise man gave this advice in the Old Testament, and said, "Whatsoever is brought upon thee take cheerfully, and be patient when thou art changed to a low estate," (153) much more ought this to be the case in the New. ... But if thou give thanks when thou art in comfort and in affluence, in success and in prosperity, there is nothing great, nothing wonderful, in that. What is required is, for a man to give thanks when he is in afflictions, in anguish, in discouragements. Utter no word in preference to this– "Lord, I thank thee!"

And why do I speak only of the afflictions of this world? It is our duty to give God thanks, even for hell itself, for the torments and punishments of the next world. For surely it is a thing beneficial to those who attend to it, when the dread of hell is laid like a bridle on our hearts. Let us therefore give thanks not only for blessings which we see, but also for those which we see not, and for those which we receive against our will . . .

Let us not then give thanks only when we are in prosperity, for there is nothing great in this . . . but whenever we are in penury, or in sicknesses, or in disasters, then let us increase our thanksgiving; thanksgiving, I mean, not in

---

(153) Sirach 2:4, "If hardship comes your way, bear it with patience, and remain cheerful when life humbles you. For as gold is tested by fire so the furnace of humiliation will try those whom God has chosen."

words, nor in tongue, but in deeds and works, in mind and in heart. Let us give thanks unto him with all our souls . . .

The ungrateful, however, and the unfeeling say, that this were worthy of God's goodness, that there should be an equality amongst us all. Tell me, ungrateful mortal, what sort of things are they which thou deniest to be of God's goodness, and what equality meanest thou? "Such an one," thou wilt say, "has been a cripple from his childhood; another is mad, and is possessed; another has arrived at extreme old age, and has spent his whole life in poverty; another in the most painful diseases: are these the works of Providence? One man is deaf, another dumb, another poor, whilst another, impious, yea, utterly impious, and full of ten thousand vices, enjoys wealth, and keeps concubines and parasites, and is owner of a splendid mansion, and lives an idle life." And many instances of the sort they string together, and weave a long account of complaint against the providence of God. . . . "But such an one," say they, "is poor, and poverty is an evil. And what (benefit) is it to be sick, and what (advantage) is it to be crippled?" Oh, man, they are nothing! One thing alone is evil, that is to sin; this is the only thing we ought to search to the bottom. . . . (154)

---

(154) These were not empty words. Most of his large income as archbishop of the cathedral at which the emperor worshipped he gave to various hospitals, and to help send missionaries to Scythia, Persia, and other lands. "His faithful reproof of vices moved the Empress Eudoxia to have him deposed and banished in 403 - first to Nicea, and then to the Taurus mountains, and

Go to the physician's, and thou wilt see him, whenever a man is discovered to have a wound, using the knife and the cautery. But no, in thy case, I say not so much as this; but go to the carpenter's. And yet thou dost not examine his reasons, although thou understandest not one of the things that are done there, and many things will appear to thee to be difficulties; as, for instance, when he hollows the wood, when he alters its outward shape. Nay, I would bring thee to a more intelligible craft still, for instance, that of the painter, and there thy head will swim! For tell me, does he not seem to be doing what he does, at random? For what do his lines mean, and the turns and bends of the lines? But when he puts on the colours, then the beauty of the art will become conspicuous. Yet still, not even then wilt thou be able to attain to any accurate understanding of it. But why do I speak of carpenters and painters, our fellow-servants? Tell me, how does the bee frame her comb, and then shalt thou speak about God also. Master the handiwork of the ant, the spider, and the swallow, and then thou shalt speak about God also. Tell me these things. But no, thou never canst. Wilt thou not cease then, O man, thy vain enquiries? For vain indeed they are. Wilt thou not cease busying thyself in vain about many things? (There is nothing) so wise as this ignorance, where they that profess they know nothing are wisest of all, and they that spend

---

finally to Pityus on the Euxine. Compelled to travel thither on foot, with his bare head exposed to a burning sun, the old man died on the way at Comana, in Pontus." (Chambers Biographical Dictionary, *in loc.*)

overmuch labour on these questions, the most foolish of all. . . .

Alas! How many things are there to teach us to bridle this unseasonable impertinence and idle curiosity; and yet we refrain not, but are curious about the lives of others; as, why one is a cripple, and why another is poor. And so by this way of reasoning we shall fall into another sort of trifling which is endless, as, why such an one is a woman? And, why are we not all men? Why is there such a thing as an ass? Why an ox? Why a dog? Why a wolf? Why a stone? Why wood? And thus the argument will run out to interminable length. This in truth is the reason, why God has marked out limits to our knowledge, and has laid them deep in nature. . . .

(Learn this), with God nothing either is inconsistent, or appears so to the faithful. Wherefore let us *"give thanks for all things,"* and let us give (God) glory for all things. (155)

ON CHURCH GOVERNANCE

Christ is the head of the body, the church. He is the beginning, the firstborn from the dead, that in everything he might be preeminent. (Cl 1:18)

Back in January 2005 I received an email query from a pastor who was concerned about several issues dealing with the structure of church government. What follows contains the gist of my reply to him, and it touches on several significant issues, which I hope you will find interesting. Since Paul

---

(155) *Homily 19 on Ephesians*; Nicene and Post-Nicene Fathers; ed. Philip Schaff; 1979 reprint by W. B. Eerdmans Pub. Co., Grand Rapids, Michigan; pg. 139.

declares in *Colossians* that Christ, and Christ alone is the ultimate Head of the church, of every church, it seems appropriate to include these thoughts in this book.

My email correspondent made several emphatic assertions about the governance of the local church, which I felt were more dogmatic than scripture warrants. So I replied –

The main difficulty arises from the awkward fact that the apostles nowhere provide any kind of consistent description of either the offices or the government of a local church, nor of the group of churches. Think about the endless contentions between Presbyterians, Congregationalists, Episcopalians, Monarchists, Theocratists, Collegiate advocates, and their ilk. Those quarrels should be enough to show anyone that the biblical data are inadequate to allow development of any infallible system of church government. Therefore, it seems, so long as no clear biblical provision is violated, we are free to set up our churches in any way that is useful or practical. At any rate, that is certainly what has happened across the past 20 centuries!

It seems fair to say, too, that the squabbles about local church and/or denominational structure and governance are in the end as unresolvable as the fruitless arguments about baptism – should we baptise infants or only believers; by sprinkling or immersion; is there an impartation of grace or not; is baptism essential for salvation or not, and so on? Similar controversies have wrapped themselves around the eucharist and around other aspects of church structure and life. Anyone who claims to have the final word on such debatable issues is either ignorant or arrogant, but certainly not truthful!

A further problem arises from the manner in which we consistently give the biblical terms meanings that may have only a loose connection with the way the apostles understood them. For example, no-one really knows what Paul meant by "pastor", "elder", or any one of several other terms. He drew his expressions from the synagogue, the secular Roman government, and from Greek culture, yet we cannot know what twist he put into each of them. Some say that all the terms (pastor, elder, overseer, presbyter, and bishop) refer to the same person, merely reflecting different aspects of that person's office or function. Others make various kinds of distinctions between them. They are probably all at least partly wrong!

Likewise, the NT offers no definitive theology of ordination, nor of how long diverse persons should be appointed to any of the offices/ministries/functions in the church, nor whether or not some element of democratic vote should be allowed, and the like. Nor does scripture show plainly whether or not "ordination" is for life. At best we have a snippet of revelation here, and another there, but nothing that allows a truly coherent and final theology to be developed.

Consequently, all systematic theologies (if there actually is such a beast) owe at least as much to human imagination as they do to divine revelation! The Bible is a wonderful book, but it is neither systematic nor coherent in the way that we westerners wish it were. Even Paul had to acknowledge that at best he was like a man peering through a piece of smoky glass, able to catch hardly more than a glimpse here and there of the scenes on the other side. (1 Co 13:12)

Back to church government. If history has any value in deciding the argument between Episcopalians and the rest, then one has to say that the former have a stronger case. The Church Fathers as early as Ignatius (who is traditionally said to have been the little child of *Mt 18:2,* and later to have become a disciple of John) staunchly defended a strong Episcopal system. However, some argue that on the contrary, the very ferocity Ignatius poured into his letters shows that there were questions about the validity of his claims! At least this much can be said – across the centuries many forms of doing church have cropped up, flourished for a while, then vanished, as still happens in our own time. But churches based upon an Episcopal system have managed to withstand horrific shocks and to struggle out of the rubble of decayed empires, collapsing kingdoms, and decaying time. I am, for example, far from agreeing with all its dogmas, but at least the Roman Catholic Church is still there!

I hope you find some food for thought in the above, and that the Lord will give you a good understanding in all things.

INDEX OF TEXTS

1:02 154	2:11 86
1:03 271	2:11, 13 83
1:03-04 11	2:12 .... 139, 142, 144, 146, 147, 151
1:04 .... 13, 18, 20	2:13 .... 77, 85, 87
1:05 .... 11, 25	2:15 8
1:05, 23, 27 22	2:16-23 11
1:09 34	2:18 94
1:09-10 .... 31, 35, 40	2:20-23 12
1:11 ..... 45, 52, 53, 137, 211, 254	2:23 196
1:12 .... 151, 271	2:5 .... 55, 56
1:13 .... 75, 76, 79, 80, 94, 151	
1:14 .... 83, 84, 151	3:01-03 .... 160, 195
1:15-17 7	3:01-04 .... 44, 122, 149, 151, 306
1:15-18 89	3:03 151
1:16 184	3:03-04 154
1:17-18 100	3:04 .... 163, 175
1:18 .... 8, 91, 339	3:05 194
1:19 .... 101, 108	3:05-09 .... 152, 170
1:21-22 151	3:06 .... 156, 195
1:22 .... 97, 151	3:08 .... 177, 178, 188, 192
1:23 .... 23, 111	3:08-09 195
1:23, 25 .... 55, 56	3:08-10 197
1:23, 27 28	3:09-10 .... 194, 198
1:26 121	3:10-11 259
1:27 .... 23, 119, 151, 277	3:11 200
	3:12 .... 201, 211, 254
2:02 127	3:12-14 199
2:03 184	3:1-3 79
2:05 .... 15, 73	3:15-16 271
2:05-07 .... 13, 20	3:16 ... 55, 56, 219, 220, 225, 230,
2:06-07 19	231, 239, 242
2:07 271	3:17 271
2:08, 18 11	3:18 .... 256, 310, 314
2:08-10 12	3:18-19 243
2:09-10 .... 101, 102, 108, 120	3:19 256
2:10 .... 151, 196	3:20 .... 257, 313

3:21 257	4:03-04 317
3:22 257	4:05-06 314
3:23 314	4:07-18 325
3:24 314	4:09 304
	4:09, 17 302
4:01 257	4:15 326
4:01, 05, 06 310	4:16 328
4:02 .... 116, 271	4:17 .... 301, 303, 307, 327
4:02-04, 12-13 315	4:18 .... 5, 218, 309, 329
4:03 287	

GLOSSARY

Abstruse – Complicated and hard to understand.
Abjure – To make a public promise to give up something, such as a belief or activity.
Aeon – A large period of time.
Amalgam – A combination or blend of diverse things.
Ameliorate – To make or become better, more bearable, or more satisfactory.
Analogy – A comparison showing that two things are similar.
Anathema – A person or thing accursed or consigned to damnation.
Aphorism – A short statement that says something wise and true.
Ascetic – Living a very simple, self–denying life for religious reasons.
Attain – To reach as an end, to gain, achieve.
Augur – An official diviner of ancient Rome. One held to foretell events by omens.
Augured – Divined, foretold.
Auspicious – Showing or suggesting that future success is likely.
Baptisand – The person to be baptised.
Brownie points – A hypothetical currency of approval from a teacher or boss.
Caldera – A large crater caused by the collapse of land following a volcanic eruption.
Canonical – Based on the laws of the Christian church.
Coign of vantage – A favourable position from which to view something.
Criterion – A standard for judging or deciding about something.

Damosel – A young woman.
Delusory – Tending to deceive, delusive, unreal.
Effulgent – Radiating, or seeming to radiate, a brilliant light.
Eloquence – Using language with fluency.
Emanation – A cosmological concept that explains the creation of the world by a series of radiations, or emanations, originating in the godhead. The theory of the origin of the world by a series of descending radiations from the Godhead through intermediate stages to matter.
Emulate – To strive to equal or excel.
Encomium – A prose or poetic work in which a person, thing, or abstract idea is glorified.
Ephemeral – Lasting one day only or a very short time.
Eponymous – Relating or being the person for whom something is, or is believed to be named; of the same name or title.
Esoteric – Relating to knowledge that is restricted to a small group.
Ethereal – Light, airy, tenuous.
Euphoric – A feeling of well–being or elation.
Extant – Currently or actually existing.
Flagellant – One who whips himself as a public penance (see penitent).
Glossolalia – Speaking in an unknown language under the influence of the Holy Spirit.
Glossolalic – Having the nature, sound, or quality of glossolalia.
Gnostic – An adherent of Gnosticism.
Gnosticism – The thought and practice distinguished by the conviction that matter is evil and that emancipation comes through knowledge.
Heavenlies – A term relating to an unknown dimension in heaven.
Impugn – Oppose or attack as false or lacking integrity.
Inarticulate – Incapable of speech.

Indictment – A formal written statement framed by a prosecuting authority and found by a jury charging a person with an offense.
Infrangible – Not capable of being broken or separated into parts.
Intuitive – Possessing or given to intuition or insight.
Irrefragable – Impossible to deny or refute.
Legend – A story coming down from the past, popularly regarded as historical but not verifiable.
Liturgies – Rites or a body of rites prescribed for public worship.
Masochist – A person who takes pleasure in being abused or dominated.
Metamorphosis – A change of physical form or substance.
Metaphor (metaphorical) – A figure of speech in which a word or phrase literally denoting one kind of objector idea is used in place of another to suggest a likeness or analogy between them.
Overt – Open to view.
Paltry – Mean or despicable.
Panacea – Cure–all.
Paradox – A statement with two parts with opposite or contradictory meanings.
Parameter – A measure, a limit affecting how something may be done.
Penitent – One who is sorry for sins or offenses.
Penury –Poverty.
Pernicious – Malicious, destructive.
Piacular – Making atonement.
Plaudits – Praises.
Pragmatic – Practical.
Pragmatism – A practical way of thinking or dealing with problems.
Prerogative – Privilege, or right.
Prosaic – Lacking imagination or excitement.
Purview – Area of responsibility or influence.

Pyrotechnics – Showpieces.
Reciprocity – a situation in which people reciprocate.
Reciprocate – Respond.
Redolent – Reminding you of something.
Relativism – the belief that things like truth and morals change depending on a particular culture or situation. Someone who believes this is called a relativist.
Resile – To spring back into the same shape or position.
Secular – Not connected with religion.
Supernal – Heavenly, or divine.
Stylites – A Christian ascetic in ancient times who lived alone on top of a tall pillar.
Surreptitious – Done or made secretly, so that others will not notice.
Syncretic – The combination of different systems of philosophical or religious belief or practice.
Syncretise – To combine aspects of different systems of philosophical or religious belief or practice.
Vernacular – The language spoken by a particular group or in a particular area, when it is different from the formal written language.
Vicissitudes – Changes and unexpected difficulties.
Volition – The power or ability to decide something by yourself and to take action to get what you want. A more usual word is 'Will'.
Warp and woof – The foundation or base of something.

BIBLIOGRAPHY

BOOKS

Anchor Bible, The; Doubleday & Co., New York, 1966.

Aesop's Fables; Pan Books Ltd. London, 1975.

Castle, Tony; ed. A Treasury of Christian Wisdom; Hodder & Stoughton, London, 2001

Chant, Ken; *The Cross and the Crown*, Vision Publishing, Ramona, California.

Discovery, Vision Publishing, Ramona. California.

Emmanuel Part One &Two, Vision Publishing, Ramona, California.

Chaucer, Geoffrey; *The Canterbury Tales* (1345-1400); tr. by Nevill Coghill; Penguin Classics, 1977.

Dryden, John; tr. Plutarch's Lives of the Noble Grecians and Romans; Modern Library, New York; reprint of the 1864 edition.

Harrison, E. F., Editor in Chief. *Baker's Dictionary of Practical Theology*, Baker Book House, Grand Rapids, Michigan, 1967.

Khayyam, Omar; tr. by Peter Avery & John Heath-Stubbs. *The Ruba'iyat*. Penguin Classics, 1983.

Malory, Sir Thomas; (died 1471) *Le Morte D'Arthur*, ed. R. M. Lumiansky; Collier MacMillan Publishers, London, 1986 edition.

Onon, Urgunge; tr. *Chinggis Khan: The Golden History of the Mongols*; rev. by Sue Bradbury; the Folio Society, London, 1993.

Ousby, Ian; ed. *The Cambridge Guide to English Literature*, Cambridge University Press, Cambridge, 2002.

Pope, Alexander; (1688-1744), *An Essay on Man*; Epistle 4.

Plass, Ewald M., compiled, *What Luther Says*, Concordia Publishing House, Missouri, 1959. Vol I-IV.

Religio Medici, ed. C. A. Patrides, Penguin Classics Edition, 1977.

Ryan, John K., tr. *The Confessions of St Augustine*; Image Books,

New York, 1960.
Wells, H. G., *The Outline of History*, (1866-1946).
Wuest, Kenneth S., *The New Testament: An Expanded Translation*; Wm. B. Eerdmans Publishing Co.
Zipes, Jack; tr. & ed. *The Complete Fairy Tales of the Brothers Grimm;* Bantam Books, London, 1987.

ANCIENT TEXTS

Bede's Ecclesiastical History, (circa 731 A.D).
Didaché, The; or, *The Teaching of the Twelve Apostles* (early 2nd century A.D)
The Metamorphoses, by Ovid, pub. in Rome, *circa*
Nicene and Post Nicene Fathers.
The Republic; Laws; Politics; by Plato, *circa* 400 B.C.

COMMENTARIES

Anders, Max., Editor. *Holman New Testament Commentary*; B & H Publishing Group; Nashville, Tennessee, 2004.
Barnes, Albert (1798-1870), *Notes on the Bible.*
Bible Background Commentary, The; Intervarsity Press, Nottingham, UK, 1993.
Calvin, John (1509-1564), *Calvin's Commentaries.*
Clarke, Adam (1715-1832), *Commentary on the Bible.*
Excell, Joseph S. & Spence-Jones, H. D. M, editors, *The Pulpit Commentary*; 1881.
Gaebelein, Frank E., editor, *The Expositor's Bible Commentary*; Zondervan Publishers, Grand Rapids, Michigan.
Gill, John (1690-1771), *Exposition of the Entire Bible.*
Hawker, Robert, *The Poor Man's Commentary On The Whole Bible;* 1850.
Hendriksen, William; *The New Testament Commentary*; Baker Book House, Grand Rapids, Michigan; 1972.
Henry, Matthew, *Commentary On The Whole Bible*; Marshall, Morgan, and Scott; London, 1953.
Hodge, Charles (1797-1878), *A Commentary on Ephesians,* Intervarsity Press.
Hubbard, David A., gen. ed.; *Word Biblical Commentary;* Word

Books, Waco, Texas; 1987.
Interpreter's Bible, The; Abingdon Press, New York, 1952.
Ironside, H. A., *Expository Commentary* (1876-1951).
IVP New Testament Commentary Series The, Intervarsity Press, Nottingham, UK.
Jamieson, Robert; Fausset, A. R; & Brown, D., *A Commentary on the Old and New Testaments,* 1871.
Johnson B. W., *The People's New Testament Commentary;* 1891.
Joplin., *The College Press NIV Commentary;* Missouri, 1996.
Macdonald, William., *Believer's Bible Commentary*; Thomas Nelson Publishers; 1989.
Nelson's New Illustrated Bible Commentary; Thomas Nelson Inc., New York; 1999.
New Testament Commentary, The, Baker's Publishing House, Grand Rapids, Michigan, 1987.
New International Commentary on the New Testament, The; Bruce, F. F., gen. ed.; Wm. B. Eerdman's Pub. Co., Grand Rapids, Michigan; 1977.
Poole, Matthew, *Matthew Poole's Commentary*; 1685
Preacher's Outline and Sermon Bible; Word Search Corporation, Nashville, Tennessee, 2010.
Preacher's Commentary, The; Word Inc., Nashville, Tennessee, 1992.
Robertson A. T., *Word Pictures in the New Testament*; 1933.
Stern, David H., *Jewish New Testament Commentary*; Jewish New Testament Publications, Inc., Clarksville, Maryland; 1982.
Tasker, R. V. G., *Tyndale New Testament Commentaries;* Tyndale Press, London; 1964.
Trapp, John., *Commentary On The Old And New Testaments* (1601-1669).
Vincent, Marvin R., *Vincent's Word Studies*; 1886
Walvoord, John & Zuck, Roy.,*The Bible Knowledge Commentary;* Cook Communications; Colorado Springs, Colorado, 1989.
Wesley, John, *Explanatory Notes on the Whole Bible*; (1703-1791).
Wiersbe, Warren W., *Wiersbe's Expository Outlines*; Publisher, David C. Cook, Colorado Springs, Colorado.
Wiseman, D. J., general editor, *Tyndale Old Testament Commentaries,* Intervarsity Press.

BIBLE VERSIONS

In addition to the *King James Version* (KJV), also called the *Authorised Version* (AV) of the Bible, the following translations are cited, or were consulted by the author of this work.

CEV – *Contemporary English Version*; the American Bible Society, New York, NY; 1995.
ESV – *English Standard Version*; Crossway Bibles, a publishing ministry of Good News Publishers; Wheaton, Illinois; 2001.
GNB – *Good News Bible*; Second Edition, by the American Bible Society; New York, NY; 1992.
GW – *God's* Word; God's Word to the Nations Bible Society; Cleveland, Ohio; 1995.
JPS – *The JPS* Bible; the Jewish Publication Society; Philadelphia, PA; 1995.
ISV – *International Standard Version*, v. 1.2.2; The ISV Foundation, La Mirada, CA; 2001.
LB – *The Living Bible*, tr. Kenneth N. Taylor; Tyndale Publishing House, 1971.
NET – *The Net Bible*; Biblical Studies Press; Richardson, Texas; 2006.
NIV – *New International Version*; Zondervan Bible Publishers, Grand Rapids, Michigan; 1978.
NJB – *New Jerusalem Bible*; Doubleday & Co. Inc; Garden City, New York; 1985
NRSV – *New Revised Standard Version*; the Division of Christian Education of the National Council of the Churches of Christ in the USA; 1989.
REB – *Revised English Bible with Apocrypha*; Oxford University Press; 1989.
RSV – *Revised Standard Version*, Thomas Nelson Inc., New York; 1959.
YLT – *Young's Literal Translation*; by NJ Young; 1898.
Wuest – *The New Testament: An Expanded Translation*, by Kenneth S. Wuest; Wm. B. Eerdmans Publishing Co; 1961.

www.ingramcontent.com/pod-product-compliance
Lightning Source LLC
Chambersburg PA
CBHW050551170426
43201CB00011B/1648